Patient Care Delivery Models

Edited by

Gloria Gilbert Mayer, RN, EdD, FAAN
Private Health Care Consultant
Huntington Beach, California

Mary Jane Madden, RN, PhD
Principal
Lawrenz and Madden
Assistant Professor
University of Minnesota
St. Paul, Minnesota

Eunice Lawrenz, RN, BS
Principal
Lawrenz and Madden
Montclair, New Jersey

AN ASPEN PUBLICATION®
Aspen Publishers, Inc.
Rockville, Maryland
1990

14020

Library of Congress Cataloging-in-Publication Data

Patient care delivery models / edited by Gloria Gilbert Mayer, Mary Jane Madden,
Eunice Lawrenz.
p. cm.
"An Aspen publication."
Includes bibliographical references.
ISBN: 0-8342-0097-X
1. Nursing--Planning. 2. Nursing services--Administration.
3. Nursing--Philosophy. I. Mayer, Gloria G. II. Madden, Mary Jane, 1936- . III.
Lawrenz, Eunice.
[DNLM: 1. Models, Theoretical. 2. Nursing Care. 3. Patient Care Planning.
WY 100 P2975]
RT84.5.P38 1989
362.1' 73' 068--dc20
DNLM/DLC
for Library of Congress
89-17755
CIP

Editorial Services: Jane Coyle Garwood

Library of Congress Catalog Card Number: 89-17755
ISBN: 0-8342-0097-X

Printed in the United States of America

1 2 3 4 5

Table of Contents

About the Editors

Preface

This book brings together operational models for restructuring patient care and key support systems that underly them. The authors address the issue of patient care in ways that enable nursing to be attractive and viable in an environment of high technology, a nursing shortage, and constant change. No single model can be adopted universally by institutions. Rather, multiple models that support professional practice offer nurses a choice, with the adoption of a particular model based on individual variables in the organization.

Chapters on work redesign and incentives for compensation present key processes used in restructuring an organization. These chapters describe organizational development tools underlying a sensitive response to the current environment and to future challenges. Critical to any successful change is the multidisciplinary approach described.

Contributors to the book represent all parts of the United States and a wide range of organizations. Some describe system-wide change, others more limited, or unit-specific ones. We assume that there are many solutions to our current dilemmas and this book is designed to present some possible answers. The authors are all experts and the systems described all contribute to the professionalism of nursing practice.

Acknowledgments

We are grateful to the many contributors to this book, for their time, expertise, and willingness to share their knowledge and experience. We are also indebted to the nursing administrators who are a part of the University of Minnesota program in patient care administration for their constant questioning—questioning that led us to bring several models together in one book. To them and to our colleagues who have participated with us in the evolution of nursing we dedicate this book, hoping that together we will continue to share our best information on how to care for patients in a world economy.

We would also like to acknowledge the assistance of the editors and to thank Debbie Christensen for her expertise and her willingness to meet rigid deadlines.

Contributors

SANDY ALDERMAN, RN, BS
Assistant Director of Nursing
Friendly Hills Regional Medical
    Center
La Habra, California

JAMES BAHR, BS, IE
President
James Bahr Associates, Ltd.
Plymouth, Michigan

PAMELA M. BECKER, RN, MS
Director of Oncology and Pedia-
    tric Nursing
Phelps Memorial Hospital
Westchester County, New York

JUDY BLAUWET, RN, MPH
Director of Nursing—Special Care
    Services
McKennan Hospital
Sioux Falls, South Dakota

PATTY BOLGER, RN, MPH
Director of Nursing—Med-Surg/
    Mental Health
McKennan Hospital
Sioux Falls, South Dakota

PAMELA BORDELON, RN, MSN
Assistant to the Vice President
    Nursing Affairs

Hermann Hospital
Houston, Texas

LINDA BURNES-BOLTON, RN,
    DRPH
Director, Nursing Research and
    Development
Cedars-Sinai Medical Center
Los Angeles, California

CAROL ANN CAVOURAS, RN,
    MS, CNAA
Vice President Nursing Affairs
Hermann Hospital
Houston, Texas

JANET CUDDIGAN, RN, MSN
COMMES Nurse Coordinator
Creighton University College of
    Nursing
Omaha, Nebraska

MARYANN DAVIVIER, PHD
Staff Specialist, Patient Care
    Services
Cedars-Sinai Medical Center
Los Angeles, California

BARBARA DIPASQUALE, RN, MS
Head Nurse
Johns Hopkins Hospital
Baltimore, Maryland

LAWRENCE J. DONNELLY, RN, MSN
Vice President, Clinical Systems
National Medical Enterprises, Inc.
Santa Monica, California

SANDRA EDWARDSON, RN, PHD
Associate Professor
University of Minnesota
School of Nursing
Minneapolis, Minnesota

Senior Consultant
Health Management Systems, Associates
Minneapolis, Minnesota

JUDITH M. FARIAS, RN, MED
Manager, Patient Care Technician Program
New England Deaconess Hospital
Boston, Massachusetts

RUBEN D. FERNANDEZ, RN, MA, PHD CANDIDATE
Vice President for Nursing
Newark Beth Israel Medical Center
Newark, New Jersey

ANNE GARNER, RN, MSN
Administrative Director Medicine/Psychiatry
Nursing Services
Hermann Hospital
Houston, Texas

KATHY HARRIGAN, RN
Staff Nurse
Cedars-Sinai Medical Center
Los Angeles, California

HELEN HOESING, RN, MPH, CNAA
Vice President for Nursing

Nebraska Methodist Hospital
Omaha, Nebraska

KATHY J. HORVATH, RN, MS
Director, Career Development Programs
Beth Israel Hospital
Boston, Massachusetts

DELMA HUGGINS, RN, BS
Professional Nurse Case Manager
Carondelet St. Mary's Hospital and Health Center
Tucson, Arizona

LINDA K. JACKSON, RN, MS
Director of Nursing Services
Friendly Hills Regional Medical Center
La Habra, California

GERRI S. LAMB, RN, PHD
Clinical Director of Research
Professional Nurse Case Manager
Carondelet St. Mary's Hospital and Health Center
Tucson, Arizona

EUNICE LAWRENZ, RN, BS
Staff Development Nurse
Principal, Lawrenz and Madden Associates
Montclair, New Jersey

SUE LOGAN, RN
Nebraska Methodist Hospital
Omaha, Nebraska

MERIDEAN L. MAAS, RN, PHD
Assistant Professor, College of Nursing
The University of Iowa
Iowa Veterans Home
Iowa City, Iowa

MARY JANE MADDEN, RN, PHD
Principal, Lawrenz and Madden
  Associates
Assistant Professor, University of
  Minnesota
St. Paul, Minnesota

MARIE MANTHEY, RN, MS
President
Creative Nursing Management,
  Inc.
Minneapolis, Minnesota

GLORIA GILBERT MAYER, RN,
  EDD, FAAN
Private Health Care Consultant
Huntington Beach, California

Executive Director, Patient Care
  Management
Friendly Hills Medical Center
La Habra, California

JUDITH R. MILLER, RN, MED
Senior Vice President/Chief
  Nursing Officer
New England Deaconess Hospital
Boston, Massachusetts

SANDRA W. MURABITO, RN,
  MSN
Vanderbilt University Medical
  Center
Nashville, Tennessee

MARY ROSE, RN, MS
Head Nurse
Johns Hopkins Hospital
Baltimore, Maryland

MARY SEROTE, RN, MS
Director for Nursing Systems and
  Resources
Catherine McAuley Health Center
Ann Arbor, Michigan

JANET P. SPECHT, RNC, MA
Director of Nursing
Iowa Veterans Home
Iowa City, Iowa

ROXANE B. SPITZER-LEHMANN,
  RN, MA, FAAN
Vice President
St. Josephs Hospital System
Orange, California

SUE TAYLOR, RN, MSN
Administrative Director Surgical/
  Renal
Nursing Services
Hermann Hospital
Houston, Texas

MARY CRABTREE TONGES, RN,
  MSN
Vice President, Nursing
Robert Wood Johnson University
  Hospital
New Brunswick, New Jersey

LORI URBANEC, RN
Clinical Instructor
Cedars-Sinai Medical Center
Los Angeles, California

MARGARET M. VOSBURGH,
  RN, MS
Director, OR Services
Cedars-Sinai Medical Center
Los Angeles, California

LYNN WALTS, RN, MSN
Administrative Director Maternal
  Child Health
Nursing Services
Hermann Hospital
Houston, Texas

JOAN I. WHEELER, RN, MSN
Assistant Administrator for
    Nursing
St. Elizabeth Hospital
Elizabeth, New Jersey

MARJORIE SPLAINE WIGGINS,
    RN, MBA
Director Medical/Surgical Nursing
New England Deaconess Hospital
Boston, Massachusetts

KAREN ZANDER, RN, MS, CS
Organizational Development
    Specialist
Department of Nursing
Director of Consultation Services
Center for Nursing Case
    Management
New England Medical Center
    Hospitals
Boston, Massachusetts

Part I

Models of
Patient Care Delivery

This book is about models for delivering patient care in acute and long-term care facilities and about the context in which this care is given. It is about bringing patients and professional nursing practice together in the midst of DRGs, prospective reimbursement, contract medicine, hospitals struggling to maintain financial viability, and information overload. It is about practicing nursing when the profession is challenged by recruitment and retention issues, budget constraints, and challenges to professional practice.

This book is the result of persons asking questions about the "best" way to deliver patient care. Historically, nurses have asked themselves, What is nursing? What is this body of knowledge unique to our practice? Theorists have contributed to our knowledge in this area, and their contribution is evident in some of the models described in this book. Authority to make nursing decisions, responsibility for carrying them out, and accountability are generally accepted as hallmarks of nursing that is practiced professionally.

Models for practice offer ways to look at professional practice within a specified context. A model is a representation or framework arranging parts in such a way as to make a whole. It organizes information and indicates what information is most relevant. It provides us with a vocabulary and a way to link and sort variables or organize them according to our experience. Models are a way of abstracting, which aids us in communication and problem solving. Often they are keys to conceptualizing and understanding a situation. They can clarify our thinking about relatively complex situations, but they can also limit it by the very fact that they filter reality.

We are all familiar with certain kinds of models, for example, models for constructing buildings and models for developing automobiles. They vary in degrees of abstraction. Indeed, in this book you will find models

1

of varying degrees of detail. Yet all of them allow the reader an opportunity to experiment, to try it on, to see how it would fit without risk.

Using models has some pitfalls. It may lead us to overgeneralize. We are often tempted to make a situation fit a model rather than trying to fit the model to the situation, and the model may not be adequately validated or understood before we adopt it. The point of presenting or using models is to achieve a goal, not just to adopt a model for its own sake. Alas, models will not prevent us from making mistakes.

It is important that an organization listens to demands from within rather than insist on a certain model. If it does not use this approach, it risks a schizophrenic crackup by putting itself off center and aligning itself from without.

The models presented here are not prescriptive. Rather, they describe what nursing leaders are doing to balance and optimize forces so that patients are best served and nurses are best able to nurse in collaboration with all other contributors to patient care.

The models presented in this book have several elements that are important independent of the models. The authors speak about the relationship of the nurse and patient and dedicate themselves to fostering this relationship. They describe environments in which patients can heal themselves. They talk of organizations that are alive with spirit, places where all parties involved design the work and the environment. Sometimes people have the notion that improvements are the result of shifting people around and changing the rules concerning who is on top and who says how things will work. This is not so. A value of far greater significance surfaces in these pages. We hope that you will read carefully and add to the models here. It is our hope that patients will have the advantage of professional practice in a context that supports that practice—whether it is called *case management, primary nursing, team nursing,* or any other name—and that these models will offer us a common language for exchanging ideas and growing.

Chapter 1

Work Redesign

Mary Jane Madden
and Eunice Lawrenz

*This chapter introduces an approach to multidisciplinary work restructure.
Since it is the editors' belief that no one system can fit perfectly into every setting,
it is hoped that each reader will explore the process of work redesign and tailor
it to achieve the goals of his or her institution.*

WHAT WORK REDESIGN IS

Work redesign is a multidisciplinary approach to restructuring the work environment for nursing within a sociotechnical systems model. Useful models link people and technology in ways that optimize the contributions of both. They become a way to do some things differently, to rethink how work is designed and how people can be organized to get things done. They act as roadmaps.

The sociotechnical approach to work design integrates the social and technical aspects of systems and makes them support one another. Most sociotechnical change projects include multiple focused interventions in the areas of jobs, rewards, physical environment, work schedules, supervisory relationships, and the creation of work groups (usually with fewer than twenty members) with shared decision making about how work is planned and executed. Focusing on the work of patient care requires a multidisciplinary approach, in contrast to the narrower vision of solving problems by individual department.

Our approach is borrowed from business and industry, where organizations (such as a General Electric plant, where workers redesigned their jobs and schedules to achieve 50 percent higher production; and Shenandoah Life Insurance Company, which increased its employee/supervisor ratio from 7/1 to 37/1 while increasing service) buried in issues of conflict, budget cuts and competition, have redefined work, tasks, and relationships to accomplish organizational goals while recognizing employees as resources and collaborators (Sherwood, 1988). The process involves creating a steering committee of key players for the purpose of organizational diagnosis and work redesign (Exhibit 1-1).

Through this multidisciplinary approach, departments can work as partners in solving patient care problems, whether unique to the organization

Exhibit 1-1 Work Redesign at a Glance: Sociotechnical Systems Model

Essence of approach	Multidisciplinary approach to people and resources
Assumptions	There is no one way to do things.
	There are many satisfactory ways to organize.
	Employees and managers make critical decisions in work flow and structure.
	Design process is open and participatory.
	Employees share in implementing options.
Key players	Senior management, department directors/managers, physicians, caregivers, steering committee, project director, design team, and consultants
Typical use	When organizations face significant opportunities/threats from the environment—shortages of workers, increased technology, acuity of patients, and length of stay
Strengths	Multidisciplinary approach based on theory of organizational development research
	Focuses on the work of patient care
Pitfalls	Requires commitment at all levels
	Assumes willingness to negotiate solutions

or shared throughout the health care industry. Work redesign makes it possible to

- reduce conflict and unnecessary competition
- develop a customized patient care model
- promote collaboration and respect among nursing staff and between departments
- increase job satisfaction
- reduce stress
- improve overall organizational communication
- minimize inefficiency and increase productivity
- reduce costs
- create a shared sense of purpose

The results of work redesign are often entirely different for each unit or division. For nursing, it may mean a different way to organize patient care; for an x-ray department, a different approach to schedule and transport to reduce patient time in the area; for a laboratory, a collaboration with the nursing department to implement a new method of obtaining blood; for finance, a partnership in problem solving; for the organization, a new model for governance. Work redesign may result in restructured work units, new teaching systems, and realigned incentive systems. Each activity in the process is geared toward creating an integrated, committed work organization.

Each work redesign project has a character all its own, depending on the specific organization's culture, goals, patient population, level of technology, and readiness for change. No one model fits all organizations. Nevertheless, the redesign process is relevant to all health care organizations because of the nurse shortage, the decreased number of health professionals in other disciplines, and the limited number of nonprofessionals in the work force. Two questions are essential for any project: (1) What tasks now being done should be done by other persons? (2) What tasks need not be done at all?

Sociotechnical principles underlying work redesign incorporate behavioral and systemic assumptions about work and the interrelatedness of work with individuals, groups, and technology. The assumptions are:

- Nursing is an open system in which internal-external boundaries must be maintained for quality patient care.
- Quality of care and service depends on giving responsibility for decisions and actions to the people who have the most relevant information and are closest to the work.
- Participation of those affected by the redesign process results in the best solutions and most empowerment.
- Teamwork must cross boundaries to other departments.
- Structure and desired outcomes must be compatible.
- Continuous learning is encouraged and rewarded.
- Technical and social systems anchored in balancing and optimizing forces underlie future strategic navigation.
- Support systems such as education, rewards, and incentives must be congruent with desired behaviors.
- Work redesign is a continuous process of review, evaluation, and redesign.

Each work redesign project has five basic elements, with the process tailored to each organization and its culture. The key elements are summarized below.

Establishing a Structure for Design

A steering committee representative of everyone affected by potential change is essential. Successful committees include senior management, department heads, staff nurses, and physicians. From this group is selected a design team of three to five people. The design team collects and analyzes relevant data and formulates a design for submission to the steering committee. The design team includes experts in design, organizational development, human resources, and nursing. This team may be complemented by ad hoc action teams of employees working on issues and portions of the total work redesign program. Focusing first on one or two units limits the variables and makes the project manageable.

Collecting Data About the Work System

Data collection is done through a mixture of surveys, interviews, onsite observations, and work sampling. Data are collected on

- efficiency in the delivery of nursing care, including overlapping functions and nonnursing tasks
- the impact of technical changes in health care on the functions and roles of nurses
- role definition and redefinition
- the relationship of nursing functions to the role of patient care
- what behaviors are rewarded, including specific data on rewards
- what occupies nurses' time
- what affects staffing and creates "chaos"
- scheduling of patient activities, such as lab tests and x-rays
- activities occurring on specific shifts
- patient management throughout total hospital stay
- physician-nurse communication
- transportation of patients, supplies, and equipment
- availability of supplies, maintenance, and environmental services
- working relationships across departments

Formulating a Work Redesign Proposal

The design team lays the foundation for future work by writing a statement of purpose for the unit(s), with business objectives and constraints. This, when compared with management objectives, generates guidelines for a new organization or affirmation of what exists. It is a framework for further evaluation and development.

Developing a Transition Plan

The design team, with the steering committee, formulates a transition or implementation plan extending to all levels of nursing and to all departments in the organization. Building ownership is a critical part of the total process, but it is especially important during this phase. Physicians, nurses, and key departments become members of ad hoc groups that solve problems affecting them.

Monitoring and Evaluating the Process

Constant monitoring and adjustment of the transition plan keeps the plan on course and offers a way to remedy unforeseen problems and to take advantage of unforeseen opportunities.

WHY WORK REDESIGN IS SUCCESSFUL

Work redesign is successful because it is based on policy design principles of innovative organizations.

Working with Operating Forces

Identifying operating forces (pressures for or against change) is one way to anticipate the acceptance of change. Given the complexity and systemic nature of organizations, change in one unit is bound to affect others: a technological change (in space or scheduling, for example) affects social systems (and therefore the relationships of people in units throughout the hospital). Identifying potential resistance to change can be useful in avoiding or reducing it.

The identification of operating forces requires reexamination of the primary purpose of the hospital, of the outcomes necessary to achieve that purpose, and of the degree of alignment and commitment to that purpose. This makes it possible to set priorities, to work with the pressures for change, and to customize the work redesign program. Individuals and departments who clearly understand and commit to patient care goals are free to set aside past norms and practices that are no longer useful. Joint problem solving has been shown to result, for example, in more timely patient medications. In another case, physicians and nurses who dropped their accusations of one another were able to focus on the patient and solve multidimensional care problems. In still another case, same-day surgery and admitting departments were empowered to resolve conflicts over preadmission testing, again by focusing on patient outcomes.

Focusing on Leverage Points

Leverage points are those few places where changes, often made with little intervention, within an underlying structure have pervasive results. Flexible staffing plans, role negotiations, nurse managers with department head status, and incentive plans are examples of leverage points that encourage the alignment of the total organization toward its goals.

Creating Functional Structures

Structures exist to bring collective efforts to a goal. Work within a sociotechnical model is redesigned in a way that recognizes the contributions of all caregivers, thus aligning them with the primary purpose of patient care. Multidisciplinary work groups of ten to twenty people make decisions about patient care. The new structures increase communication, accountability, and respect among disciplines that have previously worked as though each were a separate company. These structures empower nurses as well as housekeepers, physicians, and employees, to invest in caring for patients.

ORGANIZATIONAL EFFECTIVENESS THROUGH WORK REDESIGN

A key concern is how to find leverage points. How does one determine which structures to adopt? How does one know the operating forces and their strengths? In our experience, changes in seven primary leverage points can make a significant impact on patient care and nursing:

1. leadership
2. governance
3. staffing and scheduling
4. rewards and incentives
5. career development
6. connections between nursing and other departments
7. physician-nurse collaboration

Leadership

Nursing leaders who make a difference stand for something, articulate a vision, and are committed, even under pressure. They empower themselves and others and create organizational structures that get results; they go beyond what seems ordinary to take risks. To be a nursing leader today is to be vulnerable. To redesign the work of nursing is to be vulnerable because, in letting go of sacred cows, redefining quality, restructuring decision making, and offering incentive pay, leaders risk standing alone. Powerful leaders are those who answer the questions, Where are we going? and Who will we be when we get there? They are committed to moving forward and are comfortable with ambiguity.

Governance

Governance defines power, reporting relationships, decision making, and access to information, and it is often the basis for managing conflict. Nurses, who make life and death decisions at the bedside, cannot be governed by a structure that renders them powerless in the organization. The result of such powerlessness tends to be lack of accountability for professional decisions and rebellion against organization goals.

People who wield power must be convinced that sharing it increases the likelihood of reaching desired goals. Shared governance offers one way to shift control and the power base. For organizations contemplating shared governance models, key considerations are the readiness of nurses and the potential for using the model organizationwide. Well-executed work redesign incorporates all departments, since shared governance by nursing alone risks "backlash."

Staffing and Scheduling

Whether there are excesses or shortages of staff, staffing and scheduling are major technological issues that can result in interpersonal conflict. Clearly defining and coordinating central and decentralized functions and holding appropriate persons accountable can make significant differences in work and nurse-nurse relationships. Although this sounds simple, it is not. The key is balance. Authority and accountability for staffing must be held by the nurse manager, with some scheduling responsibilities delegated to a centralized staffing office. This office functions in a staff or consultant relationship to the manager and not as a replacement.

Combining traditional eight-hour shifts with alternative shifts optimizes nursing resources to achieve required staffing levels and gives nurses greater flexibility in their lives. The model used flows directly from the needs of each organization, but higher acuity and shorter lengths of stay generally result in a greater need for coverage on evenings, nights, and weekends. The work no longer decreases during these hours.

Essential for well-managed scheduling are competent budgetary management and reporting systems that provide appropriate information when needed, in an understandable form consistent with reports used by the fiscal department. All players need to know what it costs to provide patient care and what revenues they generate to really share in the organization's work.

Rewards and Incentives

People simultaneously seek many kinds of rewards and incentives, not just economic ones. No single factor explains behavior or reinforces it. As workers' values change, so must rewards and incentives. Organizations that have flexible plans (offering childcare as well as tuition support), that pay on the basis of performance, that use a pay scale not capped prematurely for nurses, and that recognize and promote nurses can exploit the complex needs of employees for rewards and incentives. (Chapter 18 describes an innovation in incentive pay for nurses.)

Career Development

Career development, central to recruitment and retention of nurses, must challenge nurses while preventing them from overstretching. Several authors describe models that include differentiated practice, cross-training, career ladders, and mentorships. In some instances these are combined with nurse extender models. Career development, along with training, compensation, and supervisory practices, is part of supporting and managing work.

Typically, career development practices have been fragmented and have not been compatible with creating challenging work and motivating individuals to approach their potential. Mentorships and partnerships with other practitioners are steps in the right direction, but they need to be complemented by practices such as providing regular sabbatical leaves and giving rewards for doing things differently and by structures such as those supporting "think tanks" comprising those at the bedside as well as their leaders. Career development practices must reflect the needs of "over-stretched," "fulfilled," and "growing" nurses and take into account the systemic properties of any change.

Connections between Nursing and Other Departments

The multidisciplinary nature of a sociotechnical approach to work redesign results in new relationships among all departments. Throughout the process persons negotiate on the basis of issues, not positions, and on the basis of standards, not vested interests. Work sampling provides objective information about apparently subjective problems. Issues such as reducing the amount of time between an order for medication and its administration are examined, solved, and monitored by steering committee members from involved departments. The departments directly involved have the benefit of ideas from those who are not.

Keeping the connections in place after a work redesign project and spreading connections beyond the steering committee can be achieved in several ways. Organizationwide shared governance, multidisciplinary ad hoc groups for problem solving, and having people deal directly with those with whom they have a problem are examples of methods that have made a difference. Alignment of all disciplines toward organizational goals requires that changes made in the redesign process become part of the culture of the organization.

Physician-Nurse Collaboration

Relationships between physicians and nurses are clouded by a history of issues of power, status, and gender communication, resulting in less than the best, most cost-effective care.

The issues have, in fact, a life of their own, with both parties assuming roles that may not be comfortable or productive. Nevertheless, in some instances the nature of the clinical work has helped physicians and nurses transcend the boundaries. Critical care nurses and physicians often collaborate, valuing and soliciting each other's expertise.

Work redesign offers a systemic way of resolving systemic problems. A multidisciplinary project requires the full participation of physicians who have organizational power or who provide informal leadership. As physicians and nurses share issues and "walk in each other's shoes," a foundation for mutual respect and trust is laid. Not surprisingly, nurses and physicians discover a strong, shared commitment to patient care. As the depth of the commitment to patients is uncovered and trust grows, nurses and physicians move from being adversaries to becoming *real* allies.

The process of building a collaboration can be painful and may require coaching. What has been automatic learned behavior now requires choice. Nurses who choose to empower themselves take a chance. They free themselves to work to their potential but also risk going unheard. Physicians become full partners in patient care but cease to have total responsibility for things over which they do not have total control. As the two groups negotiate roles, both are freed to uncover new solutions to issues.

Collaboration between physicians and nurses requires negotiating roles. This can be done only by the physicians and nurses involved, and it necessitates a time commitment from each person. Once begun, the process becomes part of the cultural norm and is expected and rewarded. Organizations with a reputation for collaborative relationships between nurses and physicians hold a unique market position with respect to nurse recruitment and retention.

SUMMARY

Work redesign is not the reshuffling of the same old pieces. It is a multidisciplinary acknowledgment of the past, a clear look at the present, and a creation of the future based on the design of work and the structure of the work organization. It recognizes that the patient care delivery system is complex and constantly in change, that those who give care are our best resources, and that a change in one part of the system sets other parts in motion. It is a way to unfreeze traditional roles and "investments" and to encourage collaboration in helping patients heal themselves.

REFERENCES

Hackman, J.R. & Oldman, G.R. (1980). *Work redesign*. Reading, Massachusetts: Addison-Wesley Publishing Company.

Sherwood, J.J. (1988). Creating work cultures with competitive advantages. In *Organizational Dynamics*. pp. 5–27.

Chapter 2

ProACT™: The Professionally Advanced Care Team Model

Mary Tonges

Tonges describes a complete project in work redesign, a project where the work of the unit is examined and placed within the scope of practice for the appropriate person. Patient care has been studied on the basis of professional practice, cost, personal and organizational wants and needs, and appropriateness of function. Tonges has not reshuffled the pieces of nursing once again but instead has taken a fresh look and integrated these pieces into a model driven by quality while holding costs.

The ProACT™ model, when looked at seriously, warrants attention and application to other settings. When the ongoing data collection and analysis of patient costs has been finished, the model will be enhanced.

What Tonges and her colleagues have not yet addressed is the organization of the nursing department and its impact on the unit redesign. We wonder whether such a model does not imply shared governance.

This model was created as a way of dealing with the problems of the nursing shortage. There is every indication that in redesigning the work of the unit, patient outcomes are not jeopardized and in fact may be improved. It is also likely that with costs down and the appropriate use of professional nurses, recruitment and retention would be easier.

The nursing profession is currently caught in the throes of one of the most severe manpower shortages in its history. As the economic and social

---

The author wishes to thank the following individuals for their invaluable contributions to this project: Maryann F. Fralic, RN, MN, DrPH, Senior Vice President, Nursing, whose enthusiastic interest, support, and suggestions greatly facilitated development and implementation of the model; the members of the Alternative Practice Model Development Task Force, namely, Judy Brett, RN, MSN, PhD, Al Brown, MBA, Pat Cavanaugh, RN, MSN, Joanne Hartnack, RN, MHA, Suzanne Kiniry, RN, MS, Jackie Lattany, RN, Helen Rossi, RN, ONC, Ann Sawicki, RN, BSN, Marguerite Schlag, RN, EdD, and Dave Vogel, MS, and additional members of the Implementation Task Force, namely, Greg Finnegan, MBA, Joan Gleason, RN, MA, Fred Graumann, JD, Beverly Karlik, RN, MS, and Ron Zink, MBA, for their ideas, commitment to the project, and investment of time and energy to make it happen; Helen Rossi, RN, ONC, head nurse, and the Seven Tower nursing, support services, and pharmacy staff, for living the model and transforming concepts into reality.

forces fueling the shortage intensify, the gap between the supply of and demand for registered professional nurses will continue to increase. The challenge to the profession is to assume a leadership position in managing the problem proactively before unpalatable solutions are developed and imposed externally. This can be accomplished by looking beyond the daily difficulties of the present and recognizing the opportunity to simultaneously achieve professional goals while solving the problems of the shortage.

The pressures of the current nursing shortage have created an unparalleled opportunity to restructure hospital nursing practice and care delivery and to create a system with the potential to offer nurses more autonomous clinical roles, fewer nonnursing tasks, higher salaries, and a workable transition to the delineation of two different registered nurse (RN) roles. This chapter describes the scope and causes of the nursing shortage and presents an alternative practice model that meets these imperatives. Key issues in the development and implementation of a practice model are identified and discussed. Information in this chapter should help the reader to

- describe the severity of the current nursing shortage
- list five causes of the nursing shortage in hospitals
- describe the Professionally Advanced Care Team (ProACT®) Model
- identify key issues for consideration in the development of an alternative nursing practice model (e.g., the ProACT® Model)
- outline the process of implementing an alternative practice model

DESCRIPTION OF THE PROBLEM

The magnitude and severity of the current nursing shortage can be understood through a brief review of the number and location of vacant positions, the rate of nurses' participation in the labor force, and trends in nursing school enrollments. A national survey conducted by the American Hospital Association in December 1986 revealed that the vacancy rate for RN positions in hospitals had doubled from 6.3% in 1985 to 13.6% in 1986 (Curran, Minnick, & Moss, 1987). This contrasted with an average vacancy rate for licensed practical nurses (LPNs) of 7.6% and nurse's aides (NAs) of 5.8%. Twenty-four percent of all hospitals reported RN vacancy rates of at least 15%, whereas more than 50% reported no LPN or NA vacancies (Curran, Minnick, & Moss, 1987). These figures indicate that LPNs and NAs were still relatively more available than RNs.

Regarding location of vacancies, Mid-Atlantic hospitals had the most serious shortage. Only 3.7% of hospitals in that area reported no RN vacancies, as compared with the 25% to 30% of West North Central hospitals that had no RN openings. Larger hospitals experienced higher percentages of vacancies (97.5% of hospitals over 400 beds had vacancies), and 50% of all respondents reported difficulty in filling critical care positions (Curran, Minnick, & Moss, 1987). This survey was repeated in 1987 and showed little change (American Hospital Association, 1988).

A comment frequently heard regarding the nursing shortage is that if all the inactive licensed nurses came back to work in nursing, the problem would be solved. Based on this assumption, many hospitals have offered refresher courses, hoping to attract inactive nurses back to staff their units. The reality of the situation is that 80% of RNs are employed either full- or part-time, and less than 6% are employed in other occupations and not seeking positions in nursing (Department of Health and Human Services, 1986). Given that many nurses have other responsibilities—as parents and homemakers—80% may be as high a rate as can be expected. In fact, it is one of the highest rates of participation in the labor force among predominantly female professions (Aiken & Mullinix, 1987). Thus, inactive nurses are neither the problem nor the solution.

The future supply of nurses is clearly dependent on present enrollments in schools of nursing. Enrollments in nursing programs peaked in 1983 (National League for Nursing, 1986), and combined enrollment figures for all three types of basic nursing education programs fell 13% between 1983 and 1985 and continue to decline (Miller, 1987). An analysis of these figures indicates that the impact of the decline in enrollments would affect the number of associate degree graduates in 1987, diploma graduates in 1988, and baccalaureate graduates in 1989. This projection leads to the conclusion that the worst shortage could be yet to come. Fortunately, 1988 data indicated that the decline in total enrollments was beginning to level off, and the number of first-time admissions was up by 4% (*American Nurse,* 1989).

Among the many facts and figures indicating the scope of the current nursing shortage, some of the most significant points can be summarized as follows:

- Enrollments peaked in 1983 and fell 13% by 1985.
- Inactive nurses are neither the problem nor the solution.
- The shortage is national and affects all regions of the country.

CAUSES OF THE PROBLEM

Determining the cause of a problem is an essential early step in the problem-solving process. Failure to accurately identify the cause of a problem, as opposed to its symptoms, minimizes the chances for successful problem resolution. The nursing shortage is caused by a combination of social, economic, and professional variables affecting the supply and demand for registered professional nurses. Five of the key variables affecting the shortage are as follows:

1. decreased birth rate
2. changed employment values and opportunities
3. depressed salaries
4. changed financial system
5. outdated RN role in hospitals

Decreased Birth Rate

Simply put, there are fewer young people now than there were when members of the baby boom generation were choosing careers. The demographic profile of the country is changing, resulting in a smaller cohort of 18-year-olds and an increasingly older population. This combination has led to a decreased supply of potential candidates for the nursing field and an increased demand for nursing services.

Changed Employment Values and Opportunities

Employment values among the general public and career opportunities for women in our society have radically changed in the last 15 years. Recent research found that whereas the dominant goal of college freshmen 20 years ago was "developing a meaningful philosophy of life," that goal has now been replaced by the goal of "being very well off financially" (Cooperative Institutional Research Forum, 1987). Thus, the yuppie phenomenon.

Following the emergence of the women's movement in the late 60s and early 70s, women began to consider alternatives to the traditional career options of teaching and nursing and to enter other fields in increasing numbers. In 1969, 9% of first-year medical students in America were women; in 1987, the rate was 37% (Klass, 1988). The problem is not just that many women who would have become nurses are becoming physicians. Similar increases in female enrollment have also occurred in business, dentistry, and pharmacy. To summarize, fewer of the potential candidates for nursing are interested in a career in this profession.

Depressed Salaries

Salaries that do not offer adequate compensation for the responsibility, workload, and shift work and that are not competitive with the salaries of other career options are an extremely important factor in creating this shortage. The root of the problem lies not in starting salaries, which are comparable to those for other college graduates, but in the fact that the average maximum salary for nurses is only $7,000 higher than the entry rate and that this maximum can be reached in less than seven years (*National Survey,* 1987). Thus, whereas an attorney in private practice can reasonably hope for a salary increase of 200% in a career, a staff nurse can expect an increase of less than 40% (Will, 1988).

Why is this so? Compressed salary scales in nursing can be at least partially explained by two facts. First, in most communities a small number of hospitals employ most of the local nurses, and unless nurses are willing and able to relocate, they are a "captured labor force" with few choices as to employer (Aiken & Mullinix, 1987). This situation limits the need to increase salaries based on competition.

The second reason is the labor intensity involved in utilizing RNs to provide a large proportion of hands-on patient care. Nursing is the largest department in the hospital, and at least half of the nursing staff in most hospitals consists of RNs. It has simply appeared too expensive to pay so many employees higher salaries. Consequently, despite publicity and concerns about the shortage of nurses in hospitals, nurses' wages increased only 4% in 1986, and increases for nurses lagged behind increases for all other nonphysician employees (Miller, 1987, p. 45). Given the demands of a nursing career and the employment values of today's work force, it is clear that long-term solutions to the nursing shortage must include adequate compensation.

Changed Financial Systems

Prospective payment has reshaped the health care industry by changing the financial incentives that drive it. These changes have had a tremendous impact on both nursing demand and supply. Increased utilization review and the change from payment for charges to payment per case have resulted in decreased admissions and reduced lengths of stay. Consequently, patients are now hospitalized only during the most acute phase of their illness, necessitating intensified nursing around the clock. The demand for nurses has thus increased from 50 nurses per 100 patients in 1975 to 85 nurses per 100 patients in 1985 ("Securing the Future," 1986).

At the same time that prospective payment has increased the demand for nurses in hospitals, it has decreased the supply of nurses available to work in hospitals. The drive to care for patients in less expensive settings outside the hospital has led to the creation of increased employment opportunities in alternative settings, such as surgicenters and home health agencies. While 68% of nurses currently work in hospitals, the percentage working in alternative settings continues to increase (American Hospital Association, 1987, p. vii). Prospective payment has also reduced the funds available to increase nurses' earnings, thus impacting supply by retarding salary growth.

Outdated Hospital RN Role

The last and possibly most important variable influencing the shortage and offering the greatest potential for solution is the role of the RN in the hospital. There are three primary problems with the traditional role of RNs in hospitals: (1) lack of support services, (2) inadequate incentives to stay in clinical practice, and (3) insufficient opportunities for independent decision making based on nursing knowledge and collaborative practice with physicians and other health professionals.

Despite the complexities of operating a busy nursing unit, the ratio of support personnel to professionals is substantially lower in the hospital industry as compared with other businesses. Moreover, computerization in hospitals has lagged far behind other businesses such as banking and transportation (Aiken & Mullinex, 1987, p. 645). Thus, nurses currently perform many nonclinical administrative and support functions, and nursing's universal availability is resulting in an increasing unavailability of direct nursing care.

Second, the traditional system does not offer adequate incentives to retain nurses in clinical roles. Many nurses in clinical practice have little to look forward to in terms of significant increases in compensation, more attractive schedules, and new challenges and opportunities for growth.

Finally, the traditional pattern of nurse-physician interaction does not place nurses in a position to utilize their clinical knowledge in an autonomous role. In an article on nurse retention, Weisman (1982, p. 25) noted, "Nurses' perceived autonomy, including the ability to make decisions on work conduct, is the strongest predictor of job satisfaction levels."

Hospitals have placed tremendous importance on physicians as admitters. Physicians are important, but patients are increasingly being hospitalized because they need 24-hour nursing care; otherwise, their care would be provided on an outpatient basis. As key players in the delivery of health care, nurses need more control over the independent aspects of their practice.

RESTRUCTURING NURSING PRACTICE AND PATIENT CARE DELIVERY

Numerous solutions to the nursing shortage have been proposed. The proposals vary widely in merit, practicality, and compatibility with the professional goals of nursing. They range from reemphasizing diploma education to creating a new health care position requiring nine months of training and carrying the title *registered care technologist* (Carlsen, 1988, p. 15).

Among the many solutions proposed, alternative nursing practice models offer significant potential for success. This potential is based on the fact that models can be designed to address the actual causes of the problem. Restructuring nursing practice and care delivery has the potential to affect the variables causing the nursing shortage by

- reducing demand for nurses to better match supply
- facilitating salary increases
- creating more attractive roles for nurses in hospitals

The nursing profession can also achieve at least two additional goals through development and implementation of well-designed alternative practice models: (1) the establishment of a system with two different RN roles and (2) the creation of institutional awareness of nurses' ability to manage resources and affect patient outcomes.

THE ProACT℠ MODEL

The basic features of this model are its delineation of two distinct RN roles and its restructuring of ancillary services at the unit level to provide maximum support to the patient and nurse. Its key features are

1. delineation of two distinct RN roles, primary nurse and clinical care managers (CCM)
2. creation of the CCM role combining high-quality clinical management and aggressive business management
3. supervised utilization of LPNs and NAs in direct nursing care

4. expansion of clinical and nonclinical support services at the unit level to relieve nursing staff of nonnursing tasks and enhance patient service

The model can best be described through a review of key developmental issues.

Scope of Practice

The ProACT™ Model is an expanded role. Rather than subdividing the current RN role as differentiated practice models do, this model preserves the RN role as it is known today and creates a new, expanded role for the nursing practice of tomorrow. This new role does not extend beyond the parameters of professional nursing practice but generates an opportunity to practice professional nursing more fully.

Differentiated practice is a very sensitive subject. There has been a great deal of pain generated by this issue, and, as Primm (1988) points out, much of it has been inflicted by nurses on each other. It is essential that an acceptable way be found to make the transition to two different RN roles for the future. The solution may lie in expanded role models rather than differentiated practice.

The new and restructured nursing roles in the ProACT™ Model are as follows:

1. The *clinical care manager*
   - manages the entire hospital stay of a caseload of patients through coordination of care with physicians, nursing staff, and other health professionals
   - ensures that patient outcomes are achieved within established time frames
   - completes an expanded assessment of patient and family capabilities and needs prior to hospitalization
   - acts as a role model and provides clinical direction and support to the primary nurse
   - has 24-hour accountability for patients in his or her caseload
   - assesses patients' progress through the expected hospital course, mobilizes resources, and intervenes as necessary
   - plans discharge and facilitates discharge teaching
2. The *primary nurse*
   - manages primary patients' nursing care during hospitalization on the unit
   - assesses, plans, and evaluates nursing care for primary patients and participates in direct and indirect care delivery

- consults with the clinical care manager regarding patients' conditions and problems as indicated
- assesses patients under his or her care each shift, establishes priorities, and plans care, delegating work to LPNs and NAs as appropriate
- prepares the patient and family for discharge

3. The *LPN*
   - functions as an associate nurse practicing under the supervision of an RN in providing direct and indirect care to implement the nursing care plan in the primary nurse's absence
   - provides input to the primary nurse for the nursing care plan

CCMs' caseload selection is based on diagnosis and workload and correlates with resident coverage. Primary nurses oversee the care of a group of patients that includes their primary patients, and LPNs function as associate nurses caring for patients within this group under the supervision of the RN.

Titles, Licensure, and Education

The following qualifications are required for the different nursing roles in the ProACT℠ Model:

1. The clinical care manager is licensed to practice as a professional RN. A baccalaureate degree in nursing is required and a master's degree in nursing is preferred.
2. The primary nurse is licensed to practice as a professional RN. Graduation from an accredited RN program is required.
3. The LPN is licensed to practice as an LPN. Graduation from an accredited LPN program is required.

Clinical care managers' competencies include those of the primary nurse plus advanced clinical knowledge and leadership and management competencies derived from experience in a specialized field of nursing practice.

Organizational Structure

The organization of the nursing staff is depicted in Figure 2-1.
Changes from the previous organizational structure include the addition of clinical care managers and the movement of an assistant head nurse position from the day to the night shift. The assistant head nurses receive

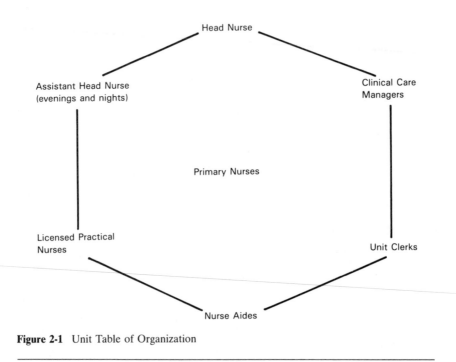

Figure 2-1 Unit Table of Organization

---

administrative direction from the head nurse (to whom they report) and are ultimately accountable for management of their shifts. Clinical care managers direct the evening and night assistant head nurses on clinical issues. The assistant head nurse position is an entry-level position on the management track and requires an aptitude for management, several years of clinical experience, and a BSN.

Patient assignments are made daily by the head nurse and assistant head nurses in collaboration with the clinical care managers. The roles of primary nurses and LPNs were discussed earlier under the heading "Scope of Practice." NAs assist the nurses in caring for patients by performing the assigned tasks delegated by the RN. Primary nurses, associate nurses, and NAs work together to care for patients; LPNs and NAs extend the efforts of the primary nurse. Unlike team nursing, however, this model is designed to provide a primary nurse role for RNs and preserve that relationship with patients. Additionally, the primary nurse is supported by the clinical care managers for nursing issues and is freed to devote more time to nursing care by expanded clinical and nonclinical support services.

One of the goals of ProACT™ is to preserve the essence of primary nursing—that is, the relationship between the primary nurse and the patient—while delegating many of the tasks. This concept is supported by Manthey (1988, pp. 54–55), who states that the essential ingredient of primary nursing is the establishment of a responsibility relationship between a nurse and a patient. The key elements of this relationship are that the nurse explains the role to the patient, provides some of the care when present, and prepares a care plan that is followed by others when the primary nurse is not on duty.

A comparison can be made between the primary nurse–primary patient relationship and the relationship of a working mother and her child. Because a working mother cannot care for her child while she is not at home, she hires a caregiver to do what she would do for her child if she were there, but the child still knows the difference between its mother and the caregiver. Similarly, others can care for the primary patient, but the patient still has a special relationship with the primary nurse.

Nurses must begin to delegate some of the direct tasks involved in patient care. Lawyers have paralegals, and they, as well as many other professionals, delegate some of their work to assistants. Nurses can too.

The Clinical Care Manager

Today's prospective payment environment mandates careful management of patient care. Nurses are excellent candidates for providing such management within the hospital setting. Implementation of nurse-managed care requires a change from simply planning care to managing care through a shift of focus from just completing tasks to attaining patient outcomes.

The clinical care manager (CCM) assumes responsibility for managing the hospital stay of a self-selected caseload of 10–11 patients. Management of the patients' hospital stay is accomplished through coordination of care with physicians, nurses, and other health professionals based upon a clinical care protocol describing key events for each day of hospitalization for a specific diagnosis. These plans are similar in concept to the critical pathways developed at New England Medical Center in Boston, and they incorporate specific outcome goals and prescribed processes to achieve these goals (Woldum, 1987). These protocols should be continually revised as new ways are found to improve care, minimize resource consumption, and maximize revenue. The financial management aspect of the clinical care manager role is a key component of the model.

Specific responsibilities of the CCM include completion of an expanded patient and family assessment prior to hospitalization in conjunction with the preadmission testing appointment. This is a broad-scope evaluation of patient and family capabilities and needs from prehospitalization through postdischarge. The assessment focuses on factors critical to achieving required outcomes for discharge, posthospitalization recovery, and health maintenance and promotion. The CCM's assessment supports the complementary admission nursing assessment completed by the primary nurse, which focuses on factors affecting the patient's nursing care during the hospital stay and preparation for discharge. All of this information is used by the primary nurse to identify the patient's individual needs during hospitalization and plan nursing interventions to meet them.

The CCM has input into staff evaluations and the authority to provide clinical direction for staff. One objective of the model's organizational structure is to preserve sufficient time for the clinical care manager's clinical practice while giving the necessary authority to direct others in the delivery of care. The CCM organizes his or her activities around the needs of the primary nurse and assists the primary nurse with assessments, care planning, and discharge preparation as necessary. CCMs also assume responsibility for unit leadership in the absence of the head nurse.

The CCM job is an exempt, nonbargaining unit position with a salary range between that of the assistant head nurse and the head nurse. Each CCM must have a minimum of a BSN and at least two years of relevant clinical experience and also must demonstrate competency for the position. A minimum of one year of experience in the appropriate specialty (e.g., orthopedics) is preferred. It is also preferred that each CCM have at least one year of experience at Robert Wood Johnson University Hospital. As certification in specific specialties becomes more available, that will be required.

The CCM primarily works a day schedule Monday through Friday but is on call for complicated admissions or unusual problems on evenings, nights, and weekends every third week. Calls concerning unusual problems of current patients are screened by the clinical supervisors to ensure that the problem cannot be handled by inhouse resources before the CCM is contacted. Examples of situations that would result in a call to the CCM for telephone consultation include the unexpected transfer of a patient out of critical care (which would require modification of the nursing plan for floor care) and the admission of an unusually complex trauma case. The CCM is called for nursing consultation rather than medical consultation.

Based on the information provided, the CCM determines whether the admission or problem can be handled over the phone or whether it is necessary to come in to see the patient. Patients' families also frequently call the CCM.

Each CCM works five out of seven days, including both weekend days during the week of on-call duty, if needed. When working on weekends, the CCM assumes a leadership position in managing the activities of the unit, takes a patient care assignment, and sees new admissions. CCMs also occasionally work holidays based on unit needs. Each CCM has a long-range pager and they share an in-house pager.

The CCMs arrange their schedules among themselves to ensure that at least one of them is working every weekday. They cover for each other in case of illness and vacation.

CCMs see patients scheduled for admission when they come in for preadmission testing to interview them and complete the assessment. The names of both the CCM and the primary nurse caring for each patient are identified on the unit assignment board and in the patient's room. The CCM gives each patient a business card and calls the patient after discharge to assess the adjustment to home, answer questions, and assist with problem resolution if necessary. If at all possible, a patient who is readmitted is cared for by the CCM and primary nurse who worked with him or her during the previous hospitalization.

CCMs are accountable to the head nurse for the quality of their practice and the quality of care delivered to all patients in their caseloads. They receive additional education through their orientation and an ongoing development program to gain the knowledge and skills necessary to collaborate successfully with physicians, nurses, and other health care workers. Periodic performance appraisals are based on specific performance standards, including clinical competence and fulfillment of role expectations, patient satisfaction, interpersonal skills and working relationships, contributions to the unit (e.g., presentation of educational programs for unit staff), and professional development through continuing education programs, readings, and participation in professional organizations. It is recommended that the performance appraisal system include both self-review and peer review input, which the head nurse uses in making the final performance rating determination. CCMs who do not consistently meet performance standards or who do not wish to remain in the role have the opportunity to transfer to a primary nurse position.

Support Services

Provision of related professional and ancillary services, such as pharmacy, housekeeping, and dietary, are restructured at the unit level to facilitate and provide maximum support to the nursing staff's efforts to care for patients and improve the quality of the service experienced by the patient.

Support services, including housekeeping, dietary, and supplies, are provided by a support service host assigned to a specific group of patients.

The support service host role encompasses traditional support service work plus a number of tasks previously assumed by various levels of nursing personnel, such as orienting patients to their rooms upon admission, distributing linen and water, making unoccupied beds, and preparing patients for meals.

Pharmacy service is enhanced by staffing a pharmacy technician on the unit to assume responsibility for all medication-related work except actual administration. For example, the pharmacy technician completely prepares all medications and organizes them for administration based on each patient's medication administration schedule. Registered pharmacists supervise the work of the pharmacy technicians and increase their clinical involvement at the unit level with both nurses and patients. Support service hosts and pharmacy technicians report through their respective departments and also to the head nurse in a matrix relationship, and they are incorporated in the organizational structure of the unit as illustrated in Figure 2-2.

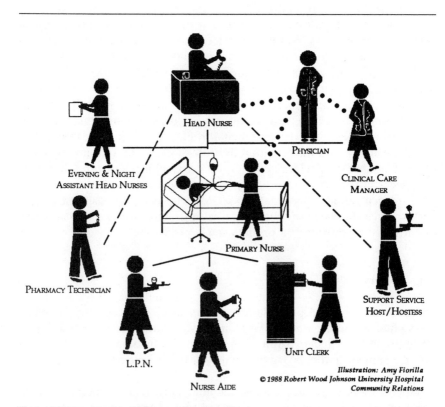

HEAD NURSE

PHYSICIAN

EVENING & NIGHT
ASSISTANT HEAD NURSES

CLINICAL CARE
MANAGER

PRIMARY NURSE

PHARMACY TECHNICIAN

SUPPORT SERVICE
HOST/HOSTESS

UNIT CLERK

L.P.N.

NURSE AIDE

Illustration: Amy Fiorilla
© 1988 Robert Wood Johnson University Hospital
Community Relations

Figure 2-2 Organization of Support Services

Staffing Patterns

The staffing pattern used before implementation of the model was significantly more RN-intensive, with RNs and LPNs providing total patient care to groups of patients. NAs gave little direct care, such as assisting with bathing and ambulating patients, and were instead assigned to distribute linen and water, take TPRs, and answer patients' lights. The revised plan includes the same number of licensed nursing personnel but the mix is less RN-intensive. This plan is based on the provision that NAs would be taught to take blood pressures and would increase their skills in areas such as assisting with physical therapy activities. The staffing standards provide for primary nurse caseloads of five primary patients for each RN on the 7–3 shift, four primary patients for each RN on the 3–11 shift, and two primary patients for each RN on the 11–7 shift. Assistant head nurses working evenings and nights are included in the complement of primary nurses. There are three CCM positions in the staffing pattern for the model.

Cost

The ProACT® Model significantly reduced the number of RNs required to staff the pilot unit. This reduction in RNs was compensated for by changes in role responsibilities, an increase in the number of LPNs and NAs, and a higher level of support services.

Despite an increased number of FTEs required for the ProACT® Model, the salary cost for the new FTEs is approximately equal to the cost of the FTEs that had been budgeted for the pilot unit prior to implementation of the model (based on a comparative analysis using current salaries for each classification). This is due to the change in the staff mix within the revised staffing patterns. Because the new staffing format includes more positions for employees more available than RNs, implementation of the ProACT® Model is more realistic than continuing to try to work with a staffing plan that is highly RN-intensive.

The fact that the budget for the ProACT® Model is approximately equal to the pilot unit's prior budget is not an accident. Equal cost was a deliberate goal, because it is very difficult to gain acceptance for a model that is significantly more expensive. Although the salary costs are planned to be budget neutral, it is anticipated that the model may result in cost savings due to the role of clinical care managers in controlling hospital resource utilization and maximizing reimbursement.

Another advantage of this model is its potential to raise salaries for a smaller workforce of nurses. As salaries continue to improve, RN-intensive staffing will become increasingly less affordable. The health care system will be able to support fewer highly paid nurses and their roles will have to be changed to make maximum use of this scarce and valuable resource.

ProACT® also includes several additional important incentives other than salary. Unlike many clinical ladder programs, which offer small pay differentials for minimally different performance expectations, this model creates a significantly different role to which the staff nurse can aspire. The rewards include new challenges and an attractive schedule as well as a higher salary.

DEVELOPMENT OF ProACT®

Recognizing the need for nursing-initiated solutions to the nursing short-age and the opportunities inherent in the situation, the leadership of the Robert Wood Johnson University Hospital Nursing Division made the decision to develop an alternative nursing practice model in late 1986. The Alternative Practice Model Task Force was organized in February 1987 with the objective of developing a model that would enable a reduced number of professional nurses to deliver nursing care within existing standards for quality while providing attractive and satisfying roles for the staff involved and at a cost not exceeding the current budget levels.

The task force was chaired by the vice president of Nursing, and the initial members were volunteers from within the nursing division. The group met every other week to formulate and accelerate the development process, and they quickly identified the six key issues to be addressed:

1. scope of practice
2. titles, education, and licensure
3. organizational structure
4. support services
5. staffing standards
6. cost

After several months of work, the first three topics were covered, and it was necessary to select a pilot unit before progressing to the development of staffing patterns and new support systems. It is essential to know the type and number of patients requiring care before staffing patterns and support systems can be designed.

The unit selected to pilot the model was Seven Tower, which is a 32-bed acute orthopedic unit with an average daily census of 30 patients. The top three DRGs are total hip replacements, total knee replacements, and back procedures, including laminectomies and spinal fusions. The patient rooms on this unit form three sides of a rectangle surrounding a central nurses' station and support facilities area, with the open side leading to a central elevator bank. A satellite physical therapy facility is also located on the unit.

This unit was selected for a number of reasons:

- The unit had a stable history of management, staffing, morale, quality patient care, and medical leadership.
- The head nurse was an experienced and capable manager and was enthusiastic about the project.
- Because of its specialization, a limited and stable group of physicians, headed by a strong chief of orthopedics, admitted to the unit.
- Despite the tertiary nature of the procedures performed, the patients on the unit had many prescribed and routine care needs that could potentially be met by staff other than RNs.
- The unit was beginning to experience problems with maintaining a full complement of RNs, thus creating difficult-to-fill vacancies that could be used to fund other types of positions.

When it was time to discuss support service systems, a subgroup was formed to look at the activities on Seven Tower, talk with representatives of ancillary departments, and recommend which departments to include. The task force ultimately decided to work with two major departments: support services (including housekeeping, dietary, and stores) and the pharmacy. Representatives of these departments then joined the task force to develop plans for the provision of expanded services at the unit level.

It was at this point that the tremendous institutional support for the project first became evident. One of the essential requirements for the successful development and implementation of this type of model is the willingness and desire on the part of other departments to move beyond traditional job descriptions and systems to find new ways to support patient care and the nursing staff. This service philosophy and cooperative spirit is overwhelmingly evident at Robert Wood Johnson University Hospital, making it an ideal environment for innovation in the delivery of patient care.

The nursing and ancillary department members of the task force worked together to develop a full set of recommendations for an alternative practice model. The outcome of the task force was the creation of ProACT™, the Professionally Advanced Care Team Model. The proposal for the model was approved for implementation in March 1988.

IMPLEMENTATION OF ProACT™

After the recommendations of the task force had been fully developed and accepted by senior management, the membership was changed to prepare for implementation. Several members of the original development group opted not to continue their participation, and a number of new members joined the task force or became involved in the project to help address the issues specifically related to implementation. The new members and the rationales for their inclusion were as follows:

1. the senior vice president of Human Resources: to offer advice and counsel regarding personnel issues
2. the psychiatric clinical specialist: to provide support for staff in managing change
3. the director of Management Systems: to assist with collection and analysis of pre- and postimplementation data
4. medical and surgical clinical specialists: to assist in the development of clinical protocols and tools and in the orientation of staff
5. the cardiovascular clinical coordinator: to help operationalize the clinical care manager role and participate in the orientation of clinical care managers
6. the administrative director of support services: to implement the support services component of the model

The reorganized task force began to meet in March 1988 to plan for implementation of the model. One of the first tasks was selection of a target date: June 6, 1988. Another important task was the development of an evaluation plan for each component of the model. The three departments directly participating in the model each developed a plan for evaluating its own services before and after implementation.

The plan for evaluating the nursing component of the model was developed by the director of Nursing Systems and includes collection and analysis of the following data both before and after model implementation:

1. average daily acuity
2. average nursing care hours provided per patient day
3. average labor costs per patient day
4. average nonsalary costs per patient day
5. average patient satisfaction scores
6. average RN and LPN job satisfaction scores
7. average number of nursing care plans completed, nursing diagnoses per patient, and nursing care plans completed within 24 hours of admission

8. number of nursing-related incidents per patient day
9. number of nursing-related infections per patient day
10. quality assurance scores
11. average length of stay of patients discharged from unit
12. average revenue generated per month
13. turnover rate
14. sick time use
15. work sampling

These data are being used to conduct a thorough evaluation of the effects of the model on cost of care, quality of care, and other important variables.

The remaining work of the task force fell into two main categories: (1) developing policies, procedures, and tools for operation of the model and (2) selecting staff and preparing all parties who would be involved in implementation. Each department formed a subcommittee to develop the structure for the implementation of its own piece of the model. The nursing subcommittee focused on the following major implementation activities:

1. recruitment, selection and orientation of the clinical care managers
2. recruitment of additional LPNs based on new staffing plan
3. development of operational guidelines for the pilot unit
4. development of clinical care protocols for the top three DRGs
5. development of an orientation program for all pilot unit nursing staff
6. development of a preadmission history and potential problem form for clinical care managers

The task force worked together to plan a series of programs to inform and prepare everyone who would either directly participate or be affected by implementation. This work fell into three main categories: preparing the staff, preparing the physicians, and preparing the institution.

Preparing the Staff

Preparation of the pilot unit nursing staff began with informal discussions with the head nurse as the model was being developed. The first formal step was a series of meetings attended by the vice president of Nursing, the director of Medical/Surgical Nursing, the head nurse, the psychiatric clinical specialist, and the staff on each shift. The purpose of these meetings was to explain the model and answer questions. Because of existing RN vacancies at this time, it was not necessary to transfer any current staff members off the unit, and an important purpose of these meetings was to stress that there was a place for everyone in the model. A written handout was distributed and served as a basis for further staff discussions with the head nurse and the psychiatric clinical specialist following the meetings.

The second important step in preparing the staff was orientation. The clinical care managers participated in a 3-week orientation program organized by the director of Nursing Education and Development. This program included content on clinical and management issues and an introduction to the roles of the clinical care managers and of key staff members with whom they would interact throughout the hospital. The clinical care managers were especially fascinated by the information about the financial aspects of patient management presented by senior members of the finance division. The cooperation of numerous staff and departments in the orientation reflected the degree of institutional support for the project.

Shortly before the pilot began, orientation classes were held for the RNs, LPNs, NAs, and unit clerks. The purpose of each class was to review the model and focus on specific role changes and expectations for each group.

The final step in preparing the staff was a brief program, followed by social time on the Friday before the model was implemented. At this meeting the importance of each group's contributions and the concept of teamwork were stressed. Each member of the staff was introduced, and the groups mingled and got to know each other better over refreshments.

Preparing the Physicians

Physician preparation began with a meeting with the chief of Orthopedics. The vice president of Nursing and the head nurse met with the chief to explain the goals of the model, review an executive summary of the proposal, and solicit his feedback, questions, and support.

At the chairperson's invitation, the vice president of Nursing subsequently presented the model at a Department of Orthopedics monthly meeting that included the attending and resident staffs. She introduced the clinical care managers to the group, answered questions, and asked for their support. The chairperson was very positive about the model at this meeting, and his and the other physicians' support has been a key factor in successful implementation.

Preparing the Institution

The model was introduced to the entire institution in a variety of ways. Many people were exposed to the model through their participation in development activities. For example, the director of Medical/Surgical

Nursing included representatives from a number of departments, including Social Services, Physical Therapy, Utilization Review, and Home Care, in the development of the clinical care protocols.

The model was also formally presented and discussed at the meetings of numerous different groups, including the Professional Affairs Committee of the Board of Trustees, administrative staff, department heads, the nursing leadership, assistant head nurses, and staff nurses.

PRELIMINARY RESULTS

Reactions to the model from patients, staff, and physicians have been very positive. The clinical care managers bring patients from preadmissions testing to the unit, give them a tour, and serve cheese and crackers during preadmission interviews. They report that patients enjoy this contact with nurses prior to admission and also respond very favorably to being called after discharge. Patients form a strong relationship with their clinical care managers and see them as advocates who actively coordinate multiple services to help the patients meet their goals. A family member who is a nurse stated that the clinical care managers were articulate, highly professional, and made her proud to be a nurse.

The nursing staff are very pleased with the assistance they are receiving from pharmacy and support services staff and report that this support is especially critical on weekends. The clinical care managers and primary nurses are working well together. The clinical care managers have relieved the nursing staff of many follow-up calls to other departments and also support them by assisting with admission assessments and care plans when needed.

Although the clinical care managers at first sometimes felt overwhelmed by the magnitude of the role change, they now enjoy their jobs. They state that they feel they are making a difference in patient care and length of stay by having time to keep track of what needs to be done and aggressively following up with other departments.

Although it is not surprising that the nursing staff are happy to receive additional help, it is interesting to find that the pharmacy technicians and support service hosts also enjoy providing this assistance. These employees report that they enjoy the diversity and challenge of their new responsibilities, feel that their work is needed and appreciated, and like being part of a team that interacts closely with patients to provide high-quality care.

Finally, physician response to the model has been quite positive. Physicians have noted a number of benefits to their patients and themselves, including: (1) better preparation of patients for hospitalization through preadmission contact with nursing; (2) increased nurse-physician collaboration; and (3) improved support services for patients and staff. Both attending and resident physicians see the CCMs as problem solvers. Residents appreciate the coordination of communication that results from sharing the same caseload of patients with a CCM. Medical attendings also find it helpful to work with the CCM as a contact person on a surgical unit and have indicated they would welcome calls for information prior to their patients' admission.

Analysis of the first set of quantitative data collected before and after implementation indicates that the model has the potential to improve quality, hold costs constant, reduce length of stay, and increase revenue. Specifically, quality scores were significantly increased, RN and LPN job satisfaction increased 10%, and length of stay for targeted DRGs decreased 9%.

CONCLUSION

Due to a combination of factors, hospitals throughout the country are facing a serious nursing shortage. One solution may lie in the creation of a new nursing practice model that would allow fewer RNs to provide high-quality care for today's patients. The Professionally Advanced Care Team Model has been developed for this purpose. ProACT™ builds on the goals of the profession to create a logical career path that preserves the primary nurse position and leads to another attractive, expanded nursing role for the future.

REFERENCES

Aiken, L.H., & Mullinix, C.F. (1987). The nursing shortage: Myth or reality? *New England Journal of Medicine, 317,* 641–646.

American Hospital Association. (1988). *1987 winter demand survey report.* Chicago: Author.

Carlsen, A. (1988, May 23). Nurses seek bigger support staffs to ease nursing shortage. *Health Week,* 15.

Cooperative Institutional Research Forum. (1987). *The American freshman: Twenty year trends.* Los Angeles: UCLA, Higher Education Research Institute.

Curran, C.R., Minnick, A., & Moss, J. (1987). Who needs nurses? *American Journal of Nursing, 87,* 444–447.

Department of Health and Human Services. (1986). *The registered nurse population, 1984* (DHHS Publication No. HRP 0906938). Springfield, VA: National Technical Information Service.

Klass, P. (1988, April 10). Are women better doctors? *The New York Times Magazine,* 32–35, 46–48, 96–97.

Manthey, M. (1988). Myths that threaten. *Nursing Management 19,* 54–55.

Miller, N. (1987). *The nursing shortage: Facts, figures, and feelings.* Chicago: American Hospital Association.

National League for Nursing. (1986). *Nursing data review, 1985.* New York: Author.

National survey of hospital and medical school salaries. (1987). Galveston, TX: University of Texas Medical Branch at Galveston.

Primm, P.L. (1988, September). *Differentiated practice: Implications for the nurse executive.* Paper presented at 20th Annual Meeting of the American Organization of Nurse Executives, Anaheim, CA.

Securing the future. (1986). *American Journal of Nursing, 86,* 832–836.

Survey shows enrollment decline is leveling off. *The American Nurse, 24,* 1989.

Weisman, C.S. (1982). Recruit from within: Hospital nurse retention in the 1980's. *The Journal of Nursing Administration 12*(5), 24–31.

Will, G.F. (1988, May 23). The dignity of nursing. *Newsweek,* 80.

Woldum, K. (1987). Critical paths: Marking the course. *Definition* [New England Medical Center, Center for Nursing Case Management], *2*(3), 1–4.

Chapter 3

Managed Care and Nursing Case Management

Karen Zander

The author describes both managed care and nursing case management and shows how these systems can be applied effectively in the acute care setting. The six components of managed care are detailed, as are the four components of nursing case management. The description of the implementation process is quite thorough and the author provides a 3-day educational outline for the concept. However, although cost of implementation is not low, the results are cost effective and it depends primarily on the internal resources of a nursing department and the extent of institutional commitment to the transition.

GOALS

Nursing case management, with its foundation of *managed care,* is a clinical system for the strategic management of cost and quality outcomes. A clinical system structures the way work is organized and processed. Thus, a clinical system has implications for the assignment of direct care responsibilities, but those implications are dependent on many factors.

Generically, case management is "a system of health assessment, planning, service procurement/delivery/coordination and monitoring to meet the multiple needs of clients" (Fuszard et al., 1988, p. 1). Although this definition is very similar to the definition of the nursing process, nursing aims to meet the multiple needs of patients in multiple settings with multiple caregivers and with fewer resources than in previous decades. With the onset of DRGs and other reimbursement and contract arrangements, nursing has to aim steadfastly for specific goals that sustain standards of high-quality clinical care, yet remain prepared to adapt to the constant changes in the industry. The realistic goals of managed care and nursing case management encompass these changes while maintaining the right of nursing

---

*Reprinted with permission from K. Zander, "Nursing Group Practice: 'The Cadillac' in Continuity," *Definition,* 3(2), 1–3.

to pursue its "destiny" as a profession (Stetler, 1988). These goals include the following:

- the achievement of expected or standardized patient outcomes
- early discharge of patients or discharge within appropriate lengths of stay
- appropriate or reduced utilization of resources
- collaborative practice and coordination and continuity of care
- professional development and personal satisfaction on the job
- encouragement of contributions by all care providers to the achievement of patient outcomes

Put another way, managed care and case management provide patients and their families with a collaborative plan based on standards of care, yet individualized by groups of clinicians who have expertise in their "case types." Continuity of care is accomplished by managed care. Continuity of providers across an entire hospital is achieved through group practices that provide case management.

COMPONENTS

To accomplish the stated goals, there must be powerful interlocking components, first in managed care and then in the larger model of nursing case management. Managed care is a unit-based clinical system that is applied to all inpatients and outpatients at New England Medical Center Hospitals. It has six components that affect tools and communication systems. Nursing case management builds on these unit-based systems and adds four additional components that affect roles, relationships, and institutionwide functioning. It is currently applied to patients in about 30 case types, involving an average of one physician and three RNs per group. The components of managed care and case management are shown in Figure 3-1 and described below.

The six components of managed care are as follows:

1. *standard critical paths,* which are used as adjuncts to care plans
2. *critical paths,* which are used as bases for change-of-shift reports
3. *analysis of positive and negative variances* from the critical path
4. *timely case consultation* for the caregiver "inheriting" a complex patient care situation
5. *health care team meetings* initiated, conducted, and followed up by nursing

Physician Involvement

Components

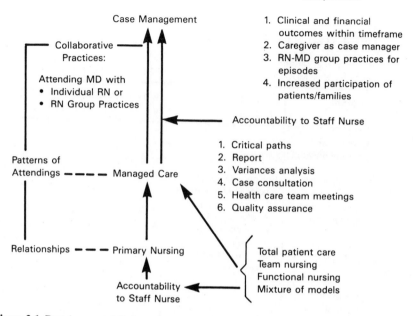

Case Management

1. Clinical and financial outcomes within timeframe
2. Caregiver as case manager
3. RN-MD group practices for episodes
4. Increased participation of patients/families

Collaborative
Practices:

Attending MD with
• Individual RN or
• RN Group Practices

Accountability to Staff Nurse

1. Critical paths
2. Report
3. Variances analysis
4. Case consultation
5. Health care team meetings
6. Quality assurance

Patterns of
Attendings ▬ ▬ ▬ Managed Care

Relationships ▬ ▬ ▬ Primary Nursing

Total patient care
Team nursing
Functional nursing
Mixture of models

Accountability
to Staff Nurse

Figure 3-1 Developmental Pathway to Case Management in Acute Care

Source: Copyright © Karen Zander, Department of Nursing, New England Medical Center Hospitals, 1989.

6. *variances aggregated, analyzed, and addressed* by the unit's nurse manager

At the core of managed care are critical paths, which are essentially project management tools based on standards of care for a case type or its subset. The standards of care, called *case management plans,* are detailed documents that highlight the nursing diagnoses, clinical outcomes for each diagnosis that are achievable within the DRG-allotted length of stay, intermediate goals and estimated dates for each outcome, and nursing and physician interventions that facilitate movement toward each goal. An excerpt from a case management plan is shown in Exhibit 3-1. Its corollary critical path is shown in Exhibit 3-2.

Critical paths are shorthand versions of case management plans. At present, preprinted case management plans replace the nursing care plan, and standardized critical paths are used in the kardex, bedside, or medication book for reports, nurse-physician rounds, and case consultation.

Exhibit 3-1 Sample Case Management Plan

NEW ENGLAND MEDICAL CENTER HOSPITALS
DEPARTMENT OF NURSING

DIAGNOSIS: Stroke

DRG: 14   MDC: 1   LENGTH OF STAY: 7 weeks

Problem	Outcome (The patient...)	Week Vst	Intermediate Goal (The patient...)
Potential for complications/self care: 1) Inappropriate medication administration and/or side effects Risk Factors: • Lack of knowledge • Lack of skill	For participants in self medication program: • And/or significant other accurately and independently administers own medications.	4 6 7	• Accurately states the prescribed medication regimen and its rationale. • States medication, action dose, frequency and side effects for each discharge medication. • Completes medication teaching plan.
	All other patients: • States rationale for prescribed treatment. • Accurately states the prescribed medication regimen: (i.e., action dose, frequency and side effects for each discharge medication).	4 - 7	• And/or significant other participates in medication teaching.
2) Injury Risk Factors: • Sensory deficits • Altered mobility • Lack of knowledge • Environmental condition	• Does not experience preventable bodily harm.	1 - 7 5 - 7 7	• Actively participates in rehab program in anticipation of pass and eventual discharge. • Completes pass evaluation form. • States community services which will be utilized post discharge.

Source: Excerpted from Case Management Plans: Designs for Transformation by C. Stetler and A.D. DeZell, 1987, Boston: New England Medical Center Hospitals.

UNIT: Rehabilitation

Week Vst	Process (The nurse...)	Week Vst	Process (The physician...)
2 - 3	• Initiates medication teaching plan. • Reviews this with family. • Provides medication cards to patient/family.	4	• Stabilizes medication regimen. Weans any unnecessary meds.
4 - 7	• Reinforces content of medication teaching plan with patient/family.	4	• Orders self meds if patient is a candidate for self med program.
1	• Assesses patient as a candidate for self meds. • Follows policy on self meds.		
4	• Initiates teaching of discharge meds to patient/significant other.		
4	• Provides medication cards to patient/significant other.		
4 - 7	• Reinforces medication teaching.		
7	• Arranges appropriate follow up with community resources for Coumadin.		
2	• Collaborates with team to identify discharge date.		
2	• Collaborates with patient to identify disposition and potential enviornmental barriers.		
4	• Prepares patient for day pass.		
5	• Prepares patient/family for weekend pass.		
5	• Reviews pass evaluation form and intervenes to resolve any problems.		

Exhibit 3-2 Sample Critical Path

NEW ENGLAND MEDICAL CENTER HOSPITALS
DEPARTMENT OF NURSING

EMBOLIC STROKE CRITICAL PATH

Patient _____
MD _____
Case Manager _____
Date Critical Path Reviewed by MD _____
Date _____

Case Type _____
DRG _____
Expected LOS _____

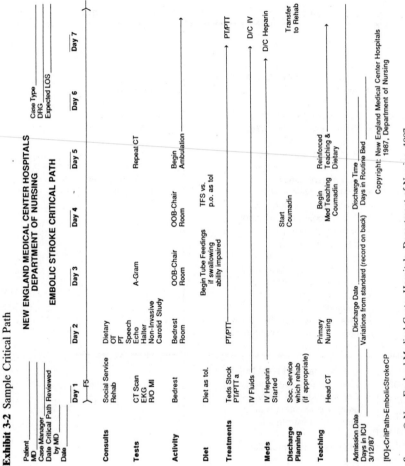

	Day 1	Day 2	Day 3	Day 4	Day 5	Day 6	Day 7
Consults	Social Service Rehab	Dietary OT PT Speech					
Tests	CT Scan EKG R/O MI	Echo Halter Non-Invasive Carotid Study	A-Gram		Repeat CT		
Activity	Bedrest	Bedrest Room	OOB-Chair Room	OOB-Chair Room	Begin Ambulation ——→		
Diet	Diet as tol.		Begin Tube Feedings if swallowing ability impaired	TFS vs. p.o. as tol			
Treatments	Teds Stock PT/PTT a	PT/PTT —————————————————————→					PT/PTT
	IV Fluids ——————————————————————→						D/C IV
Meds	IV Heparin Started ————————————————————→			Start Coumadin			D/C Heparin
Discharge Planning	Soc. Service which rehab (if appropriate)	Primary Nursing					Transfer to Rehab
Teaching	Head CT			Begin Med Teaching Coumadin	Reinforced Teaching & Dietary ——→		

Admission Date _____   Discharge Date _____   Discharge Time _____
Days in ICU _____   Variations from standard (record on back)   Days in Routine Bed _____
3/12/87

[IO]<CritPath>EmbolicStrokeCP

Copyright: © New England Medical Center Hospitals
1987, Department of Nursing

Source: © New England Medical Center Hospitals, Department of Nursing, 1987.

Not only do they assist each caregiver each shift in placing the patient in a context, they provide clear guidelines to full- and part-time, and temporary staff and serve as excellent orientation tools.

Individualizing, for each patient, the standard pattern of care indicated in a critical path occurs after the initial assessment. Even multisystem patients benefit from critical paths that relate to their central reason for admission. When the condition of a patient changes (e.g., if a surgical patient has a myocardial infarction) or the length of stay is extended, a new, more specific (often entirely nursing-related) critical path is devised. The action of formulating a critical path (e.g., Failure to Wean) speaks to the prevalent but underresearched phenomenon of relative chronicity in acute care settings. However, even with major variances, critical paths convert the passivity often seen with complicated clinical and psychosocial situations into hopeful activity.

Critical paths become part of practice when they are easily accessible and when they are included in shift reports. Using them as a basis for reports is probably the single most dramatic change in the way nursing staff communicates its values and workload around the clock. Whether the reports are in person or taped, using shift sheets, such as the one shown in Exhibit 3-3, can greatly enhance continuity of information and the on-coming caregivers' ability to "zero in" on their assignments.

Variance analysis is another term for ongoing evaluation of care. Variances are written on a log on the back of the critical path and generally fall into three categories: system (e.g., CAT scan breakdown), clinician (e.g., teaching not initiated), and patient/family (e.g., refuse nursing home placement). When noted, the cause (if known) and corrective action are written in the log and reported at the change of shift. Patient/family variances are also documented in progress notes in the medical record. Analysis of variances every shift puts action-oriented quality assurance in the hands of the staff RN. Problems cannot so readily be passed on and on without resolution. Progress notes regarding patient/family variances are enhanced due to the continuous comprehensive evaluation of care. Other than the variances created by clinicians and larger hospital systems, when a patient is at variance with a critical path, it indicates that his or her clinical condition is changing.

Case consultation, the fourth component of managed care, is helpful when the same variances are reported but nothing is changing. In this situation, the nurse manager or charge nurse will suggest that a brief (10–15 minute) consultation be held immediately following the report or at a designated time during that shift. Thus, the mode of active problem solving is maintained.

At times, the most appropriate advice given the current caregiver during consultation is to pull together a meeting of the key clinicians involved

Exhibit 3-3 Sample Intershift Report and Shift Sheet

Figure 1
Script for Intershift Report

Mr. _____ , a _____ year old patient of Dr. _____

with _____ , DRG # _____ , is on Day # _____ of a _____

Length Of Stay. Past medical/surgical history _____ , Critical Path update

_____ , variances and actions taken _____ .

Figure 2
Managed Care Shift Sheet

RM #	Patient Age	Serv-ice	Diagnosis Surgery	DRG	PT DAY # / LOS	PMH* PSH	VITAL SIGNS	I & O / IV	MEDS	CRITICAL EVENTS	VARI-ANCES	OTHER**
771D	Murphy 12	Ortho	Osteotomy Add Releases	212	7 / 7	Anoxia Sz g tube	VSS	I Isomil O OK IV O	tyl x 1 Fe So4 Colace	turn q 4	N.H. Placement Mon.	Referrals done SPICA TURN CSM COOL
771W	Shepard 16	Heme Onc	Chemo	410	1 / 1	Osteo Sarcoma Appe	VSS RR 14-20	I NPO O OK 1.014 IV D5 1/2NS @ 150	Vincristine Cytoxin Anti-emetics	D/C ☐ D/C Anti RT ☐11A		Lab urine VOM x 2 Sleepy Mom here
773D	Jones 4	Card	VSD Repair	108	3 / 6	VSD / URI	5↓3 ® 39▼38 AP 116-124 RR 24-32 BP 100-108/P	I 120 O 240 IV H.L.	tylenol Oxa Genta	CXR ☐ CBC CPT Q 4	Antibiotics x 2 wks	Wt ↓7kg BS clear Dysuria heme ⊖

Copyright NEMCH 1988
Christine Price RN, BSN

* PMH = Past Medical History
PSH = Past Surgical History
** Other = Includes psychosocial issues

Source: Chart developed by Christine Price, 1988. From "Why Managed Care Works," 1988, *Definition*, 3(4). Copyright 1988 by New England Medical Center Hospitals. Reprinted by permission.

with the patient and family of concern. Health care team meetings, then, constitute the fifth component of managed care. Although not necessary for all patients, health care team meetings are crucial for the resolution of patient problems that in some way confound the larger system. Often, when such problems are defined at first glimmer, they do not create compound problems in case management down the road.

Quality assurance via the attention of unit managers to patterns of variance is the sixth component of managed care. Through this method, the fund of clinical knowledge about groups of patients is increased, and new interventions and programs can be instituted. Rather than a retrospective quality review, managed care monitoring is concurrent and the feedback loop is shorter.

Managed care may be used in any care delivery system to improve productivity, management of care, and nurses' sense of control. It involves all staff in outcome-oriented patient care, and when used with primary nursing, it tangibly extends the primary nurse's authority around the clock. Without managed care, any case management model will lack ultimate effectiveness, because the actual caregivers will not be influenced.

Nursing case management relies on the unit-based systems of managed care but goes one step further to identify the specific nurses and physicians who will be accountable for the financial and clinical outcomes of designated patients. The four components are as follows:

1. accountability for the clinical and financial outcomes of patients' entire episodes of care
2. the use of caregiver (staff primary nurse) as case manager
3. formal RN-MD group practices
4. increased patient and family participation in and control of health care

The first component, accountability for outcomes, is achieved at the staff nurse level through a combination of primary nursing, managed care, and formal group practice. Rather than add a layer of "checker-uppers" to an already overly layered acute care setting, the better alternative—and the principle of this model—is to use those providing direct clinical care as case managers.

Paramount to the nursing case management model is the use of caregiver as case manager (except for training or volume-overload situations). This component differentiates the model of New England Medical Center Hospitals from others in which the case manager may be a nurse but is not involved in the direct care of the patients being managed. *Nursing case management results in ultimate decentralization inasmuch as it delegates accountability for clinical and financial outcomes to specific staff nurses.* To accomplish this, the staff nurse, as case manager, is placed in a case-based matrix at the patient care level (see Figure 3-2). The staff nurse works with certain physicians individually or as a member of a multiunit group of primary nurses. The case manager is both a member of a unit-based staff and a member of the group practice.

As in other matrix organizations, a "matrix demands new behavior, attitudes, skills, and knowledge," because people are expected to function in new ways (Davis & Lawrence, 1977, p. 103). In essence, a matrix creates new interdependencies that necessitate new communication patterns within the institution. Of course, in health care the interdependencies have always existed, but rarely have they been given formal structures. Case management creates a structure and requires a commitment to the strategic management of cost and quality outcomes. Understanding case management as a formal patient-centered matrix within the institutional setting can be helpful in implementing this model (Zander & Etheredge, 1989).

The fourth component encompasses new methods for actively involving patients and their families in every phase of care. This includes pre- and posthospitalization phone calls, giving patients copies of their critical paths, using patient portfolios, including patients (when indicated) in team meetings, negotiating meaningful outcomes and discharge plans, and involving them in audits of their responses to interventions. To achieve the full potential of this fourth component, there needs to be increased understanding of what being ill means to patients and how they experience being healed.

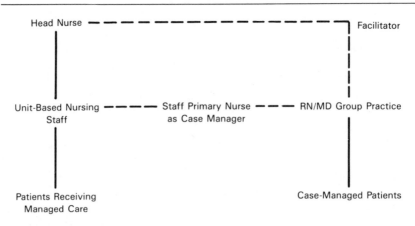

Figure 3-2 Patient Care Level Matrix

All components put together result in a structure. The ground rules for case management and the role description of the case manager are presented in Exhibits 3-4 and 3-5.

UNDERLYING ASSUMPTIONS

There are numerous assumptions, derived from 20 years of observing many models, on which managed care and case management are built. The chief assumptions are that (1) nursing is a business with products rather than a service; (2) individual staff nurses in the role of primary nurse or

---

Exhibit 3-4 Ground Rules for Case Management

1. Every designated patient will be admitted to a formally prepared group practice composed of an attending physician and staff nurses from each of the units and clinics likely to receive the patient.
2. Each nurse in the group practice will give direct care as the patient's primary or associate nurse while the patient is on his/her geographic unit.
3. Every group practice will assign one of its nursing members to be the case manager who works with the attending physician in evaluating an individualized case management plan (CMP) and critical path for each patient.
4. A critical path for the whole episode of care will be used to manage the care of every designated patient, both at change-of-shift report and during group practice meetings.
5. The nurses in the group practice will meet on a weekly basis at a consistent time and place and maintain a patient roster.
6. Each nurse member of the group practice will communicate immediate patient care issues with the attending physician while the patient is on his/her own unit. The assigned case manager will work through the group and the attending physician for nonemergent issues.
7. Negative variances from critical paths and/or CMPs require discussion with the attending physician and possibly a case management consultation.
8. The group practice will meet to discuss care patterns, policies, specific patients and variances, research questions and updated knowledge at their own predetermined intervals, e.g., monthly, bimonthly. Minutes will be taken for reference by members who cannot attend.
9. Nurse members of the group practice will negotiate a flexible schedule that accommodates the needs of their case-managed patients and collaborative practices *as well as* the needs of their units.
10. Responsibility of the case manager begins at notification of patient's entry into the system and ends with a formal transfer of accountability to the patient, family, another health care provider, or another institution.

Source: Copyright © Karen Zander, Department of Nursing, New England Medical Center Hospitals, 1988.

case manager should be held accountable for the products of nursing, which consist of individualized sets of clinical outcomes for patients in their caseload; and (3) to achieve these outcomes, nurses need to use all steps of the nursing process in a continuous loop of assessment, goal setting, initiative, skilled intervention (including collaboration with physicians), follow through, and active evaluation.

Exhibit 3-5 Role Description for Case Manager

1. Establishes a mechanism for notification when a new patient enters the caseload (this includes determining which patients he or she will case manage).
2. Introduces self to the patient or family and explains the role of case manager and group practice.
3. Gives patient and family the group practice card.
4. Contacts physician(s) to begin sharing assessments, goals, and plans for the patient's episode of illness.
5. Knows the anticipated diagnosis-related group (DRG), length of stay, and transfer or discharge dates.
6. Discusses ongoing and future care with the other nursing staff on units (inpatient and ambulatory) to which the patient will most likely be transferred.
7. Negotiates work schedule with the nurse manager to attend weekly group practice meetings.
8. Compares the standard case management plan against the patient's individual needs in such areas as social and economic data, family resources, functional abilities, knowledge needs, potential risk factors and complications, and special issues.
9. Identifies a critical path for the patient and places it in the nursing kardex.
10. Reviews and revises the individual critical path with the physician(s) within 24 hours of admission.
11. Contacts other key members of the patient's team (e.g., the social worker, dietitian, physical therapist, community resources personnel, and others, as needed).
12. Gives and monitors the delivery of care and the patient's responses to care every day that the patient is on the case manager's unit.
13. Arranges for continuity of plan and provides coverage during short, long, and unexpected absences.
14. Gives the patient and family a time schedule and tells them who to contact during the case manager's absence.
15. Documents the achievement of intermediate goals and clinical outcomes as they occur.
16. Integrates case management information and revised interventions (processes) into intershift report and group practice meetings.
17. Requests consultation and feedback before a crisis occurs.
18. Plans, participates in, and follows through with health care team meetings, as needed.
19. Manages the patient's transitions through the system and transfers accountability to the appropriate person or agency upon discharge.
20. Completes a follow-up evaluation.

After 12 years of solid primary nursing, with audits conducted every 4 months with every staff nurse concerning his or her charts, patients, and managers, there were still weak areas in the accomplishment of patient-family outcomes. For example, nursing care plans alone were inadequate to provide continuity, especially when patients progressed between several inpatient units as well as ambulatory clinics. In addition, the authority base of a staff nurse in the complex acute care setting was not structured as firmly as needed to help the nurse truly make the system work for patients, families, and physicians. Physicians and nurses functioned in parallel rather than in formal collaborative groups, and shared outcomes were not a conscious aspect of practice.

Managed care can be used with any care assignment method, but it is especially useful in strengthening coordination and continuity of primary nursing around the clock. Case management provides patients and families with physicians and nurses who perceive themselves as members of a team that work together from patients' entries to exits. *To use either managed care or case management, nurses must stop assuming that other groups know better what to do for patient care and that other groups do more important work.* Nurses must seek out accountability rather than shun it out of fear of an increased workload or increased frustration.

IMPLEMENTATION

The Nurse Manager's Role

As in all other systems that require behavior changes among nursing staff, the role of the nurse manager (head nurse) is of ultimate importance. Managed care and case management will not work unless the nurse managers understand the models and support their use 24 hours a day.

Nurse Managers need to develop the initial case management plans and critical paths with key physicians. They also need formal coaching as they discover answers to the following questions:

1. Design Process
   - What is the nursing product?
   - What is the current nursing production process?
   - What is the time line associated with the production process?
   - What are the factors that influence length of stay and resource utilization?

- What revisions can be made to the production process that will lower length of stay and cost while achieving satisfactory patient outcomes?
- How can those revisions be implemented?

2. Managed Care Implementation
   - How can I revise shift reports and shift sheets, making sure each staff member is oriented to managed care?
   - What do the staff need to know about variance analysis and how do I expect them to act on variances?
   - What is the best time for case consultation and how do I make sure it occurs and is helpful?
   - Which skills does each nurse need (see Exhibit 3-6) and who will teach them?

Exhibit 3-6 Managed Care Skills Checklist

Assessment, Case-Specific
  Initial
  Ongoing
Use of Critical Paths
Outcome Identification
Variance Identification
Variance Analysis
Identification of Goals for Shift
Focus Care toward Shift Goals and Outcomes
Prediction of Patient Needs beyond the Immediate Shift
Follow-up
Documentation of
  Progress toward outcomes
  Variance identified
Identification of Issues for Case Consultation
Collaboration with
  Physicians
  Other health care team members
Identification of Patients'
  Discharge needs
  Resources (including payer benefits)
Negotiation
Communication
  Use of report for managed care
Running a Health Care Team Meeting

Source: Copyright © K. Bower, Center for Nursing Case Management, New England Medical Center Hospitals, 1988.

- How can I help each RN identify the need for and conduct health care team meetings?
- What actions are expected by the nursing department in response to the variances I aggregate?

3. Case Management Implementation
    - Which case types and physicians could most benefit from case management?
    - Which other units and nurses would be involved in specific group practices?
    - How do I educate myself and the staff about case management?
    - When do I approach the physicians about their involvement?
    - How can I facilitate the group practice's operations and development?
    - What are the supports and resources available to me as we continue to implement case management?
    - How do I assist in resolving "system" and "clinician" variances?
    - What can I do to give genuine and consistent support to the staff nurses from my unit who are in group practices?

Staffing

The staffing ratio for managed care can be any ratio deemed adequate for providing humane care. Staffing for case management should resemble that for primary nursing, which means a caseload of 2–6 patients for each full-time (32–40 hours per week) RN. Thus, if a unit handled 28 patients, a budget for 7 day and evening RNs, 2 night RNs, and 6 LPNs or aides would be adequate for case management, because each RN (not including permanent nights) would have an average caseload of 4 patients at all times. Of course, the shift assignment might include more than 4 patients, but that does not alter the caseload number.

It should be noted that managed care is a standard for all patients, but not all patients must be case managed. For instance, an orthopedic unit with the budget above may provide managed care to all patients but choose to case manage only fractured hip patients. Suppose such patients add up to 5 of the 28. In this situation, two RNs of the seven may case manage them (2 or 3 per caseload), which would allow them to take care of other types of patients as well during a shift's assignment.

Scheduling

Scheduling for managed care is no different than regular scheduling. However, scheduling for case management requires a commitment from the nurse manager and unit staff to allow each representative to each group practice to go to an hour meeting every week. Arranging for these meetings is easier if the group meeting day, time, and place is the same each week. For example, a rehab unit may have the staff nurse in the stroke group practice off the unit on Tuesdays from 11 AM to 12 PM and another staff nurse from the rhizotomy group off the unit Fridays from 2 to 3 PM. Group members are expected to negotiate their schedules accordingly and arrange for coverage of their patients. They are not expected to come in on days off or to spend overtime "doing" case management. This form of case management enables nurses on 50% shift rotations and other flextime schedules to be part of the model.

Selection of Personnel

Once the roles and practices have been designed, the staff nurses who will be members of the group practices can be chosen by the nurse managers involved. Although it would be ideal to require a master's degree and many years of experience, this is neither practical nor necessary given a good curriculum and ongoing support. What is required is a minimum of 1-year's experience and an above-average evaluation as a primary nurse. A BSN is preferable, but equivalencies in the following areas could serve equally well: (1) knowledge and use of the nursing process; (2) collaborative relationships with other nurses, with physicians, and with patients and their families; and (3) excellent management skills as shown by management of self, shift charge responsibilities, and caseloads.

In addition to the academic and practice criteria, the candidate should be assessed for a track record of (a) taking initiative and following through with complex problems, (b) effective communication skills, (c) ability to be either a follower or a leader in group, and (d) interest in the welfare of the institution and the community it serves.

Anyone embarking on Case Management should be able to work interdependently in, at times, highly ambiguous situations. Potential case managers should be interested in the model and ready to make a new level of commitment to patients, colleagues, and the well-being of the institution. "Greater emotional energy is required because people must be open, take more risks, work at developing trust and trusting others." (Zander & Etheridge, 1989).

Education and Training

Managed Care entails training in the skills listed in Exhibit 3-6. It also entails the change in mindset discussed above in the section "Underlying Assumptions." All RNs at New England Medical Center Hospitals must pass a DRG test during orientation and attend 3 days of mandatory management training during their first year of employment.

When appointed to a group practice for case management, there is an additional 3-day curriculum required. Although each institution would tailor certain parts, there are many subjects common to all settings and case types. The goal of the curriculum is to provide (1) a description of and rationale for case management; (2) advanced-level nursing process skills; (3) case type–specific knowledge; (4) system-specific information; and (5) collaboration and team-building experiences.

The following is an overview of the topics covered in the case management education series.

Day 1

I. Introduction to case management
   (administer pretests)
   A. Definition and rationale
   B. Case management background
   C. NEMCH model
II. Defining our business
   A. Case management plans
   B. Critical paths
   C. Moving from planned care to managed care
III. Defining the group practice
   A. Identifying the RNs, MDs, and patients
   B. Team building of the group practice (Part I: Who Are We?)
IV. Updating assessment skills
   A. Physical assessment
   B. Functional assessment
   C. Family assessment
   D. Case type–specific issues

Day 2

I. Realistic outcomes with time frames
   A. Predicting and individualizing outcomes from experience
   B. Reimbursement and continuing care
   C. Helping patients survive at home
II. Making professional commitments
   A. To patients and families
   B. To career growth
III. RN-MD collaboration
   A. Five building blocks of collaborative practice
   B. How to run a health care team meeting
IV. Team building of the group practice (Part II: What Is Our Work?)

Day 3

I. Concurrent review
   A. Tracking and documenting care
   B. Case type–specific variances
   C. Use of telephone and other systems
   D. How to provide case consultation to peers
II. Formal evaluation
   A. Identifying trends for groups of patients
   B. Using research and resources
   C. The change process and being "system savvy"
III. Landmarks of a well-functioning group
   A. Case example
   B. Team building (Part III)
IV. Putting it together
   A. Authority, autonomy, accountability
   B. Time and stress management
V. Summary and future directions
   A. Series evaluation and posttest

Reward Systems and Governance

Currently, being a member of a group practice is considered an honor with many advantages. Case management is a patient-centered shared governance model which encourages staff nurses to "connect" differently with each other, attending physicians, and the entire delivery system.

Ideally, case managers should be on the top step of a clinical ladder of the career-tracking plan. They and the attending physicians should also be acknowledged beyond salary by bonuses that are given to the group practices and that reflect their contribution to the cost-effective care of specific case types.

Support Systems

The central support for managed care and case management is the nurse manager on each unit. In the case management model, the nurse manager is a group practice facilitator. Even if other people are facilitators, the nurse manager is still the gatekeeper of the unit, reinforcing institutional goals and department objectives.

To implement managed care or case management, a project manager and steering committee are needed for at least 2 years. Members of the steering committee should include nurses involved in management, education, documentation and computerization, and clinical specialties.

Of course, behind the whole development effort must be the knowledgeable commitment of the vice president for nursing. Because case management involves such a major integration of nursing, physicians, patients, and the rest of the institution, the vice president must stay realistic and responsive and yet take risks—and encourage others to be the same way. Perhaps the toughest aspect is to convert clinical systems while maintaining the usual departmental operations.

FINANCIAL ESTIMATES

Managed care and case management do not change the budget, cost per patient to deliver care, hours of care per patient day, acuity points, or other measures used in tracking nursing manpower. This is due to the matrix structure of the model, which does not separate the staff nurse (as case manager) from his or her unit. Rather, case management forms a "unit without walls" with no additional expense.

The start-up expenses of implementing managed care and case management are mainly education and development costs. Minimum estimates of time frames are shown in Table 3-1.

COST BENEFITS

Paradoxically, it has been true that whenever cost issues have been addressed by the actual clinicians giving medical and nursing care, quality

Table 3-1 Start-up Time Frames

	Managed Care	Case Management
Design (including all leadership personnel)	2 days (with consultation)	2 days
Nursing manager training	3 days	2 days
Staff nurses training	3 days	3 days
Implementation	3–6 months	6–9 months

has also been enhanced. The cost benefits of managed care and case management fall into two large categories and take numerous, sometimes more subtle forms. The two main categories are decreased length of stay (at least one day per case type) and decreased resource utilization per case type (when appropriate). For example, by not admitting every patient with a stroke to the neuro ICU from the emergency room, patients reached equal or better outcomes in less time with less cost. Their families did not have the added anxiety of an ICU stay, and the patients went to rehabilitation 7–12 days sooner than before the institution of case management. This combination of changes converted stroke patients from money losers to income producers (Zander, 1988).

The beauty of the model is that as it develops and the group practices mature, continual cost benefits, paired with quality improvements, can be seen. Nurses have made major strides in systemwide interventions that aim at the resolution of patient problems (nursing diagnoses) only now beginning to be understood. These key diagnoses have the potential for complications related to treatment, complications unrelated to treatment, complications arising from self-care, and complications related to the extension of the disease process (Stetler & DeZell, 1987, pp. 26–32). These problems truly highlight nursing's specific and dynamic contribution to quality and cost-efficient care. Cost benefits for each outcome per case type need to be calculated. This work has only just begun.

CASE STUDY

If you are admitted for an abdominal aortic aneurysm repair, you become a patient of a collaborative practice composed of two vascular physicians and four staff nurses who treat you throughout your entire episode of care. In fact, you probably are already followed by the physicians and L. Isaacson, the ambulatory nurse in the group practice. Now that you are entering acute care, she will notify her group of your special needs and work with the physician to facilitate a smooth pre-op course.

The group uses the critical path for DRG 110 (Major Vascular Surgery; length of stay 10–13 days) to plan, track, and evaluate your progress. The critical path is based on a case management plan, a larger document that outlines the cause and effect relationship between problems, intermediate goals and the corresponding interventions by physicians and nurses, and desired and specific clinical outcomes within the 10-day length of stay time frame.

When you arrive on the inpatient unit, J. Clark, the inpatient nurse in the group practice, becomes either your primary nurse or associate primary nurse. She will discuss your critical path with you and your family and will help you become familiar with the sequencing of events. She will give you direct care before surgery and after your SICU stay. She will also coordinate your transitions with J. Martz, the OR/RR nurse in the group practice, and J. Hayes, the nurse member from the SICU. In fact, J. Hayes will meet you before surgery, offer to take you on a tour of the SICU, and answer any questions you or your family may have.

The group practice communicates often with your surgeon and meets formally for about an hour a week to discuss their 30 active patients. Although these nurses are part of the regular staff on each of their units, they take vascular patients of specific physicians within their primary caseloads and shift assignments. When any one of them is not on duty, his or her peers on the unit continue to follow the critical path in a way similar to following a nursing care plan.

When you are ready for discharge, L. Isaacson will again meet with you to reinforce your follow-up appointments in the ambulatory setting. With the surgeon and the rest of the group practice, she will assess your achievement of the outcomes as well as analyze any variances from the critical path that may have occurred. By doing this, the group can better anticipate your future needs and can also improve the way the system works.

This group practice has demonstrated in several ways that "the whole is more than the sum of the parts." By viewing the whole episode of care as the responsibility of each, they can uncover problems and effective solutions. For instance, several surgeries a week were being cancelled because patients who were already admitted and scheduled were not passing a thallium-Persantine scan (stress test). The group practice suggested that these scans, as well as angiograms, be done on an outpatient basis. They were able, through their head nurses and with C. Blaney as facilitator, to negotiate a set time for these scans reserved by the vascular service. They then wrote a letter to patients explaining the importance of the scans and noting the scheduling. By this one change, they have saved OR time and eliminated unnecessary patient anxiety over surgery that might not even be performed. They have gained more control over their time and their environment. Through enhanced communication between the nursing group and the physicians, they have cut SICU days from a range of 4–5 days to 3–4 days in the past year—without compromising standards and yet saving an estimated $20,000 per year. In addition, they have managed their caseload of patients through early intervention so well that the patients who tend to have complicated and chronic conditions and to be on Medicare (an estimated 70%) do not frequent the emergency room.

The physicians are pleased with group practice and zero in on the staff nurses who care for the same patients that they are treating. They are getting more comfortable sending some patients to the recovery room instead of the SICU. One physician from another collaborative practice, alluding to the way nursing group practice makes the system work, referred to it as the "Cadillac treatment."

The nurses express more satisfaction in using their nursing knowledge, more respect for the work of those in other areas, and more connection with patients and the institution. "It takes the anxiety out for the nurse when you know what happens everywhere and that makes you a better teacher." The group helps them be realistic about their expectations regarding themselves and their patients. The group alerts them about potential problems, such as substance abuse, and helps them anticipate action. Overall, the group decreases a nurse's isolation while providing a stimulus for professional growth.

PROS AND CONS

Managed Care

Pros	Cons
1. Managed care establishes nurses as the managers of the acute care business and concurrent quality assurance every 8 hours.	1. It requires major mindset changes that can only occur from departmentwide commitment, and must be managed from the top.
2. Case management plans and critical paths bridge conceptual maps between nursing and medical models, showing independent and interdependent functions.	2. Each discipline may have political and philosophical reasons to be hesitant in committing practice patterns to paper.
3. Managed care can be used in any care delivery system (team, functional, total patient care, and mixed methods) without changing staffing mix, budget, and so on.	3. Without primary nursing, the nurse manager is accountable for all outcomes for all patients and must manage all critical paths.

Pros	Cons
4. Managed care increases the productivity of all nursing staff and more equally distributes workload and outcome-based practice across all shifts.	4. It initially adds one more piece of paper (the critical path) to the shift, even though writing is only required when there is a variance.

Case Management

Pros	Cons
1. Case management empowers the staff nurse through increased authority in the system.	1. It requires additional training.
2. It establishes a truly collaborative practice at the caregiver level.	2. Staff nurses work through attending physicians, which, depending on the institution's medical organizational structure, may put them in the middle of the conflict.
3. Case management retains experienced, motivated staff and encourages them to make commitments.	3. It requires group practice members to be off their units an hour a week and to contact other nurses or patients (as needed) throughout the week.
4. Case management decreases prejudicial barriers between units (ICU, floor, OR/RR, ambulatory areas, etc.), thus smoothing transitions for patients and increasing the knowledge of nurses and physicians.	4. It requires facilitation to get the group off the ground.

EVALUATION

It can be seen above that every pro has a con, which is not necessarily an unworkable situation. Unlike other care delivery models, managed care and case management force all levels of a nursing organization to focus less on predominantly internal concerns and more on institutional structures and problems. Although the model concretely brings accountability, authority, and autonomy together, that represents a "quantum leap" for most nurses. Therefore, the usual recommendation is to establish managed care before specific staff nurses are placed in group practices for case management.

Initial outcomes (0–3 months) might show mixed results, as would the outcomes of any new system. A project director who assists in setting reasonable target dates and stays responsive to problems as they arise will smooth the transition.

The model is currently being evaluated on all parameters, and previous audits of staff primary nurses, leadership practices, charts, and patient and family interviews continue. Case management plans are being tested for validity and reliability, and strategies for evaluating outcomes postdischarge are being developed. Financial outcomes are reviewed concurrently, and experimental budgets using critical paths and other indicators are being considered.

Managed care is in place when the following base line criteria are met:

1. Every patient has a critical path in use that is monitored every 8 hours during the shift report.
2. Variances are analyzed and acted on quickly.
3. Case consultations and health care team meetings occur frequently.
4. Head nurses aggregate variances from the critical paths and use the data for quality assurance.

Case management is firmly in place when the group practices are meeting regularly and evaluating the quality and cost of care for all patients within their defined caseloads. The signs of a well-functioning group are

1. resolved membership issues, with smooth personnel changes
2. timely and frequent case consultations between RNs and MDs
3. rapid feedback
4. identification and involvement of "junior partners" (staff nurses who are currently giving care to case-managed patients during the absence of "senior partners" but who are not principals in the group)
5. formation of research hypotheses
6. integration into practice of new literature on related subjects
7. formation of new programs for patients
8. changes in the way the total institution responds to the group practice's patients
9. new formal links between the institution and external agencies and programs
10. publishing, speaking, consulting by group practice members

SUMMARY

Managed care and nursing case management show great potential, and there is some initial hard evidence that they can provide quality care within cost constraints. As clinical systems, they merge the best contributions of nursing and physician groups. They are practical and adaptable and can be implemented within a relatively short period. Given their underlying assumptions, it is clear that managed care and case management are rooted in the nursing process as it relates to outcome-based practice. With improved tools, systems, and relationships, staff nurses become empowered, which in turn empowers the individuals who constitute their reason for existence: the patients and their families.

REFERENCES

Davis, S. & Lawrence, P. (1977). *Matrix.* Reading, MA: Addison-Wesley.

Fuszard, B., et al. (1988). *Case management: A challenge for nurses.* Kansas City, MO: American Nurses' Association.

Stetler, C. (1988). Goals of case management and managed care. Adapted from unpublished manuscript.

Stetler, C., & DeZell, A.D. (1987). *Nursing case management: Designs for transformation.* Boston: New England Medical Center Hospitals.

Zander, K. (1988). Nursing case management: Strategic management of cost and quality outcomes. *Journal of Nursing Administration, 18*(5), 23–30.

Zander, K. (1988). Why managed care works, *Definition, 3*(4), 3.

Zander, K., & Etheredge, M.L. (Eds.). (1989). *Collaborative care: Nursing care management.* Chicago: American Hospital Association.

Chapter 4

Organizing a Nursing System through Theory-Based Practice

Ruben D. Fernandez and Joan I. Wheeler

Fernandez and Wheeler, like Manthey, begin their chapter by defining common terms used in describing patient care delivery systems. This provides an excellent background for their descriptions of two different hospitals that utilized Orem's self-care theoretical foundation as the basis of their nursing care delivery systems.

A theory-based practice model for nursing provides the structure for understanding all the practice components of nursing service delivery. It lays the foundation for nursing practice by providing a framework that organizes knowledge and delivery of care based on that knowledge, thus creating a bridge between nursing theory and nursing practice.

The need for practice-oriented theory and conceptual models for nursing practice has long been identified in the literature (Fawcett, 1978; Flaskerud, 1980). However, the implementation of a conceptual model in the practice arena often creates some difficulties due to the incongruence of hospital systems; medical models superimposed on nursing practice; and the lack of understanding of the phenomenon of nursing, including its dimensions and coherence. In order to provide a sense of unity, the model's focal point must be defined, described, and explained and its dimensions must be understood.

In order to fully understand the nature, function, and value of models, it is necessary to examine their relationship to theory. Often the terms *model* and *theory* are used interchangeably. This is confusing and prevents the precision that science seeks to attain. Although a model primarily expresses structure (Bush, 1979, p. 16), theory provides substance in addition to structure. Theory is a conceptual system, "a set of interrelated construct [concepts] definitions, and propositions that present a systematic view of phenomena by specifying relations among variables, with the purpose of explaining and predicting the phenomena" (Kerlinger, 1973, p. 9). Thus, theory represents a set of interrelated concepts, definitions, and propositions that present a systematic view of phenomena by specifying relationships among variables.

THE SELF-CARE MODEL

Nursing has a mandate from society to use its specialized body of knowledge and skills for the betterment of humans. The mandate implies that knowledge and skills must grow so as to keep up with the changing health goals of society. Furthermore, nursing must regulate its own practice, control the qualifications of its practitioners, and develop and implement systems that are grounded in nursing theory. In recognizing the societal mandate and the need to implement new knowledge, the nursing departments of Newark Beth Israel Medical Center and St. Elizabeth Hospital embarked on a visionary action plan to facilitate practice, stimulate learning, enhance patient care, and ultimately cost out nursing services. This visionary master plan called for the selection of a theory or a practice model that was congruent with each department's philosophy, each institution's mission, and the evolution of nursing practice. Both departments chose the concept of *self-care* as elucidated by Dorothea E. Orem as the theoretical foundation for their practice.

Self-care is an approach that focuses on patients' perceived needs and preferences regardless of whether such needs and preferences conform to professional perceptions of patients' needs (Levin, 1978). Patients determine, in this model, the desired outcomes in accordance with their decisions as to which risks they choose to contend with or avoid. This approach shifts the decision-making responsibility to the patients. The responsibility is based on patients' perceptions of the risks involved in their illnesses and in possible treatments (Chang, 1980). Patients' choices may not always conform to professional values. In medical and nursing literature, patients whose choices do not coincide with professional values are said to be noncompliant. In this model, there is no such thing as a noncompliant patient, but there may be patients who do not adhere to their health care plans (patient decision making may or may not be involved in the formulation of these plans).

Self-care, with its goal of promoting health and preventing disease and its emphasis on patients as active participants and decision makers, requires that nurses assist patients in arriving at informed decisions and in developing behaviors to improve health. A contractual agreement exists between the patient and the nurse as to the level of participation and the expected outcomes (see Exhibit 4-1). It was this contractual concept, with its emphasis on participating knowingly, that moved both nursing staffs to select the Orem model. In addition, the concreteness and straightforwardness of the model were identified by the staffs as influencing their selection.

Although there were significant differences in the way the two agencies went about assessing their needs, evaluating options, and selecting a model, certain commonalities did exist. The staff at both institutions identified the need for

1. a common nursing language
2. a framework based on concepts unique to the discipline of nursing
3. a nursing system that could allocate resources based on patients' needs
4. a model that would direct nursing actions
5. a model that would closely fit the practice of nursing
6. a model that would allow nurses to practice nursing as a learned profession
7. a nursing system that would best reflect the values of the staff and the philosophy of the nursing department

After serious deliberations, both departments agreed to explore further, develop timetables, and initiate the process of implementing a theory-based practice model (namely, the Self-Care Deficit Theory of Nursing elucidated by Dorothea E. Orem [1980]).

The selection process, goals, timetables, priorities, and tool design selected by each agency provide alternatives for those interested in implementing a conceptual framework.

ST. ELIZABETH'S EXPERIENCE

Selection Process

St. Elizabeth's experience with the self-care model has been ongoing since 1982, when the hospital became the first acute care facility in New Jersey to commit itself to a theory-based practice model. Prior to 1982 the authors of this chapter, at that time both working at St. Elizabeth, expressed the need for nursing to define its practice through a conceptual framework or theory. This definition process did not begin until 1982 due to lack of support from the administrative staff.

Reorganization of the administrative staff in 1982 was the first step toward the implementation of a theory-based nursing model. The administrative staff supported a participative management model. The Council on Nursing Practice was created. The council was charged with standard development and evaluation of practice. In order to facilitate involvement,

Exhibit 4-1 Newark Beth Israel Medical Center

The following contract has been designed to assist the nurse and ancillary staff in helping you meet your needs to prepare for discharge. This is not a legal contract, it is a tool to aid us in providing care to you as a patient while in Newark Beth Israel Medical Center.

My goal is: _____

_____

_____

Please answer the following questions:

1. I feel I will need:
   Complete nursing care (unable to do anything for myself).   _____ _____

   Partial nursing care (can do some things but need help).   _____ _____

   Only support, encouragement and education as to why I'm in the hospital.   _____ _____

2. I agree to notify the nurse of any changes in the way I feel.   _____ _____

3. I will maintain a record of my intake and output.   _____ _____

4. I agree to abide by the unit's regulations for visiting hours and the smoking policy.   _____ _____

5. I agree to utilize the patient dining areas for meals.   _____ _____

   I agree to be responsible for the care and the prompt return of borrowed games and activities from the Patient Activities Room.   _____ _____

   I agree to respect and not deface any hospital property or equipment.   _____ _____

6. I understand that the nurse will consider my needs in relation to other patients' needs.   _____ _____

_____   _____

Patient's Signature   Date

Nursing Component:

1. I consider this patient to require the following level of care:

   Wholly compensatory nursing care.   _____ _____
   Partly compensatory nursing care.   _____ _____
   Supportive educative nursing care.   _____ _____

(If the nursing assessment differs from the patient's stated need – please explain in Nursing Comment section.)

2. I agree to teach this patient about his/her diagnosis/reason for admission.   _____ _____

Exhibit 4-1 continued

The goals negotiated with this patient are:

_____

_____

_____

3. I agree to abide by the mutually determined goals: _____ - _____

Length of stay: _____

_____   _____
Nurse's Signature   Date

Patient's Comments

_____

_____

_____

_____

_____

_____

Patient's Signature: _____

Nurse's Comments

_____

_____

_____

_____

_____

_____

Nurse's Signature: _____

Date: _____

the staff members held an election to select representatives. The council's membership consisted of one professional staff nurse from each nursing unit (selected by the professional staff of that unit). The council reported to the director of nursing and the nursing administrative staff. This afforded the council the authority and structure to impact the decision-making process and policy setting at the hospital.

The council's charges, as defined by the director of Nursing and administrative staff, were to

1. create a ladder of clinical excellence
2. develop a patient classification system
3. identify and implement a theoretical framework for practice
4. integrate the theoretical framework within the department so as to define both the concept and practice of nursing

The selection process for a theory-based nursing model began in mid-1983. The Council on Nursing Practice identified 13 nurse theorists for review. The field was then narrowed to 7. Each member or a group of members selected a theorist. Through review of the literature, each group acquired basic knowledge of a specific theory to determine if it was consistent with nursing. The council presented each theorist's model to the nursing and administrative staff. Following presentation to and discussion with staff members, a consensus was reached in mid-1984 to utilize Orem's self-care model to frame nursing practice at St. Elizabeth Hospital. By incorporating the nursing staff in the process of selection, the administration gave them ownership of the model and generated a commitment to succeed.

The process of selection took 2 years, a length of time that could result in diminishing the commitment to the model. The process provided the staff, not with immediate gratification, but with long-term satisfaction.

Implementation

To implement this framework within the nursing department, the process began by looking at the department as a whole and then at the patient-specific integration of the model.

In June 1985, the Council on Nursing Practice "Oremized" the philosophy and objectives of the nursing department. Using Orem's model, belief statements, objectives, and application statements were developed for each level of practitioner.

The council presented the completed philosophy and objectives to the nursing staff in mid-1986. The staff were very receptive and expressed a desire to learn more and to practice within the model.

To facilitate practice within the model, support had to be developed. These supports took the form of tools documenting the nursing process from the initial nursing assessment. The council selected the assessment as the point to begin development. A nursing history and assessment tool was created in August 1986 (Exhibit 4-2).

The council developed an eight-page form to record the basic conditioning factors and to assess the universal care requisites. The original form was piloted on two nursing units. The staff requested a less comprehensive

Exhibit 4-2 Nursing Assessment Tool

ST. ELIZABETH HOSPITAL Elizabeth, N.J.	NURSING ADMISSION ASSESSMENT (Page 2)

AIR

Temp.		BP	Right	Left
Apical Rate	Rhythm	Respiratory Rate		Rhythm

Breath Sounds: Clear   Congested   Other

Cough: Productive   Non-Productive   None

Problems: Asymmetrical   Use of Accessory   None
     Chest   Muscles

Color: Pale   Pink   Normal
     Cyanotic   Jaundice

Problems Edema   Varicosities
     Calf Tenderness   None

Description of Sputum:

Pulses: O=Absent to 4=Bounding

Carotid	R_____ L_____	Femoral	R_____ L_____
Brachial	R_____ L_____	Popliteal	R_____ L_____
Radial	R_____ L_____	Pedal	R_____ L_____
		Posterior Tibial	R_____ L_____

Describe the self-care agent's abilities and/or limitations to maintain an adequate amount of air:

Nursing Diagnosis:

Initials		Date

FOOD/FLUIDS

Diet	Appetite	Problems With:
		Chewing Swallowing Nausea Vomiting Gas
IV, NG, Gastrostomy Tube Feedings	None	Weight Gain Weight Loss None Other

Exhibit 4-2 continued

Describe the self-care agent's abilities and/or limitations to maintain a sufficient intake of water and food:

Nursing Diagnosis:

Initial _____ Date _____

ELIMINATION

Bowel Pattern	Color	Remedies	Problems With: Constipation Diarrhea Bleeding None Hemorrhoids Other
Bowel Sounds		Presence of: Distention Pulsations Tenderness	Ostomy None Other
Bladder Pattern	Color	Catheter Size:	Insertion Date

Problems With:
Burning   Frequency   Urgency   Hesitancy   Genitourinary Discharge   Nocturia   Incontinence   Hematuria   None   Other

Describe the self-care agent's abilities and limitations to regulate elimination:

Nursing Diagnosis:

Initial _____ Date _____

NORMALCY

Reproductive History:

Menarche   Menopause   Menses

Problems With:
Vaginal   Breast   Breast Exam   Date   Date of Mammography

Dysmenorrhea   Bleeding   Discharge   None   Other   Self   Physician   None

Describe the self-care agent's abilities and/or limitations to maintain a level of normalcy:

Nursing Diagnosis:

Initial _____ Date _____

Source: Courtesy of St. Elizabeth Hospital, Elizabeth, NJ.

tool. The council was able to condense the eight pages to four. The advantage of the new form is its compatibility with the computer format.

During this process, the council also developed a patient classification system framed using Orem's Universal Self-Care Requisites. This system not only defined self-care deficits but also assisted with the definition of the nurse agency and the nursing system required to meet the therapeutic self-care demands.

As the nursing staff begins to practice and document within the nursing model, the final stage of the process of implementation has started. This stage involves defining the standards of care and standards of practice within the model, which will lead to quality assurance programs (Exhibits 4-3 and 4-4).

Exhibit 4-3 Standards of Care

ST. ELIZABETH HOSPITAL
NURSING DEPARTMENT
STANDARDS OF CARE

The Standards of Care are applicable to all self-care agents (SCAs) and dependent care agents (DCAs) throughout St. Elizabeth Hospital. These are:

Air: The SCA or DCA demonstrates the self-care ability to provide and maintain an adequate intake of air.

Foods/Fluids: The SCA or DCA demonstrates the self-care ability to provide and maintain an adequate intake of food and fluids.

Elimination: The SCA or DCA demonstrates the self-care ability to regulate and maintain elimination.

Activity/Rest/Sleep: The SCA or DCA demonstrates the self-care ability to maintain an appropriate activity/rest level.

Solitude/Social Interaction: The SCA or DCA demonstrates the self-care ability to maintain a balance between interactional behavioral patterns.

Protection From Hazards: The SCA or DCA demonstrates the self-care ability to prevent injury and harm to well-being.

Normalcy: The SCA or DCA demonstrates the skills to maintain his or her individual perceptions of self, self-worth, and integrity of values.

Knowledge: The SCA or DCA demonstrates the knowledge to manage self-care requisites.

Treatments and Medications: The SCA or DCA demonstrates the psychomotor skill to manage self-care requisites.

Hygiene: The SCA or DCA demonstrates the self-care ability to manage activities of daily living in order to promote physical well-being.

Exhibit 4-4 Unit Standards of Care

ST. ELIZABETH HOSPITAL
NURSING DEPARTMENT

UNIT STANDARDS

4N

1. Nurse agent of 4N assesses the following parameters of each self-care agent (SCA): air, food and fluids, elimination; hygiene; solitude and social interaction; normalcy; activity, rest, and sleep; hazards; knowledge and skills; and treatments and medications.

2. Vital signs (temperature, pulse, respiration, blood pressure, height and weight) are noted on admission.

   Weights are taken, when ordered, at 6 a.m.

3. Nurse agent notes bowel pattern daily on graphic sheet. Elimination pattern is assessed in the AM.

4. Nurse agent records intake and output postoperatively × 48 hrs and per physician order.

5. Nurse agent performs AM care on all totally dependent SCAs, which includes bathing, range of motion, linen changes, and skin assessment.

   Skin assessment includes observations of the following: presence of hematoma, abscess, rash, discoloration, or injury.

6. Nurse agent performs AM care to all partially dependent SCAs, which includes back care with lotion.

   Nurse agent performs PM care for all postoperative and immobilized dependent SCAs, which includes turning and positioning, back care with lotion, linen change (if necessary), and mouth care.

   Nurse agent provides pull pads and eggcrate mattresses for orthopedic, immobilized, and incontinent SCAs.

7. Nurse agent documents urinary output q shift for all SCAs with a foley catheter.

8. Nurse agent turns and positions all dependent SCAs once per shift.

9. Nurse agent encourages all SCAs with a physician order for out-of-bed activity to be out of bed BID.

Education has been ongoing throughout the process. The staff received an intensive Orem workshop. Each new employee in the department receives a similar workshop during orientation. This enables the new employee to begin right away the process of thinking about nursing in terms of Orem's theory.

Since June 1987, the Council on Nursing Practice, with the assistance of the clinical specialists and unit staff members, has developed nursing department standards, divisional standards, unit-based standards, specific patient population standards, standardized care plans, and teaching plans for universal care requisite knowledge (Exhibit 4-5). A patient information letter was developed to introduce patients to the self-care model at St. Elizabeth Hospital (Exhibit 4-6).

The ongoing development process generated a computerized database that combined the Orem components of the existing manual patient classification system with a costing methodology developed by Caternicchio (1984), the outcome being Nurse Executive.

Nurse Executive links paid hours by cost center elements of cost (position types), reconciled with GL or payroll, to patient-specific information derived from the medical abstract (e.g., DRG, acute care days, special care unit days, discharge status, patient account number, etc.). These actual labor hours and costs are prorated to the patient given the patient's actual days of stay within a given DRG, with the days of stay weighted for relative acuity differences and such factors as unit type, living arrangements, discharge status, and so on.

Acuity differences are derived for each hospital by linking assessment models to days of stay by DRG. For example, self-care deficit requirements, nursing diagnoses, traditional care indicators or tasks, or nursing treatment protocol weights are accumulated and assigned to days of stay within each DRG. These weights are used to allocate hours as a function of patient care requirements or challenges to the nursing process (Caternicchio, 1984).

At the present time, several staff members are involved in computerization of the model. This will provide the staff with a nursing information system consistent with the process of nursing within the model. It will allow for communication of nursing outcomes that are consistent across agencies. Regulatory agencies will be measuring nursing practice by patient outcomes within a few years.

NEWARK BETH ISRAEL'S EXPERIENCE

The process for theory selection at the Newark Beth Israel Medical Center took into consideration the needs of the patients, the educational background of the nursing staff (most of the nurses at the medical center come from education centers where Orem is utilized as the framework for the curriculum), and the philosophy of the nursing department. Although a number of staff nurses voiced their preference for this particular model, the ultimate selection was done by the management staff. The Council on Nursing Practice was in the process of defining its mission and was later

Exhibit 4-5 Sample Teaching Plan

OPERATIONAL STANDARDS OF PRACTICE
FOR
PREOPERATIVE TEACHING PLAN

Area of Assessment	Nurse Agency Responsibility	Scientific Rationale
STANDARD I Air	—Demonstrate deep breathing exercises —Explain purpose and benefits pre- and postoperatively —Encourage three cycles of ten repetitions qh	Deep breathing exercises help to: —prevent accumulation and improve mobilization of bronchial secretions —improve the efficiency and distribution of ventilation —improve cardiopulmonary reserve using exercise techniques to promote physical conditioning
STANDARD II Food/Fluids	—Reinforce menu plan as ordered by MD for preoperative preparation —Explain purpose and benefits of intravenous therapy pre- and postoperatively —Inform SCA about changes in meal schedule on nursing unit	IV fluids are given sometimes prior to OR because of the amount of fluids (body) lost during surgery to perspiration, hyperventilation, and vomiting. Some patients need IV fluids to hydrate them prior to OR. Also, in the event of an emergency, the IV provides a route for immediate infusion of medications, blood, or other solutions. Restriction of food and fluids may be ordered to decrease risk of vomiting or aspiration. Meal patterns vary from unit to unit depending on dietary schedule of distributing meals.
STANDARD III Elimination	—Encourage SCA to report changes in bowel patterns and urinary output —Inform SCA of the use of I/O Sheet postoperatively and encourage SCA participation in this activity	Both trauma of manipulation during surgery and anesthesia, as well as changes in food intake and activity level, can cause changes in bowel/voiding patterns. Close monitoring of I/O aids in detecting fluid shifts and volume overload.

Exhibit 4-6 Patient Information Letter

ST. ELIZABETH HOSPITAL ELIZABETH, N.J.	PATIENT INFORMATION LETTER

The nursing staff of St. Elizabeth Hospital welcomes you.

Our philosophy of nursing practice supports your active participation in care activities. Our goal is to provide you with the best nursing care possible to enhance your well-being.

We invite you, the Self-Care Agent, and your family to participate in the planning of your care. This shared responsibility will foster interactions between you and your nurse.

Information about basic care needs that are universal to all Self-Care Agents is identified below:

AIR/FOOD/FLUIDS are essential for life and well-being. The three-meal plan is instituted in compliance with your physician's orders. Our dietary department shall teach and assist you as needs are identified in this area.

ELIMINATION processes are part of everyday living. Bathroom facilities are provided for your convenience. Bathroom privileges are instituted in compliance with your physician's orders.

ACTIVITY/REST cannot be overlooked during your hospitalization. The importance of a balanced activity and rest routine will be maintained during your hospital stay. We encourage your participation in daily care activities. We welcome your family to visit during your stay in the hospital. For your benefit, visiting hours on the general nursing units are from 11:00 AM to 8:00 PM. For special care areas, please check at the front desk.

SOCIAL INTERACTION/SOLITUDE can contribute to your health. Families are encouraged to assist you with your care upon your request. TV and telephone services are available for a nominal fee (see Cashier, first floor).

HAZARDS are controlled during your hospitalization. For your safety, there are call bells and side rails at each bedside. These devices are used for your protection.

HYGIENE is part of everyone's daily routine. You will receive an Admission Kit when you arrive in your room on the nursing unit. Toothbrushes, toothpaste, lotion and soap are available upon request. Your nurse will assist you with your daily hygienic needs if you require this service.

TREATMENT/MEDICATIONS will be a routine experience for you during your stay. Your nurse will give your medications as prescribed by your physician. Special treatments and therapies will be provided by our skilled staff to assist you in achieving optimal health.

NORMALCY in lifestyle pattern is encouraged. You will be encouraged to verbalize any concerns or fears about the hospital experience to the staff. Chaplains are available to all during the day and night.

Before you are discharged from St. Elizabeth Hospital, we will provide you with the necessary learning experiences and skills required for your return to an optimal level of functioning and health.

Nursing Department

Source: Courtesy of St. Elizabeth Hospital, Elizabeth, NJ.

consulted as to the advantage of the model and the process of implementation. Once the goals were made clear to all levels of personnel, a consensus as to the advantages of a theory-based practice model was reached. Both management and nursing staff agreed that a theory-based practice model was advantageous to everyone in terms of the direction in which nursing as a practice profession is moving, as well as the overall evaluation of nursing practice at the medical center. Everyone agreed that the Self-Care Deficit Theory of Nursing best met the needs of the medical center, since the model

1. can be utilized to justify nursing actions
2. provides certain measurable outcomes for which quality can be measured
3. provides a structure that the nursing department can use to operationalize its action plan
4. can cost out those interventions that are germane to nursing practice
5. provides a value system that the staff can identify with, integrate, and interpret to others

The nursing administration agreed that in order to make the project a success, certain investments were required:

1. A dedicated specialist in Orem and nursing theory needed to be hired as a project director and facilitator.
2. Other manpower resources needed to be allocated for the purpose of education and implementation.
3. Collaboration with schools of nursing that used the model needed to increase.
4. An Orem library needed to be developed.
5. The nursing department needed to become known locally and nationally as an Orem center of nursing excellence and practice.

The goals became set as investment factors were operationalized: An Orem coordinator was hired to spearhead the process of education and implementation and to formulate a 5-year action plan; the Council on Nursing Practice was charged with standard setting, tool development, and progress communication with staff; the Quality Assurance Committee was charged with the development of monitors within the model; and the Nursing Education Department agreed to incorporate in all its presentations aspects of the model and how the actions or interventions were to be interpreted according to self-care deficit. The Nursing Education Department has increased its collaboration with various institutions that practice using this model, and it currently has, in conjunction with Seton Hall University, a critical care grant through which two of the department's instructors have been released from 50% of their work to teach a graduate course. This course was designed by the participants in the grant, and its curriculum was framed using the Orem model. An Orem Center of Nursing Excellence was inaugurated at the same time as the Orem Library, which was dedicated to Dorothea Orem and formally opened by her. The Orem Library became a reality thanks to donations provided for that purpose by the Newark Beth Israel Medical Center Alumnae Association. In addition, the nursing department committed itself to host the Eastern Region Orem Self-Care Deficit Conference. The nursing department has been collaborating with national scholars in the field, including Dr. Orem, in planning the regional conference.

The vision and 5-year plan calls for the development of an Orem-based computer system. The department elected to sponsor and provide access to Nursing Systems International in developing the first Orem theory-based computerized nursing system. The medical center became the first nursing department to contract services, provide data, and become a national testing and demonstration center for the purpose of advancing development of the model.

THEORY-BASED PRACTICE AND DELIVERY OF CARE

In order for a theory-based practice model to functionally operate, a multilevel forum must exist where ongoing evaluation, free discussion, and planning take place. The communication process must encompass the unit level, the middle management level, and the nursing administration level. The overall concerns of the staff, the overall action plan, and the mission during the various transitional phases must be clearly articulated.

The transitional phases include, but are not limited to,

- the identification phase (selection of a theory-based practice model)
- the education phase (everyone in the nursing department is educated about the model)
- the transition phase (the staff attempt to incorporate the model into their daily activities as seen in care plan documentation; the beginning of tool and standard development takes place and accelerates midway through this phase [Exhibit 4-7])
- the implementation phase (the department practices according to the theory and true integration begins to occur)

Exhibit 4-7 Patient Care Flow Sheet

PATIENT CARE
FLOW SHEET

DATE:		7 AM – 7 PM	7 PM – 7 AM
	BLOOD PRESSURE		
	PULSE: RATE/QUALITY		
	RESPIRATIONS: RATE/RHYTHM		
	LUNG SOUNDS		
	APICAL RATE/RHYTHM		
AIR	HEART SOUNDS		
	SKIN: TURGOR/APPEARANCE		
	SKIN: COLOR/TEMPERATURE		
	WEIGHT		
	EDEMA		
	INTRAVENOUS THERAPY SITE		
FOOD & WATER	SITE APPEARANCE		
	IV DRESSING CHANGE		
	TYPE SOLUTION		
	RATE		

Exhibit 4-7 continued

DATE:		7 AM – 7 PM		7 PM – 7 AM	
FOOD & WATER	LIB—BEGIN SHIFT				
	LIB—END SHIFT				
	IV INTAKE				24°
	PO FLUID INTAKE				24°
	DIET				
	% TAKEN				
	SELF/ASSISTANCE				
ACTIVITY REST & SLEEP	ACTIVITY				
	TOLERATION				
	RANGE OF MOTION				
	SLEEP/REST PATTERN				
ELIMINATION	VOIDING				
	URINE APPEARANCE				
	OUTPUT				24°

Exhibit 4-7 continued

DATE:		7 AM – 7 PM	7 PM – 7 AM
ELIMINATION			
	ABDOMEN/BOWEL SOUNDS		
	STOOL		
SOLITUDE & SOCIAL INTERACTION	COMMUNICATION		
	LEVEL OF CONSCIOUSNESS		
	ORIENTATION		
	VISITORS		
PROTECTION FROM HAZARDS	SAFETY: SIDE RAILS		
	CALL LIGHT WITHIN REACH		
	WOUNDS: LOCATION		
	TYPE		
	APPEARANCE		
	TREATMENT		
	DRESSING CHANGE		

Exhibit 4-7 continued

DATE:		7 AM – 7 PM	7 PM – 7 AM
PROTECTION FROM HAZARDS			
	PAIN: TYPE/LOCATION		
	INTERVENTION		
	RESPONSE		
	EQUIPMENT		
NORMALCY	HYGIENE		
	ORAL CARE/ BACK CARE		
	BEHAVIOR		
KNOWLEDGE & SKILLS	TEACHING		
	PROCEDURES		
	SIGNATURES		

Source: Courtesy of Beth Israel Medical Center, Newark, NJ.

- the evaluation phase (although the evaluation process is dynamic and continuous, there is a need, after the model is fully implemented, to evaluate desired outcomes and movement toward theory development; the theory is further refined by those staff members that understand it and have integrated it into their practice)

During the various phases, the role of the patient needs to be evaluated. Patient education about the model must start from the moment the patient is admitted to the unit. A common misconception is that "self-care" means that no care or support will be provided. This misconception must be eliminated. The patient is to be given an information flyer explaining the philosophy of self-care deficit. The patient's role as independent agent, partner in care, recipient, and provider must be incorporated into the overall plan of care. When the patient participates knowingly within this framework, control is taken from the nurse and shared responsibilities are clearly delineated. A contractual relationship comes into being. This can be threatening to some nurses who feel the need to be in control of all patient care outcomes.

CONSIDERATIONS REGARDING IMPLEMENTATION

Although both institutions continue to progress toward their goals, a strong move toward the implementation phase is indeed evident. When an institution is moving toward or considering the implementation of a theory-based practice model, the nursing management must be cognizant of these issues:

1. Any model represents an alternative system of care grounded in a nursing theory, and it is not to be considered as the sole answer to refining and defining nursing practice.
2. There is a need to validate through nursing research some of the variables that the staff may identify as requiring further development and refinement.
3. Ultimately the model must provide a mechanism to cost out that which is uniquely defined as the practice of nursing.

REFERENCES

Bush, H.A. (1979). Models of nursing. *Advances in Nursing Science, 1*(2), 16.

Caternicchio, R. (Ed.). (1984). *DRGs: What they are and how to survive them: A source book for professional nursing.* Thorofare, NJ: Slack, Inc.

Chang, B.L. (1980). Evaluation of health care professionals in facilitating self-care: Review of the literature and a conceptual model. *Advances in Nursing Science, 3*(1), 43–53.

Fawcett, J. (1978). The what of theory development. In *Theory development: What, why and how* (pp. 17–33). New York: National League of Nursing.

Flaskerud, J. (1980). Areas of agreement in nursing theory development. *Advances in Nursing Science, 3*(1), 1–7.

Kerlinger, N. (1973). *Foundations of behavioral research.* New York: Holt, Rinehart & Winston.

Levin, L.S. (1978). Patient education and self-care: How do they differ? *Nursing Outlook, 26,* 170–175.

Orem, D. (1980). *Nursing concepts of practice* (2nd ed.) New York: McGraw-Hill.

Chapter 5

The Johns Hopkins Professional Practice Model

Mary Rose and Barbara DiPasquale

The authors present a model for professional practice that pays attention to the environmental factors that make this practice possible. They describe how organizational issues and governance are related to the values that underlie primary nursing.

In the development of their model, the authors address a common incongruity: nurses practicing primary nursing in hierarchical organizational structure. Rather than use the term shared governance, *they define how nurses make decisions that govern their work as well as their clinical practice.*

This chapter describes the philosophy, objectives, basic assumptions, implementation, maintenance, and outcomes of the Johns Hopkins professional practice model. An analysis of benefits and costs, as well as firsthand experiences with the development and actual workings of two models, is presented by the authors, who are both head nurses at Johns Hopkins Hospital. It is important to note that the specific examples are limited to the Meyer 7 practice model, which is used on a 22-bed acute care neuroscience unit, and the Meyer 3 practice model, which is used on a 22-bed acute care psychiatric unit. The Meyer 7 model was the first model developed at Johns Hopkins Hospital and was implemented in 1981. The Meyer 3 model was implemented in 1984.

DESCRIPTION AND GOALS

The Johns Hopkins professional model of nursing practice is a nursing care delivery system that is based on the philosophy that nurses are professionals and should therefore govern the environment in which they practice nursing.

It can be defined as a unit-based system that employs the concepts of shared governance and group practice. It supports the tenets of shared governance through its decentralized structure of decision making, whereby the nurses on the unit have control over their work environment and practice. Within this practice group, power, authority, accountability, and decision making are vested in the membership. Inherent in this system is

85

a management philosophy that fosters autonomous function and accountability for patient care. The unit is managed by professional staff who assume responsibility both individually and collectively for the adequacy and safety of the nursing care provided. The goals of this model are improved patient care, increased autonomy, increased professional development, increased job satisfaction, and professional accountability.

Although there is no legally binding contract, the members of the practice model enter into an informal agreement with the hospital. According to this agreement, nurses assume responsibility as a group for the provision of nursing care to a particular unit over a specified time frame in exchange for shared governance and professional compensation.

The first reference to a professional practice model for nursing practice appeared in the nursing literature in 1978, in an article by Virginia Cleland, a professor of nursing and an employee-management relations consultant. Cleland (1978) presented a professional model of shared governance in an attempt to explore ideas that could move nursing toward attainment of its professional goals: (1) to control the practice of nursing, (2) to implement the standards enunciated by the profession, (3) to secure conditions of employment that would attract able persons to careers in nursing, and (4) to secure conditions of employment and a climate of practice that would foster a lifetime career attachment to nursing (p. 40).

The creation of a professional practice environment requires that the unit have sufficient autonomy and budgetary control to be able to assume accountability for the quality of nursing practice (Cleland, 1982). Thus, individual nurses in the practice model agree to provide nursing service on their unit for a specific salary amount and are fiscally accountable for the expenditure of these "labor" dollars. In planning the budget, variable levels of patient needs, occupancy, and staff competence are considered. Incentives are built into the model. If the practice group is able to contain costs and spend less than projected, they share in the financial rewards at the end of the fiscal year.

ASSUMPTIONS

Specific assumptions, beliefs, and values have shaped the design of the Johns Hopkins professional practice model. The most fundamental assumptions revolve around the belief that nursing is a profession and that nurses should partake in all the responsibilities, rights, and privileges that accompany professional status. It is believed that the traditional structure, in which the nursing administration assumes responsibility for the staff nurses, prevents these nurses from developing accountability for practice.

An organizational system of shared governance is necessary to allow professional nurses to share responsibility with their nursing administrators for decisions that affect nursing practice in hospitals.

Additionally, it is assumed that the empowerment of staff nurses in hospitals is necessary to broaden nursing's overall power base. True empowerment of staff nurses involves holding nurses individually accountable for practice. Thus, the highly decentralized unit-based approach to professional practice attempts to bring accountability down to the bedside or to the individual nurse providing care for the patient. In this model, the bedside nurse is valued as the most essential person, since he or she is the provider of care to the patient. The true valuing of nurses is demonstrated by providing intrinsic rewards to the nurse who remains at the bedside.

This leads us to another assumption of the model, namely, that professional nurses are motivated by intrinsic rewards such as achievement, the work itself, recognition (status), and autonomy as well as by professional compensation. It is believed that a fundamental wrong occurs in nursing when the only way to be intrinsically rewarded is to leave the bedside. Therefore, Johns Hopkins system rewards the most educated and competent nurses so that they will remain in clinical nursing, which is where they are most needed. The professional practice model recognizes staff nurse competence and advanced education in practice, allows for professional fulfillment, and, most importantly, eliminates the old assumption that someone is obviously not very important if he or she is "just a staff nurse."

Another assumption unique to this philosophy of practice is that nursing administrators must trust in the abilities of staff nurses and allow them to be accountable professionals. In an environment in which there is trust and clear expectations of professional behavior, nurses will perform up to and exceed established standards of practice. In other words, excellence in nursing practice can only occur if the environment supports it. In the professional practice model environment, the administrator relinquishes accountability for practice to the nurse (this takes trust!) and assumes accountability for providing an environment that supports nursing practice at the bedside.

COMPONENTS

The basic components of the Johns Hopkins professional practice model are a primary nursing delivery system, standards of care, standards of practice, staffing standards, clearly defined roles for nurses, eligibility criteria for membership, quality assurance monitoring, peer review, self-scheduling, and salary compensation. These basic components are complemented by a set of operationalizing elements essential for the unit-based model. Together, the basic components and the operationalizing elements form the framework for the professional practice model.

The operationalizing elements are empowerment of staff nurses, decentralized decision making, individual or shared staff nurse authority, control over practice (autonomy), accountability for practice, group problem solving, team cohesiveness, commitment, ownership, professional values, ongoing evaluation, support, and feedback. The basic components can be considered the building blocks. The staff's participation in embracing the operationalizing elements provides the cement that holds the structure together and creates a professional practice model.

It is important to realize that the basic components have been uniquely operationalized by the efforts of staff nurse work groups at the unit level. This has allowed for differences in the nursing services provided and in the creativity of the individual nurses on a particular unit. In exploring these components, each unit has looked at what other units have done and asked, How does that fit here? What needs to be different? What's missing? What's unique to or characteristic of the nursing service we provide?

This approach has caused positive development of the original ideas and encouraged nurses to think creatively and become excited about having a say in the way nursing will be practiced on their unit. It is an example of the decentralized decision making that occurs in this model.

It is important to note that the aforementioned listing of basic components and operationalizing elements is not exhaustive but will provide a basic foundation for the successful implementation of the professional practice model.

STRATEGIES FOR SUCCESSFUL IMPLEMENTATION

It was apparent that to develop strategies to meet nurses' higher-level needs, a restructuring of how the unit was organized and managed would need to occur. It was time to rethink the traditional employer-employee relationship that exists between the hospital and the staff nurses. Prior to planning the specifics of the change, nursing management examined its preparedness to respond to the nurses' expectations. Was it ready to allow nurses to practice with a sense of accountability to the recipients of their service and not to it? Was it ready to allow staff to monitor and evaluate practice from a peer group rather than from the traditional organizational orientation? Was it ready to have nurses participate in decision making? Nursing management needed to reexamine what it had to control and what could be relinquished. In the final analysis, the answer was clear. It had no reason to believe that nurses were incapable of managing their practice and working life. It had to reaffirm its belief that nurses are indeed professionals and should therefore be managed and compensated as such.

Consequently, it was recognized that change strategies would need to focus on the intrinsic needs of nurses. The specific objectives of the model are to increase job satisfaction levels among nurses; to decrease turnover, absenteeism, and the costs associated with recruitment and replacement of staff nurses; and to improve nursing practice. The strategies implemented to meet these objectives are shared decision making, primary nursing, a peer review process, decentralized staffing and scheduling practices, salaries for nurses, and financial incentives.

Staffing and Scheduling

Staffing and scheduling are decentralized, and decision-making authority is vested in the staff nurse. Every nurse is given the authority to plan his or her own schedule in accordance with guidelines set forth by the scheduling committee. Equity in scheduling is maintained through peer review rather than administrative control.

The scheduling committee circulates a blank schedule with the required staffing patterns; practice model participants post their time using the unit's staffing standards as guidelines. The final draft of a schedule is subject to committee approval.

As a professional group, the nurses within a particular unit submit a yearly proposal that they will provide staffing on a 24-hour basis. They submit that there will be no utilization of purchased nursing, nor will they expect additional coverage from another unit. The only exception to this occurs if the staffing levels fall below 12% of the budgeted RNs for that particular unit. This mechanism insures a "safety net" for the nurses as well as for hospital administration.

The group and hospital also agree that no nurse will be reassigned to another unit to provide coverage. Because of this agreement, the unit develops its own on-call system.

Every nurse is responsible for being on call for a specific number of shifts per month. The number of on-call hours is developed on a monthly basis by the scheduling committee. The methodology used is as follows: The number of shifts (per 4-week schedule) is divided by the number of nurses in the model. For example, suppose the coverage needed for days, evenings, and nights for a 28-day schedule equals 84 shifts. Eighty-four divided by 17 (the number of nurses on the unit in PPM) equals 4.9. Thus, each RN is responsible for 5 on-call shifts per month. (The number of on-call shifts is prorated for part-time RNs.) This system allows the unit to be self-sufficient in maintaining adequate coverage when a nurse is ill or the acuity level of the unit increases.

Every nurse on the unit commits to stay for the entire duration of the fiscal year. In this way resignation can be planned in a manner that allows the unit to provide safe, cost-effective care. Nursing resources are planned on a yearly basis in accordance with budgeted occupancy and projected acuity. At the end of the fiscal year, every nurse can share in any money saved by the unit. If, for example, a vacancy rate of not more than 12% occurs, or the patient volume increases and the nurses provide additional coverage, 90% of the salary dollars saved will be divided among them at the end of the fiscal year. This is an incentive that does not exist for nurses on a traditional nursing unit. Consequently, there is an increase in the nurses' willingness to provide additional hours when necessary and to do their part in keeping the occupancy at or above the budgeted rate.

Compensation

The compensation structure is redefined. Nurses become salaried employees. There is no additional money for overtime, holiday differential, or shift differential. All compensation is built into the annual salary. The compensation structure is computed on a base rate, plus money for actual rotational patterns, holiday time, and projected overtime. The cost is approximately 10% above the salaries of nurses who are not in a practice model within the hospital. The method of compensating the professional nurses allows for effective utilization of resources. They are not locked into the traditional 40-hour work week. This allows for flexible scheduling. Nurses can plan their time in accordance with patient needs. During times of decreased occupancy or acuity, nurses may choose to work less than 40 hours. Conversely, when the need for resources increases, they are available to meet the demand.

Primary Nursing

Giving authority, autonomy, and responsibility to nurses within a primary nursing system is the most logical way of providing nursing care. Such a care delivery system was not new to Meyer 7 or Meyer 3 prior to the inception of the practice model. Since the implementation of the model, primary nursing has taken on a new dimension. Nurses within the model are not only accountable for patient outcomes but also have the authority to set standards of care and practice within their units. Staff, individually and collectively, hold each primary nurse accountable for meeting these standards. To maintain this process, there is a primary nurse committee that meets on a regular basis in order to review and monitor the standards and implement corrective action when infractions occur. This committee also defines the educational and eligibility criteria for primary nurse candidates.

Peer Review Board

The peer review group on Meyer 7 is composed of a senior clinical nurse, three other clinical nurses, and the head nurse. Staff members of this group are elected annually by all practice model participants. This body assists in upholding established standards of practice; evaluates, through the use of eligibility criteria, the readiness of nurses to enter the model; participates in performance appraisal; and provides counseling to model members where discipline, probation, or removal from the model may be at issue due to standards infractions.

Requirements defining eligibility to join the model reflect the philosophy of the unit as well as that of the nursing organization. Criteria for acceptance consist of multiple factors that guide peers in weighing an individual's readiness to enter the model. The Meyer 7 model criteria include experience in the nursing specialty, the length and nature of previous clinical practice, performance appraisals, acceptable negative time patterns, a commitment to work in the model 1 year, a demonstrated ability to communicate effectively and to work collaboratively, and a willingness to assume individual accountability for professional practice.

The following is an example of the membership process for entering a model. After 6 months of active employment on the Meyer 3 inpatient unit, a nurse becomes eligible to join the professional practice model. First, the nurse candidate will be asked to review the eligibility criteria and make a commitment to the group based on an individual willingness to meet the expectations of professional practice.

The second step includes consideration by the peer review group whether to allow the candidate entry into the practice model. All current professional practice model members will review the eligibility criteria and vote for or against the candidate's request to enter the model. The review board will collect the results and inform the candidate of the decision.

If entry into the practice model is denied by the group, the candidate will be given specific feedback about performance problems and will be asked to correct these behaviors. The individual will then be given 3 months to demonstrate correction of problematic behaviors. The group will again vote on whether to allow the individual entry into the practice model. If the individual is still unable to meet the expectations of the group, he or she will be asked to consider employment elsewhere.

Additionally, all professional practice model members will be held individually accountable for upholding their agreements on an ongoing basis. In the event a member is unable to meet the expectations of this professional practice model group, it is his or her personal responsibility to inform the group and take necessary actions.

Peer Review

Peer review on the Meyer 3 unit is a formal process that supports the professional development of the nursing staff. Every nurse is required to participate in a peer review group. There are five groups, and each one consists of a senior clinical nurse, who acts as coordinating leader, and three to four other clinical nurses. All members have been randomly assigned to their groups. The groups meet monthly to develop a working relationship in a small group setting. Each member completes a written form that requests a statement of that member's overall developmental goals, the objectives intended to help achieve these goals, target dates, and actual outcomes. A supportive environment is fostered to allow nurses to exchange ideas and expertise. Every 6 months a formal review of each member's objectives is done through self-evaluation and solicitation of peer feedback; changes in objectives and new areas for development are identified at this time. This peer review process is an adjunct to the formal hospital evaluation that is done each year.

Quality Assurance

Quality assurance monitoring exists within the professional practice model to provide a means for staff nurses to systematically assess, monitor, and make judgments about the quality of care provided to their patients as measured against established standards of care.

All professional practice model units have developed an internal quality assurance program. At present on the Meyer 3 inpatient unit, there are two quality assurance committees. One committee is responsible for concurrent chart auditing to evaluate documentation in light of Joint

Commission of Healthcare Organization guidelines. The second committee was devised to coordinate evaluative research efforts.

A senior clinical nurse developed and pilot tested a 16-item consumer questionnaire evaluating the effectiveness of primary nursing and patient satisfaction. This tool is given to every fifth patient at the time of discharge. Results have yielded valuable information, which is shared with all nursing staff and assists in making changes to enhance nursing practice on the unit. This unit-based approach had made quality assurance meaningful to the nurses. At present, the quality assurance committee is exploring other creative ways to ascertain outcomes that will assist in modifying practice to better meet the goal of providing quality patient care. It is expected that nurses working in the practice model are professionally accountable for evaluating the outcomes of their practice.

ROLE FUNCTIONS

Clearly defining the roles of the nursing staff within the practice model is essential for articulating professional accountability and for eventually redefining the roles to make them more effective. All of the nursing staff participate in this process. Professional accountability of clinical nurses is defined in the areas of practice, competence, professional development, quality assurance, and peer review.

Each staff nurse is expected to (1) meet or exceed the established standards of care and practice; (2) function at a minimum basic level of competence in all clinical practice situations or determine when clinically incompetent to care for particular patients; (3) actively pursue professional development; (4) evaluate outcomes of clinical practice by participating in quality assurance monitoring; and (5) solicit feedback on practice and identify areas for growth through a system of peer review.

A competency-based structure of performance identifies three levels: basic, master, and expert. Once at the expert level of clinical practice, a staff nurse may decide to remain at the clinical nurse level—with the option of expanding his or her practice in the areas of unit operations, research, advanced practice, or education—or seek a senior clinical nurse promotion.

The role of the senior clinical nurse is defined as a leadership position in the practice model. The senior clinical nurse functions as an expert clinician in the areas of professional nurse accountability previously described and additionally is expected to function as a coordinating leader of a peer review group and of the maintenance committees of the practice model.

A brief digression may be useful here to describe this in more detail. For example, the Meyer 3 unit has five ongoing maintenance committees, which are in the areas of nursing practice, environmental and nursing resources, staffing standards, quality assurance, and marketing. Each committee consists of four to five nurses from the unit. The senior clinical nurses are expected to coordinate and facilitate the activities of these committees, and the clinical nurses are expected to participate in the activities. Some senior clinical nurses have found it useful to rotate leadership responsibilities to the clinical nurses to facilitate their development and their participation in the committees.

Each committee establishes goals for the year, resolves problems that arise, and reports on its activities to the entire staff at the practice model meetings that are held six times a year. Attendance at these meetings by all practice model members is expected, and coverage for the unit is arranged by the clinical manager (head nurse). When a committee recommends major changes in practice, a discussion occurs and a vote is taken. Although the group aims for a consensus, often majority rule will be accepted. It is important to note that there are no hard and fast rules and that flexibility and ongoing evaluation have been key to keeping the system thriving.

Senior clinical nurse role development is fostered through monthly meetings with the clinical manager and the unit-based clinical specialist. The focus of these meetings is on the status of practice on the unit, the development of the nursing staff, peer review, unit morale, and planning for the practice model meetings.

The unit-based clinical specialist role is unique to the Meyer 3 professional practice model and evolved out of the advanced professional development that occurred on this unit. The unit-based clinical specialist holds a master's degree in nursing, functions at the highest level of competence in practice, and is coordinating leader of the nursing practice committee. The role is operationalized as 75% clinical practice and 25% staff development. The staff development activities focus on facilitating the peer review process and on mentoring nurses interested in a clinical specialist career track.

The role of the clinical manager results from the redefinition of the traditional head nurse role. The areas of accountability specific to this role are resource management, organization, support, vision, and marketing. Included are the procurement and utilization of several types of resources (e.g., nurses, monies, materials, and supplies); unit operations, including environmental and support service issues; organizational structure, support, and communications; visionary planning that is based on an awareness of emerging health care trends; the identification of nurses' educational needs that will guide development and definition of practice on the unit; the assessment of patient needs; and the promotion of the staff's ability to meet these needs.

Operationally the clinical manager functions as a role model for nursing service administration, represents the nursing staff at the departmental and central organizational levels, and is coordinating leader of the nursing, environmental resources, and marketing committees. Additionally, the clinical manager remains clinically competent in practice and mentors nurses who have an administrative career development focus. The primary role of the clinical manager is to help integrate professional practice on the unit and to provide leadership that encompasses facilitating, supporting, mentoring, consulting, articulating clear expectations, fostering development by encouraging risk taking, rewarding success, promoting collegial relationships, and holding nurses individually accountable for professional practice. The previously described unit-based practice model structure allows every member of the staff to be a valuable, indeed essential, contributor to the success of the unit.

BENEFITS

This model provides benefits to (1) nurses, (2) patients, (3) the health care organization, and (4) the nursing profession. The benefits to the nurse have been referred to throughout this chapter. They include increased job satisfaction, increased morale, increased professional autonomy, improved collegial relationships, enhanced professional development, increased professional compensation, increased retention, and decreased negative time use.

The benefits to patients are predominantly related to improved quality of care. Although no formal research studies to measure quality of care outcomes have been done to date, it seems reasonable to believe that highly motivated professional nurses who establish and define standards of care, evaluate effectiveness through quality assurance measures, and are empowered to make changes that can improve care do provide a better quality of care to patients.

The benefits to the health care organization include quality care, nurse retention, stabilization of nursing costs over time, an improved hospital image, and a reduced threat of nurse unionization. Quality care provided by professional nurses who maintain a consumer-focused approach to care and who review outcomes of patient satisfaction at the time of discharge serves to enhance the hospital's image and marketability. Cost savings occur due to decreased turnover, decreased use of agency nursing, enhanced productivity, and decreased negative time use. Lastly, nurses who are empowered and valued and who share in organizational decisions that affect nursing practice are unlikely to need a union to represent them in dealing with the administration.

Finally, the nursing profession benefits from professional practice because it allows nursing to attain professional status within the health care organization. This enhances nursing's professional worth and creates a positive image of nursing. This serves to attract able persons to careers in nursing and assures nursing's viability in the future health care market.

NEGATIVES

Two major considerations when deciding to implement a model are the time needed for development and the cost per unit. Obviously, implementation calls for a major transformation as the staff nurses take on additional responsibility and nurse managers allow the process of empowerment to occur. The length of time required can vary from 1 year to 18 months, and the associated cost is an additional 10% above the base salaries of nurses on traditional units. This initial start-up cost is neutralized over time because of the decreased recruitment training dollars and decreased utilization of purchased nursing services.

Additionally, one must consider that decentralized communication, group problem solving, and shared decision making take longer. However, once a change in practice is made, the results are positive and long lasting.

SUMMARY

It is important to note that the restructuring process is a "grass-roots" endeavor. Although the impetus for change at Johns Hopkins Hospital came from the administration, the actual planning and implementation of the practice model was accomplished by nurses at the unit level. A transformation of ideas and philosophies must come from both the nursing administration and the individual nurse. Each nurse contributes to the planning, implementation, and maintenance of the models and thus has a vested interest in and commitment to its success. A change of this nature cannot be imposed. It must come from the individuals who will be accountable for its success or failure—the bedside nurses.

The time frame for developing a model varies from 1 year to 18 months. During this time nurses learn to trust that the tenets of the model will be supported by the peer group, the head nurse, and the administration. This trust is the foundation upon which the model is based.

The practice model is a decentralized management system that delegates authority and accountability for patient care to those at the staff level. Its intent is to provide structure while simultaneously allowing flexibility and creativity in designing models that are congruent with the diversity of patient and staff needs. The professional practice model is applicable to staff in most settings. Since its initial implementation on Meyer 7 in 1981, it has been implemented in various departments at the hospital: the cardiac operating room, the emergency room, outpatient areas, surgery, pediatrics, psychiatry, and the neuroscience critical care unit. This represents approximately 25% of the 1500 nurses employed by Johns Hopkins Hospital. Because of the length of time it takes to implement the model, different units are at various stages of development. The process cannot be hurried.

In view of the nursing shortage and the current and anticipated economics of health care, one of the most significant challenges facing hospitals is to attract and retain professional nurses. It is time to depart from the traditional responses to this challenge and to identify and address the real issues: autonomy and parity for nursing practitioners within the organizational structure. Implementing the professional practice model is a way of addressing them that holds out the promise of success.

REFERENCES

Cleland, V.S. (1982). Nurse's economics and the control of nursing practice. In L.H. Aiken and S.R. Gortner (Eds.), *Nursing in the 1980's: Crises, opportunities, challenges.* Philadelphia: J.B. Lippincott.

Cleland, V.S. (1978). Shared governance in a professional model of collective bargaining. *Journal of Nursing Administration, 8*(6), 39–43.

Chapter 6

Cooperative Care: A Common-Sense Approach for Patient Care Delivery Systems

Sandra W. Murabito

Murabito's chapter analyzes a model for patient care that shifts the focus of practice from what health care professionals can do to get the patient well and home to how the patient can get him- or herself well and home. This approach involves a reversal of the patient role and the professional roles that support it. Patients in this project have a moderate acuity, but they do require hospitalization. Nurses, selected on the basis of competency and source of satisfaction, tend to be more mature and seasoned.

A key component of the model's success is the care partner, a family member who must agree to become involved in the hospitalization. Environmental factors also contribute to the model's success. These include shared governance (i.e., nurses participate in organizational decisions that affect them), the sharing of physical spaces by patients and care partners, and nursing support services (including management support).

The dramatic changes experienced by the health care industry over the last decade are forcing administrators to carefully evaluate the efficiency and productivity of their patient care delivery systems. Characteristics of an ideal program include the generation of quality health care in a cost-effective fashion, utilization of human resources to their fullest potential, and creation of an environment conducive to the satisfaction of consumers

I would like to express my deep appreciation for the support of my husband and family throughout the writing of this chapter. Without their help and patience, it would not have been possible. A special thanks also goes to my colleagues who assisted in editing this chapter: Sharon Adkins, Adrienne Ames, Linda Betz, Rebecca Culpepper, Barbara Holzclaw, and Cheryl Schmidt. My gratitude is also extended to Kelly Hollis, my typist, who persevered through my rough drafts.

Correspondence regarding the contents of this chapter should be addressed to Sandra W. Murabito, RN, Nurse Coordinator, Cooperative Care Center, P.O. Box 120134, Nashville, Tennessee, 37212.

and health care professionals. The Cooperative Care Center at Vanderbilt University Medical Center (VUMC) offers a viable way to achieve the ideal.

THE CONCEPT

The basic concept of *cooperative care* is not new. In fact, acute care institutions have been experimenting with similar forms of care for over 25 years. In the literature, units providing such care have been classified under descriptors such as *self-care, progressive care, interactive care,* and even *minimal care.* Still others are denoted by the predominant diagnosis of the unit (e.g., *diabetes center*). The major patient populations served in those units are characterized by minimal to moderate acuity, chronic illness requiring massive life style changes, or the need for extensive rehabilitative therapy.

Cooperative care is a method of delivering nursing care to patients who require hospitalization but not necessarily intensive, 24-hour nursing observation. A self-care philosophy, intensive patient education, and a wellness-oriented atmosphere are crucial to a cooperative care center's operation. Cooperative care centers differ from the other types of self-care units previously mentioned. The discriminating characteristic is the joint involvement of the patient and family as active participants in the care during the hospitalization. Nursing interventions are provided, but the patient maintains a more proactive role in seeking the assistance and guidance of health care professionals.

The number of cooperative care centers in the United States is surprisingly small. These centers vary widely in terms of size, populations served, admission criteria, and scope of practice. The most prominent is the cooperative care center at the New York University Medical Center. Many institutions, including VUMC, used this program as a paradigm in creating their own centers. A partial list of existing cooperative care programs, including addresses, is in Appendix 6-A.

ASSUMPTIONS

The cooperative care concept is grounded in self-care principles. Central to the VUMC model is the belief that hospitalized patients wish to be active participants in their care. This assumption may or may not reflect reality. Personal preference, culture, past experiences, and the current physical ailment may influence acceptance of responsibility in an institutional setting. The patient's initial response may be one of "culture shock," since expectations regarding traditional hospital services are contradicted (Stewart & Ufford, 1981). Comprehensive patient orientation programs are essential in order to avoid incongruity and promote positive relationships.

Second, the model assumes that individuals have the capacity to learn. Patient education is a primary therapeutic tool in the cooperative care system. Theoretically, those persons with mental disabilities, sensory deficits, and age limitations should be excluded from the center. However, the cooperative care model provides a built-in support system for these situations—the incorporation of a family member as a *care partner*. Any patient who is alert, oriented, and clinically stable and has a care partner could conceivably be a candidate for this unit.

Third, the model suggests that a homelike environment is therapeutic to a patient's convalescence. Through simulation of a more familiar atmosphere, the negative connotations of hospitalization are expected to decrease. This is achieved through room decor, provision of privacy, and reduction of restricted patient areas on the unit. Units that have utilized patient satisfaction tools have found scores related to environmental factors in cooperative care to be extremely high (Gibson & Pulliam, 1987; Grieco, 1987; Jenna, 1986).

HISTORICAL DEVELOPMENT

The VUMC Cooperative Care Center, licensed for 50 beds, first opened its doors in September 1982. The unit was one of three centers involved in a broader expansion called the *Stallworth Rehabilitation Center Project*. The other units were a 30-bed rehabilitation facility and a regional burn center for middle Tennessee and the bordering areas of Kentucky and Alabama. The desire for diversification and expansion of services within the VUMC complex was the major impetus for this project. The possibility of utilizing existing space in an area vacated as a result of the medical center's relocation to a newly constructed facility was an additional consideration.

A special task force of nurses, physicians, administrators, and financial managers created a committee to plan the entire implementation process for the Stallworth project. After careful research, discussion, and site visits, the New York University Cooperative Care Center was chosen as the model for the VUMC unit. The committee chose to alter the New York University model's admission criteria so as to encourage the presence of care partners without requiring them. A limit on the acceptable acuity level was an additional guideline for admission to the unit.

The unit began as a 20-bed pilot program in a portion of the student health building. A separate group called the *Cooperative Care Advisory Committee* was formed at this time to address issues regarding the center's utilization, marketing strategies, and additional program needs. The project gained momentum, and by January 1984 the center had moved to a larger renovated area in the Round Wing of the hospital. It occupied two patient care floors and had a 34-bed capacity. The entire planning and implementation process, including the operation of the pilot unit, required approximately 3 years. (Note: The unit has since been reduced to 16 beds. See the section "Current Operations" at the end of the chapter.)

GOALS

The initial goal of the VUMC Cooperative Care Center was to provide patients and family members the unique opportunity to be active participants in the health care process and to provide quality, cost-efficient health care. Many hospitalized patients do not require intensive, 24-hour nursing services. By grouping these selected cases into one unit, a reduction in costs can be realized (Glass & Warshaw, 1978). Many other benefits, ranging from patient satisfaction to staff nurse retention, can also be attributed to the implementation of this model. These will be discussed later in this chapter.

COOPERATIVE CARE COMPONENTS

The components of cooperative care at VUMC currently include patient and family participation, education using a multidisciplinary approach, and a wellness-oriented environment. A thorough understanding of these program values by all involved staff is critical for successful implementation. The specific methods by which the center's staff promotes these concepts will be discussed.

Patient Participation

The evolution of the parental medical model and unprecedented growth in technology have resulted in "asymmetrical relationships between health care professionals and patients contributing to a condition of learned helplessness among many consumers" (Johns, 1985, p. 153). Twenty-five years ago, Parsons (1951) described the typical patient role as passive and compliant. Lack of cooperation was explained by patient deviance. Unfortunately, this traditional view continues to be accepted by many health care professionals.

Patients have not always been mere passive recipients of care. Before the 18th century, sick persons treated themselves with folk remedies and family members assisted their recuperative efforts. The traditional health care system as we know it breeds and reinforces dependency. Health care professionals possess the ultimate control. This phenomenon is manifested in activities such as dispensing medications and construction of schedules for activities of daily living. Tasks are performed on the patient with no consideration given to the individual's role in promoting recovery and wellness.

Active patient participation can be an effective strategy for alleviating the negative implications of the illness and giving autonomy to the patient (Caporael-Katz, 1983). Shared responsibility between the patient, the care partner, and health care professionals is essential. The goal is to incorporate the patient's perspective, thoughts, and actions into the plan of care. Participation begins with the admission process and continues throughout the hospitalization. Research indicates that patient participation can promote positive patient-nurse interactions, satisfaction with medical care, and even enhancement of patient performance (Langer & Rodin, 1976; Littlefield & Adams, 1987; Lum et al., 1978; Pool, 1980). Therefore, this strategy could have long-term positive implications for patients in all health care settings and populations.

Family Participation

Family members involved in the cooperative care experience are called *care partners*. A care partner's responsibilities include assisting the patient with activities of daily living, participating in the learning process regarding required life style changes, and being a supportive companion throughout the hospitalization. This role is different from a care*giver* role. The care partner and patient share responsibilities. As the patient regains physical health, the care partner gradually decreases participation. The ultimate goal is for the patient to independently assume all health care responsibilities. In the case of patients who are chronically, physically, or mentally incapacitated, a care partner may evolve into a permanent caregiver.

In the VUMC cooperative care system, a care partner is required only for patients who are not able to perform activities of daily living with minimal assistance. Otherwise, a family member's attendance is encouraged but not essential for admission to the center. The patient's physical and emotional needs partially determine the care partner's length of stay. When no relative is available, a close friend or companion may be chosen to fulfill the care partner role.

Patient Education

Patient education is a primary therapeutic activity in VUMC's Cooperative Care Center, and it is a component of virtually all program areas and interventions. The staff nurses, pharmacists, and dietitians join together to provide information to patients and care partners. The primary objective is to get each individual to function independently and confidently within the prescribed life style parameters by the time of discharge. All patient care activities are carried out in a manner that promotes self-care. Medications are self-administered (if appropriate). Any other treatment regimens, such as dressing changes, gastrostomy feedings, or insulin injections, are explained and demonstrated to the patient and care partner. Gradually they accept responsibility for performing these tasks. Instruction in techniques for dealing with any alteration in activities of daily living also occurs.

Formal classroom instruction takes place individually or in groups in the education center. This room is solely dedicated to patient education and is unique to the Cooperative Care Center. A variety of patient education materials and pamphlets, which are either developed internally by VUMC or commercially prepared, are available. Additional teaching resources include printed handouts, self-help booklets, relaxation tapes, slides, videos, and replicas for return demonstrations. Instructional aids can be as simple as an empty food box used for learning how to read labels to determine sodium content. The subject matter of the structured classes ranges from diet and health promotion activities to information about chronic disease processes. Instruction frequency is determined by the patient's needs and interest. Standardized teaching plans are available to the staff nurses, since they are primarily accountable for classroom education.

The pharmacists and dietitians are invaluable resources for patients and family members. The dietitians teach all group education classes regarding diet restrictions, meal planning, and healthy diet tips. Individual counseling is also available. Referrals can be made to ascertain food preferences, complete comprehensive diet histories, or offer suggestions for nutritional management.

The pharmacists that serve the Cooperative Care Center are located in a satellite unit separate from the central department in the main hospital. This pharmacy provides medications in multiple-dose pill bottles rather than unit doses. One-on-one consultations occur regularly for patients who are started on new drugs or have questions concerning their current medication therapy. Education regarding the purpose, method, and time of administration and potential side effects is also given. Another benefit is the ability of this department to assist in checking the progress of patients involved in the self-administration program. Written patient information sheets are available for commonly prescribed medications. These materials were developed and produced within the pharmacy department.

Nursing is central to the successful education of the patient and family. Primary nursing is the patient care delivery modality used in the VUMC Nursing Department, and it is incorporated into the Cooperative Care Center. Patient–primary nurse relationships tend to support the cooperative care model. In addition, the nursing staff has access to other consultants in the hospital, such as social services and clinical nurse specialists.

Coordination of multiple disciplines and resources then becomes a major responsibility for the cooperative care nurse. Weekly discharge conferences are held with all team members to determine each patient's progress, response to treatment, and need for continued interventions after discharge.

Wellness Environment

Generally hospitals are regarded as unpleasant places to be, and few people are unconcerned about the prospect of admittance to a facility (Roth, 1972; Tagliacozzo & Mauksch, 1972). The environment is totally foreign, with uniform-clad caregivers, intimidating machinery, and confinement to one room (except when escorted by a health care employee). Levin (1978) has characterized the hospital setting as hostile and contradictory to the espoused goal of patient independence. Patients are expected to have their baths between 8 AM and 12 PM every morning, wear hospital-provided garments, take medications on unrealistic time schedules, and unquestioningly accept orders from any health care worker dressed in white. On the other hand, health care professionals expect patients to automatically perform all of these duties and more upon discharge. In essence, double messages are sent. Greico, founding medical director of the cooperative care center at the New York University Medical Center, concurs with Levin's opinion. He states, "The traditional acute care hospital setting with its concentration of technological devices and its reliance on staff members to deliver all services to the bedside of each patient breeds dependency rather than stimulating the independence to return home. The stress and dependency engendered by hospitalization can itself be an impediment to recovery" (1987, pp. 2–3).

Health care institutions did not intend for their environment to impede the recovery of hospitalized patients. However, in planning facilities, many professionals have ignored the basic principles regarding human needs and satisfaction in order to promote sterile, efficient, and organized environments.

The Cooperative Care Center at VUMC is designed in such a manner that many of the aforementioned barriers to recovery are eliminated. The center is keyhole shaped and consists of 16 spacious patient rooms. Each of these rooms has large windows to accommodate scenic views of the Nashville skyline or Vanderbilt campus. In addition, each room is carpeted and has homey furniture in earth colors and with wood finishes, including a bed, desk, several chairs, and a sofa bed for the care partner. Telephones, televisions, and call lights for emergency needs are also provided. The oxygen, suction, and sphygmomanometer wall units provide the only indication that the patient is in a hospital room.

Patients are free to go anywhere on the unit. The nurses station is open and accessible to all persons. There is a nutrition room directly behind the station, complete with microwave, ice machine, canned drinks, juices, crackers, and soups. In addition, patients have access to the linen closet and supply rooms. The patient lounge provides a pleasant atmosphere for group dining at lunch and dinner. Recreational activities are provided weekly by a hospital volunteer. The television, stereo, tape deck, game closet, magazines, and well-stocked refrigerator make this an enjoyable relaxation area for patients, care partners, and visitors.

Patients are encouraged to wear their own clothes or pajamas. A washer and dryer are also available on the unit for patient use. The nursing staff wear street clothes and white lab coats in an effort to reduce the regimented atmosphere often found in health care institutions.

UNIT STRUCTURE

The Role of Nursing in Cooperative Care

The nursing staff is a vital link in the successful implementation of the VUMC model. The overall decentralized nursing service philosophy of the medical center also applies to cooperative care. Primary nursing is central in the daily practice of staff nurses. Shared governance principles are implemented by means of clinical service councils, staff action committees, nursing bylaws, and a clinical ladder advancement program. Staff nurse participation on committees (sometimes as chairpersons) and in the development of patient education materials and protocols for nursing standards is encouraged. Research and educational activities, in addition to clinical practice, are respected at all levels in the institution. Figure 6-1 indicates the chain of command and communication flow for the center.

Nursing Staff Characteristics

Nursing professionals are essential in the cooperative care model. Staff nurses must possess a registered nurse license, a wide knowledge of various medical and surgical specialties, excellent communication skills, and the ability to instruct people in individual and group settings. In addition, staff nurses must be comfortable in relinquishing control to the patient in such a fashion that the patient does not feel abandoned. Those nurses who derive satisfaction primarily through the performance of tasks and doing things for patients are probably not appropriate for this clinical practice

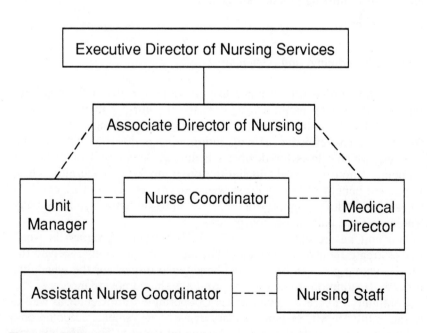

Figure 6-1 Chain of Command

setting. For these reasons, only experienced and well-rounded, mature professionals should be considered in selecting personnel.

Educational background and years of experience are also important factors to consider. Theoretically, baccalaureate-prepared individuals are preferred, as their background is consistent with the teaching responsibilities of the center. However, associate degree and diploma nurses with at least 2 years of medical or surgical experience and good clinical judgment skills have demonstrated that higher education is not essential. Multiple patient populations and the need to present health information clearly to laypersons make new graduates less likely candidates for the center. A strong unit-based orientation given by a senior staff preceptor, combined with an emphasis on self-care principles, has proven to be the most successful method of training.

At present, the cooperative care nurses are all female, with a mean age of 35.7 years. The staff is equally divided among those with associate degrees, baccalaureate degrees, and diplomas. Approximately 25% of the nurses were on the original charter staff of the Cooperative Care Center. Resignation rates are significantly lower than for the overall hospital. Reasons stated for leaving the unit include changes in personal life situations (e.g., retirement, motherhood, and family relocation) and the desire to leave clinical nursing practice altogether.

Staffing, Scheduling, and Assigning

The Cooperative Care Center has positions for 10.4 FTE registered nurses and 3.0 FTE medical receptionists. The nurse:patient ratio is 1:8 for all shifts, 24 hours a day, 7 days a week. This staffing pattern allows for a more cost-effective unit operation. The majority of the staff are salaried, which allows for flexible scheduling. As a result of the recent implementation of a weekend staffing program, 75% of the nurses have the added benefit of having every weekend off. The staff involved in the weekend scheduling option work 12-hour shifts on Saturday and Sunday. The nurses are paid on an hourly basis.

The unit has recently developed a self-scheduling program in which nurses create their own schedules. The staff have generally received this project with a positive attitude and heightened respect for the scheduling process. In addition, this program promotes shared governance.

Continuity of care is valued in the Cooperative Care Center as well as in the entire VUMC system. Primary or associate patients accepted on a voluntary basis dictate the patient assignment process. The remaining patients are divided equally with regard to acuity, nursing expertise, and interest. Each nurse's previous assignment is also considered. Application of the primary nursing philosophy fosters trusting and satisfying relationships between patients and nurses.

Nursing Support Services

Support services, such as supply distribution, housekeeping, patient transport, phlebotomy, and IV therapy, are accessible to the Cooperative Care Center. However, the medical receptionists contribute the most vital services to the center. In VUMC, they fall under the supervision of the nursing service. Routine tasks, such as transcribing physicians' orders, answering the telephone, and facilitating the scheduling of tests, are standard throughout the hospital.

As for cooperative care, communication with patients and family members is the medical receptionists' most crucial function. A receptionist is often a patient's initial unit contact, and making a good first impression is paramount. Screening telephone calls, communicating with ancillary departments, and completing time-consuming paperwork frees the RNs to deliver direct patient care and engage in teaching activities.

Nursing Management

The nurse coordinator has 24-hour accountability for the delivery of quality patient care. Nursing services at VUMC are decentralized, with many responsibilities located at the unit level. Common areas of nurse coordinator accountability throughout the hospital include the management of personnel, unit cost, equipment, and supply resources. The nurse manager in the Cooperative Care Center must also market the unit within the medical center as well as to the community and other interested parties. This requires commitment, time, and energy. The cooperative care philosophy is often unfamiliar to health care professionals. Inadequate understanding of the philosophy seems to breed misperceptions. It is largely the nurse manager's responsibility to make it clear to other nursing units, physicians, and ancillary personnel.

Maintenance of the education center is another important responsibility of the nurse manager. Reordering pamphlets, updating materials, and identifying potential resources that could benefit the program are among the required activities. Until the summer of 1987, maintaining the education center was the responsibility of a clinical nurse specialist, who also gave formal classroom instruction and promoted staff development. Economic constraints, coupled with the untimely resignation of the clinical nurse specialist, resulted in the deletion of the position. The staff nurses then assumed the major responsibility for patient education. Although this required a period of adjustment and reeducation, participation in educational activities has been viewed as worthwhile. The nurse coordinator is accountable for all tasks not taken over by the staff nurses. Clinical nurse specialist consultation is still available to the center through the main hospital.

Management Support Services

The VUMC nurse coordinator has four support persons to assist and support her in administrative activities. They include an associate director of nursing, medical director, assistant nurse coordinator, and unit manager. Each has specific tasks that facilitate the functioning of the center.

The associate director of nursing is the nurse coordinator's direct link to the executive director of nursing services and other hospital administrators. Decisions regarding policy and unit guidelines are made in conjunction with the associate director. General troubleshooting of management issues and long-range planning are also important functions of this position.

The medical director's primary responsibilities are marketing the cooperative care unit to other physicians and consulting on administrative and policy-related decisions. At the VUMC Cooperative Care Center, the medical director is also instrumental in soliciting donations from drug companies to financially support maintenance of the education center.

The assistant nurse coordinator is philosophically a management position, yet 75% to 95% of the work time is involved in direct patient care. This position helps the nurse coordinator maintain communication ties with the day-to-day unit operations. It is also designed to groom nurses with leadership potential for future management opportunities.

The unit manager assists the nurse coordinator in routine plant operation maintenance and ordering of equipment and supplies. Minor clerical accounting duties constitute an additional responsibility. The unit manager in the Cooperative Care Center has more tasks to complete than normal, as the center has many appliances to keep in working order. Examples include maintenance of audiovisual equipment and washer-dryer facilities.

ECONOMIC ASPECTS OF COOPERATIVE CARE

The Concept

The Cooperative Care Center achieves cost savings primarily through reduction of the nurse:patient ratio. Its ratio is 1:8 compared with the 1:4 ratio in the main hospital. The resulting workload is possible for several reasons. First, patient–care partner responsibilities decrease the amount of task-oriented activities for the nurse. Second, many of the patient activities are centralized, specifically group teaching and dining. Third, the unit generally draws a lower acuity patient, because admission criteria require clinical stability. Continuous observation is therefore not required. All of these factors result in the decreased need for traditional bedside nursing care.

In view of these factors and New York University Medical Center's preliminary reports of a 30% to 40% savings in cost, the VUMC administration made the decision to offer a reduced room charge for cooperative care. This distributed the majority of the cost savings to the valued customers—the patients. The room rate is one-third less than the rate in the main hospital.

On the other hand, one could easily justify charging the regular room fee. In many ways, patients and families actually receive more for their investment. Benefits range from a homelike atmosphere and individualized learning opportunities to the ability of the families to stay with the patients at no additional cost.

Financial Description

The 16-bed cooperative care unit has an average daily census of 12 patients (an average occupancy rate of 75%). The minimal accepted staffing level for both low and maximum occupancy is identical. Approximately 93% of the unit's budget is dedicated to salary and benefit expenses, and the remaining funds are allocated for the routine operation of the center. The past fiscal year proved to be profitable in terms of revenue for the unit. This broke the trend of budget deficits in past years.

Revenue is achieved through patient billing. Third party reimbursement is not difficult, since all cooperative care patients must first meet hospital admission criteria to gain entrance. The patient mix in terms of payers is similar to that of the overall hospital.

Patient Classification Tool

The patient classification tool is closely associated with monitoring budgetary and staffing activities. The Medicus NPAQ package is utilized throughout the VUMC nursing department (*Manual for Medicus,* 1972). The tool consists of a computer scantron sheet with 37 descriptors relating to patient care activities. Each criterion has a standard assigned point value. Each patient is evaluated daily with this tool. Preset ranges of scores provide guidelines for classification of each patient's acuity into one of five types. Nursing hours required for each patient type are also assigned in this system.

The target hour-per-workload index selected by this institution is 4.0 hours. The budgeted acuity for this center averages 0.8 and ranges from 0.6 to 1.1. Table 6-1 offers a breakdown of patient types and nursing hours required in the Cooperative Care Center.

The majority of patients are classified as Type I or Type II. A Type III patient is a candidate for the unit only if the condition is temporary (4 hours or less) or a care partner is present. The nursing-hours-per-workload index for the center typically ranges from 5.4 to 6.9 hours. This occurs due to the small unit capacity and the requirement that two nursing professionals be present regardless of acuity or occupancy rates.

The preceding information is beneficial to facilitate objective comparisons between this center—other VUMC units, and even to similar health care facilities. Identification of general trends in acuity and nursing hours is another advantage. Presently, VUMC's center is the only cooperative care center that uses the Medicus tool.

CASE STUDY

The following description is intended to give the reader an idea of how the cooperative care process might take place. The results are positive and

Table 6-1 Patient Classification Description for the Cooperative Care Center

	Type I	Type II	Type III	Type IV	Type V
Category %	52	37	11	0	0
Hours of Care	(0–3)	(3–5)	(5–10)	(10–16)	(16+)
Acuity					
Values	.5	1.0	2.3	3.8	5.5

uncomplicated in this example, but it should nonetheless provide a broad view of the process.

Mrs. J. is a 48-year-old, obese black female with hypertension and recently diagnosed diabetes. She presents in the emergency room with complaints of headaches and dizziness. On examination, her blood pressure is 196/114 and her blood glucose level is 410. She is admitted to the Cooperative Care Center for evaluation and treatment of hypertension and diabetes. She is fearful and worried over the prospect of being admitted to the hospital.

Upon arrival to the floor, Mrs. J. and her husband are greeted by the medical receptionist and escorted to their room. Their nurse, dressed in street clothes and a lab coat, introduces herself and orients Mr. and Mrs. J. to the room. Mrs. J. is surprised by the spacious accommodations and is pleased her husband will be able to stay with her on the sofa bed during her stay. After an initial nursing history and assessment, the tour proceeds as the nurse explains the concept of patient-family participation. She describes how the center is different from the hospital and the benefits they will achieve during the hospitalization.

Joint exploration of the unit is the next step in the orientation process. Specific highlights include an introduction to the education center, lounge, self-service linen closet, washer, dryer, and snack room. Upon return to their room, Mr. and Mrs. J. unpack their belongings. Mrs. J. voices concern that she will not be able to care for herself alone. Mr. J. offers reassurance and optimism.

Upon examination of Mrs. J.'s history, along with pertinent information provided by Mr. J., it is discovered that Mrs. J. only takes her hypertensive medication when she "feels bad" and has no idea of the names of her medications or their intended purposes. Her diet is high in sodium and cholesterol, and she gets no regular exercise. She is presently 75 pounds over her ideal body weight. Her primary nurse begins to plan her care, with a heavy emphasis on educational principles regarding hypertension, diabetes, and cardiac risk factors.

During Mrs. J.'s 5-day stay, she and her husband spend a majority of their time in the education center. They attend classes on diabetes, insulin injections, and foot care and also review principles of hypertensive care. Validation of acquired knowledge is assessed daily by the nursing staff.

Mr. and Mrs. J. work together to ensure Mrs. J. is taking her medications. She is given a simplified medication record to document the times she administers her medication. All pills are delivered in bottles with multiple doses. Mr. J. assists her in administration of her insulin, since her eyesight is poor. The pharmacist provides Mr. and Mrs. J. with written information regarding the medications and answers any questions they may have.

Mr. and Mrs. J. attend a class on 2-gram sodium diets. They are given cooking tips to reduce sodium and learn foods to avoid. The dietitian asks Mrs. J. to plan a weekly menu to document her understanding of the information provided.

Throughout the hospitalization, Mrs. J. becomes stronger and more confident. She is discharged with a knowledge of her disease process, medication therapy, and routine treatments and care. Mr. J. is able to assist her with any tasks that require sharp eyesight and with general troubleshooting activities. No other assistance is required, since Mrs. J. performs all other responsibilities.

Although this is an idealized example, the process is typical. Some patients are initially unsure, pessimistic, and even dissatisfied at the prospect of performing their own treatments. In these cases, the staff's expertise in communication becomes essential. Each patient and each care partner must be assessed in order to determine how to present the self-care concept and how much responsibility to assign. This is crucial for a successful hospitalization.

PROGRAM RESULTS

The self-care concept has been the focus of considerable interest over the past decade. However, few institutions in the United States have incorporated the concept into their health care delivery systems. Examination of the potential impacts may offer insight. The benefits and drawbacks of implementing this concept are varied. The program's impact will be described in relation to the patient, the staff, and the organization as a whole.

The Patient

The VUMC Cooperative Care Center is patient-centered. Therefore, the patient is likely to receive the majority of benefits through participation in the cooperative care system. Perhaps the most striking of these positive outcomes is consumer satisfaction. Many individuals prefer being independent and in control. As a result, patients are often comfortable and confident in caring for their health—whether preventively or during an illness and convalescence. The environmental "creature comforts" of the center make the hospital stay more bearable, even pleasant. Patient comments on discharge questionnaires include "I'll never go to a regular hospital again," "My family could stay with me!" and "I could even take my own medicines!" All of these indicate the consumers surprise and their satisfaction with the cooperative care experience.

There are patient populations for which the cooperative care delivery model is not appropriate. Examples include patients who require intensive nursing care or who possess mental deficits that inhibit learning. In some cases, an individual may prefer not to enter the center. Such persons generally feel that being hospitalized necessitates the "full service" of nurses doing tasks for them. The VUMC unit does not accept patients who adamantly oppose the philosophy.

The Staff

The unit is designed for the mature, experienced nursing professional who values the opportunity to incorporate self-care philosophy into daily practice. The cooperative care delivery system allows nurses to devote the majority of their efforts to educating patients to help themselves. The regimented policy, the restricted patient areas, and the focus on task-oriented priorities found in traditional settings are eliminated.

The major drawback is the increased demand for clinical experience, communication skills, and professionalism. Today's health care environment, with its inadequate supply of nurses, makes meeting this demand difficult. In addition, education at the associate degree or diploma level may not prepare nurses for this type of clinical experience.

The Organization

The health care institution reaps varied benefits through implementation of the cooperative care concept. One positive outcome is satisfaction for both patients and the nursing staff. With stiff competition among hospitals, patients' contentment with the health care experience becomes increasingly important. Hospital administrators continue to rate nurse retention and recruitment as a top priority. Thus, nurses' job satisfaction is paramount. Nurses generally compose the largest labor force within the institution. Therefore, providing alternative and enjoyable practice settings may be an advantageous strategy for administrators to employ.

Cost savings is also of interest to hospital management. Cooperative care allows cost reductions in several ways besides a decreased nurse:patient ratio. For example, there are reduced construction costs. According to administrators at New York University Medical Center, construction expenses were decreased 30–40%, primarily because oxygen and suction outlets were not needed. In addition, a nurses station might only be needed on one floor (Basting, 1984). At VUMC, a previous hospital ward was renovated, negating the need for costly construction. Oxygen and suction outlets were already in place and a nurses station was only needed on one of the two floors. Therefore, the majority of costs were for employee salaries and benefits, equipment, and furniture. Construction costs were estimated to be $8,000 per bed (Gibson & Pulliam, 1987).

Savings may also be realized in decreased lengths of stay for patients under DRG payment systems. In cooperative care, patient education begins upon admission and continues throughout the hospitalization. This should hasten recovery and prepare patients more effectively for discharge.

Increased nurse retention may also prove to be an unexpected cost benefit. Decreased turnover can save many dollars as a result of lower orientation costs.

Drawbacks depend on the setting, implementation, and emphasis of each individual center. Perhaps the major drawback is the need for total project support from the unit level to the top ranks of hospital administration. Lack of understanding or commitment at any level can sabotage efforts. Staff nurses must be able to communicate and practice within the model's assumptions and concepts. Nursing administrators are essential in providing support to the staff and marketing the unit concept to the institution and throughout the community. Well-respected physicians within the facility who are willing advocates for innovative health care delivery models are of vital importance. Hospital administration must be willing to allocate start-up budgets for construction, staffing, and marketing plans. A cooperative care program requires everyone to work together for success. Getting such total commitment in large health care facilities having varied interests can be difficult. Before beginning a cooperative care center, doing an assessment of the institution's political and economic climate and values is imperative.

The unknown legal liabilities of cooperative care constitute another disadvantage. At this time, self-care issues have not been tested in courts of law. This makes decisions regarding the limits of patient participation even more complex.

Current Operations

Many cooperative care centers have decreased beds, changed program goals, or been terminated. The VUMC Cooperative Care Center has found that being flexible is a necessity for successful operation. After about 2 years of permanent operation, the center began to have a pattern of unpredictable declining census. This phenomenon was due to several factors. The first was the implementation of the DRG system. Since admission to the unit was based partially on minimal acuity, occupancy rates vacillated downward. The major services affected were dermatology, arthritis, and radiation oncology. Most of the unit's previous population are now seen in ambulatory and outpatient settings. The reluctance of physicians to utilize a nontraditional unit located in a facility separate from the main hospital also seemed to play a role in the decreased census. In response, an administrative decision was made to decrease the bed capacity to 16, deleting one floor from the center. The need for additional outpatient clinic space also hastened this decision.

Other changes made in the center include deletion of treatment rooms for nurse-patient visits and deletion of the observation center. These components were identical in purpose to components of New York University Medical Center's cooperative care center. Reduction of space to a single floor, in addition to staff reduction, made continuance of these components costly.

Although census rates increased slightly, the center's inconsistent utilization persisted. In the summer of 1987, the unit altered its admission criteria to accept patients with a higher level of acuity (such patients were required to have care partners). A marketing plan was developed and became an ongoing responsibility of the center's management staff. Currently, occupancy rates average between 70% and 75%, compared with previous figures of 65% to 70%. This includes weekend and holiday census statistics, which are characterized by a 30% to 50% drop in occupancy.

Implementation of the cooperative care concept involves a calculated risk. Few centers have been in operation long enough to produce financial analyses that indicate the implications for manpower or cost-benefit reports that suggest that commitment to such an endeavor would be profitable or even feasible. Lack of adequate measuring tools, interaction of multiple intervening variables, and the difficulty of selecting appropriate outcome indicators to demonstrate patient response obstruct quantification of the effects of cooperative care (Gallicchio, 1977).

CONCLUSION

Our nation's health care must be dynamic and responsive to society's ever changing needs and attitudes. Coile (1986) suggests that the surviving health care institutions in the year 2000 will be those who purposely delineate their future rather than becoming victims of the current competitive and hostile environment. Implementation of innovative patient care delivery systems such as the cooperative care model may prove to be a viable and even lucrative option for administrators to consider in controlling their destiny.

REFERENCES

Basting, T. (1984, June). Cooperative care benefits may go beyond initial cost savings. *Health Care Systems,* pp. 25, 32.

Caporael-Katz, B. (1983). Health, self-care and power: Shifting the balance. *Topics in Clinical Nursing, 10,* 31–41.

Coile, R.C. (1986). The new hospital: Future strategies for a changing industry. Rockville, MD: Aspen Publishers.

Gallicchio, J.D. (1977). *Consumer self-care in health* (Report No. NCHSR77-154). Hyattsville, MD: Department of Health, Education, & Welfare, National Center for Health Services Research.

Gibson, K.R., & Pulliam, C.B. (1987). Cooperative care: The time has come. *Journal of Nursing Administration, 17*(3), 19–21.

Glass, A.L., & Warshaw, L.J. (1978). Minimal care units: Mechanisms for hospital cost containment. *Health Care Management Review, 3*(2), 33–40.

Grieco, A.J. (1987, May). *Home care/hospital care/cooperative care: Options for the practice of medicine.* Paper presented at the Section of Medicine of the New York Academy of Medicine.

Jeanna, J.K. (1986, May-June, July-August pt. 2). Toward the patient-driven hospital. [Parts 1 & 2] *Health Care Forum, 29*(3), pp. 8–18, *29*(4), pp. 52–59.

Johns, J.L. (1985). Self-care today—in search of an identity. *Nursing and Health Care, 6*(3), 153–156.

Langer, E.J., & Rodin, J. (1976). The effects of choice and enhanced personal responsibility for the aged: A field experiment in an institutional setting. *Journal of Personality and Social Psychology, 34*(2), 191–198.

Levin, L.S. (1978). Patient education and self-care: How do they differ? *Nursing Outlook, 26*(3), 170–175.

Littlefield, V.M., & Adams, B.N. (1987). Patient participation in alternative perinatal care: Impact on satisfaction and health locus of control. *Research in Nursing and Health, 10*(3), 139–148.

Lum, J.L., Chase, M., Cole, S., Johnson, A., Johnson, J.A., & Link, M.R. (1978). Nursing care of oncology patients receiving chemotherapy. *Nursing Research, 27*(6), 340–346.

Manual for Medicus System Nursing Productivity and Quality (NPAQ) Tool (1972). Evanston, IL: Medicus System Consulting Firm.

Parsons, T. (1951). *The social system.* Glencoe, IL: The Free Press.

Pool, J.J. (1980). Expected and actual knowledge of hospital patients. *Patient Counseling and Health Education, 2*(3), 111–117.

Roth, J. (1972). The necessity and control of hospitalization. *Social Science and Medicine, 6,* 425–446.

Stewart, K.P., & Ufford, M.R. (1981, November-December). Patient education plays integral role in innovative acute care unit. *Promoting Health,* pp. 4–6.

Tagliacozzo, D.L., & Mauksch, H.O. (1972). *Patients, physicians and illness* (2nd ed.). New York: The Free Press.

BIBLIOGRAPHY

Alfano, G.J. (1971). Healing or caretaking—which will it be? *Nursing Clinics of North America, 6*(2), 273–279.

Bartkowski, J.J., & Swandby, J.M. (1980). Charting nursing's course through megatrends. *Nursing and Healthcare, 6*(7), 375–377.

Beckman, R. (1971). The therapeutic corridor. *Hospitals,* pp. 73–80.

Beglinger, J.E. (1987). Designing tomorrow. *Journal of Nursing Administration, 17*(4), 4–5.

Bells, S.S. (1986, May-June). Cooperative care: An educational ideal whose time has come. *Promoting Health,* pp. 8–11.

Chang, B.L. (1980). Evaluation of health care professionals in facilitating self-care: Review of the literature and a conceptual model. *Advances in Nursing Science, 3,* 43–58.

Cousins, N. (1979). *Anatomy of an illness.* New York: W.W. Norton.

DeVries, A. (1970, June 16). Progressive patient care. *Hospitals,* pp. 43–48.

Duff, R.S., & Hollingshead, A.B. (1978). *Sickness and society.* New York: Harper & Row.

Green, K.E., & Moore, S.H. (1980). Attitudes toward self-care. *Medical Care, 18,* 872–877.

Green, L.W., Werlin, S.H., Schauffler, H.H., & Avery, C.H. (1977). Research and demonstration issues in self care: Measuring the decline of mediocentrism. *Health Education Monographs, 5*(2), 161–189.

Krantz, D.S., Baum, A., & Wideman, M.V. (1980). Assessment of preferences for self-treatment and information in health care. *Journal of Personality and Social Psychology, 39,* 977–990.

Levin, L.S. (1981). Self-care: Towards fundamental changes in national strategies. *International Journal of Health Education, 24*(4), 219–228.

Linn, L.S., & Lewis, C.E. (1979). Attitudes toward self-care among practicing physicians. *Medical Care, 17*(2), 183–190.

Mullin, A. (1980). Implementing the self-care concept in the acute care setting. *Nursing Clinics of America, 15*(1), 177–189.

Naisbitt, J. (1982). *Megatrends.* New York: Warner Books.

Roter, D.L. (1977, Winter). Patient participation in the patient-provider interaction: The effects of patient question asking on the quality of interaction, satisfaction and compliance. *Health Education Monographs,* pp. 281–315.

Sarver, S.C., & Howard, M. (1982). Planning a self-care unit in an inpatient setting. *American Journal of Nursing, 82,* 1112–1114.

Seeman, M., & Evans, J.W. (1982). Alienation and learning in a hospital setting. *American Sociological Review, 27,* 772–782.

Seeman, M., & Seeman, T.E. (1983). Health behavior and personal autonomy: A longitudinal study of the sense of control in illness. *Journal of Health and Social Behavior, 24*(6), 144–160.

Steiger, N.J., & Lipson, J.G. (1985). *Self care and nursing: Theory and practice.* Bowie, MD: Brady Communications Company.

Sturdevant, M., & Mickey, H. (1966, February 16). An experiment in minimal care: Part 1: Determining eligibility and demand. *Hospitals,* pp. 44–50.

Sturdevant, M., & Mickey, H. (1966, March 1). An experiment in minimal care: Part 2: Patient and staff acceptance. *Hospitals,* pp. 50–54.

Sturdevant, M., & Mickey, H. (1966, March 16). An experiment in minimal care: Part 3: Nursing time and costs. *Hospitals,* pp. 70–74.

Taylor, S.E. (1979). Hospital patient behavior: Reactance, helplessness, or control? *Journal of Social Issues, 35*(1), 156–184.

Vertinsky, I.B., Thompson, W.A., & Uyeno, D. (1974). Measuring consumer desire for participation in clinical decision making. *Health Services Research, 9*(2), 121–134.

Weiss, S.J. (1986). Consensual norms regarding patient involvement. *Social Science and Medicine, 22,* 489–496.

Weiss, S.J., & Davis, H.P. (1983). The health role expectations index: A measure of alignment disparity and change. *Journal of Behavioral Medicine, 6*(1), 63–75.

Appendix 6-A

Cooperative Care Resource List

This is a partial list of cooperative care centers in the United States. Health care facilities whose cooperative care units are not mentioned are encouraged to contact Barbara Giloth, Manager, Patient Education, Center for Health Promotion, American Hospital Association, 840 North Lake Shore Drive, Chicago, IL 60611.

Good Samaritan Hospital and Medical Center
Wilcox Cooperative Care Unit
1015 NW Twenty-Second Avenue
Portland, OR 97210
503 229-8394

Greater Southeast Community Hospital
Alternative Care Unit
1310 Southern Avenue, SE
Washington, DC 20032
202 574-6971 or 202 574-5455

Medical Center Hospital of Vermont
Cooperative Care Unit
Colchester Avenue
Burlington, VT 05401
802 656-5125

Mercy Hospital
InterActive Care Unit
Pride & Locust Streets
Pittsburgh, PA 15219
412 232-8111

Methodist Hospital
Cooperative Care Program
1604 North Capital Avenue
Indianapolis, IN 46206
317 929-3533

New York University Medical Center
Cooperative Care Center
530 First Avenue
New York, NY 10016
212 340-7201

Plantree Model Hospital Project
2040 Webster Street
San Francisco, CA 94115
415 923-3681

Vanderbilt University Medical Center
Cooperative Care Center
1161 21st Avenue
S-7400 Medical Center North
Nashville, TN 37232-2210
615 322-6203

Chapter 7

New York University Medical Center Cooperative Care Model

Pamela M. Becker

The author describes a large, self-care, acute inpatient unit that has grown over 10 years. The length of experience gives credibility to the model. The author reports a cost savings that is worthy of note, particularly because the majority of nurses are well prepared and experienced. A key to the cost savings is the use of care partners. In addition, the number of clerk typists and their value to the unit suggest that they play a larger role than in other units. Costs are compared to those of a traditional medical inpatient unit.

The author reports a decrease in complications related to adherence to medical regimes. Other significant outcomes include increased satisfaction by the nursing staff and high levels of satisfaction by patients and care partners.

The Cooperative Care Unit of New York University Medical Center is a 104-bed acute care unit. It was the first, and is the largest, cooperative care unit in the United States. Established as a pilot program in 1979, the unit is a success as far as patients, physicians, and nurses are concerned. Patients enjoy greater independence and a greater sense of control over their lives and health care. Physicians enjoy the patients' increased knowledge and preparation. Nurses enjoy the opportunity to teach and to make a lasting change in the health care patterns of individuals.

The Cooperative Care Unit philosophy is that patients have both a right and a responsibility to participate as full partners in their own health care during their hospitalization. Participation in decision making produces a feeling of "being a part of" rather than just "agreeing to." It also allows patients to become more capable of and comfortable with the management of their care at home after discharge. To assist this process, a *care partner* stays with the patient from admission to discharge. The care partner might be the spouse, another family member, or a friend who will have an ongoing significant relationship with the patient. All visits with physicians and nurses and all educational sessions are attended by both the patient and the care partner.

Although patients with many diagnoses are admitted, the majority are medical patients needing intermittent intravenous drugs, chemotherapy, invasive procedures such as endoscopy, cardiac catheterization, or coronary angioplasty. In 1979, more than half the patients admitted were transfers from other acute care units (frequently they were recuperating from various surgical procedures). The luxury of a several-day stay in a cooperative care unit to recuperate and gain strength and independence after illness or surgery—during which time patients could enjoy health education concerning, for example, reduction of risk factors—is rarely possible. Today, the majority of patients are direct admissions and only 10% are transfers from other acute care units.

When first admitted to the Cooperative Care Unit, the patient and the care partner are seen by the nurses in the Education Center. The initial assessment focuses on the learning needs of the patient and care partner. Their understanding of the current health problem and its anticipated impact, their knowledge of the philosophy of cooperative care, and the availability of the care partner are assessed. An initial health care education plan is jointly developed. The patient and care partner are scheduled for classes (or individual sessions, if needed) from among the comprehensive assortment offered by the Education Center.

Educational sessions with a nurse educator are likely geared toward orientation to the Cooperative Care Unit (reinforced by a 15-minute videotape) and toward the procedure for which the patient was admitted. Care partner responsibilities are emphasized, and outpatient follow-up is suggested (if applicable).

Nutrition education is given a high priority, as many patients are nutritionally at risk due to complications of their disease or treatment. Supplements and snacks are available on order by the nutritionist. For patients or care partners who need diet counseling beyond what they receive during their hospitalization, there is the option to see a nutritionist in the Education Center as an outpatient.

Social workers in the Education Center are available to assist in care during and after hospitalization. Arrangements for care partners can be facilitated by the social workers if family members are not available. Assistance with discharge planning includes making referrals to appropriate agencies, counseling, and making arrangements for medical follow-up.

The staff of the Education Center consists of 4.5 full-time master's-prepared nurse educators, 2.5 nutritionists, and 3.0 social workers. A part-time movement therapist and a full-time recreation therapist are available. In addition, closed circuit television channels guide patients through progressive relaxation and imagery for stress reduction. A full-time master's-prepared nurse is the supervisor of the inpatient side of the Education Center. The busy outpatient side is staffed by a supervisor and numerous per-session professionals and nonprofessionals.

After the initial meeting in the Education Center, the patient and care partner are seen by a nurse in the Therapeutic Center for a physical and nursing assessment. A health history, including coping skills and home management of health-related problems, is obtained. The current medical plan, schedule of tests, medications, and treatments are discussed. A copy of the plan, revised when necessary, is given to the patient. The patient and care partner are then assigned to a room.

Patient rooms are on the 9th to 13th floors of the 15-floor Arnold and Marie Schwartz Health Care Center. These rooms are more homelike than hospitallike. The attractive decor, twin beds, and lack of suction, oxygen, and medical equipment create an atmosphere similar to that which the patient will experience after discharge. A small refrigerator and sitting area permit the patient and care partner to have visitors at their convenience in the comfort and privacy of their own room. Nursing staff is available 24 hours a day by telephone and by an emergency call system, but there are no nurses actually present on the patient floors.

The 14th floor contains the Education Center and the Therapeutic Center. Nurses are there 24 hours a day. Patients and care partners are given appointments with their primary nurses in the Therapeutic Center or scheduled for classes in the Education Center. Physicians see their patients in the examination rooms of the Therapeutic Center. The 15th floor contains the dining room, recreation area, and lounge, which has a magnificent view of the New York City skyline and the East River.

Although all patients must meet the standard criteria for admission as inpatients to an acute care hospital, cooperative care patients must also be strong enough or mobile enough to move independently from their rooms to the 14th and 15th floors, since all services are centralized there. Patients use wheelchairs, canes, or walkers as necessary. Assistance is provided by the care partners. The only other requirement for admission is that the patient not need continuous nursing observation, since only the care partner is available to observe and assist the patient on the patient floors.

Because of the centralized services and the elimination of costly medical equipment in each patient room, costs of delivering service are approximately 30% less than in other acute care units at the medical center.

Support services from other departments include a satellite pharmacy and a satellite admitting department, which are located on the 14th floor. The pharmacy is staffed with two physicians daily. A laminar air flow hood is used to mix the many chemotherapeutic and investigational agents used. In addition, a pharmacist is available each afternoon in the Education Center to teach patients and care partners the pharmacology of their drug regimens, warn of possible side effects or interactions, and assist in the management of the plan of care.

The satellite admitting department handles the 20–30 daily admissions and discharges. Occupancy of the unit has increased yearly to the current 89% average. During the week, when all hospital departments are fully operational, occupancy is 97% to 99%, with an active waiting list of 10–20 people.

New York University Medical Center has a four-step clinical ladder program. Nurses with 3 or more years of experience are senior nurse clinicians and eligible to apply for a position in the cooperative care setting. Since there is no medical house staff support, it is essential that the senior nurse clinicians feel confident in their skills and judgment. Although it is not mandatory, 50% of the 34 senior nurse clinicians are or are in the process of becoming master's prepared. Senior nurse clinicians in the Therapeutic Center independently assess each of their 13–15 primary patients daily, discuss progress with the health care plan, make recommendations (including the initiation of patient self-medication and symptom management), and evaluate the patient's readiness for discharge.

Since the patient population includes a wide range of clinical areas and each nurse is expected to function with a high degree of autonomy, orientation usually involves 6–8 weeks with a preceptor. Nurses orienting to cooperative care are experienced practitioners, many from critical care backgrounds. The change from following directions to giving directions requires support and guidance. In addition, all physician contact is with attending physicians rather than house staff. For those nurses who have had few encounters with the attending physicians, instruction in the appropriate etiquette eliminates anxiety and fosters cooperation.

The professional nursing staff in cooperative care also includes 4 full-time master's-prepared oncology nurse specialists and 3 third-level nurse clinicians. In addition to the administration of chemotherapy, the oncology nurse specialists assist the senior nurse clinicians and the patients and care partners in symptom management, education, and support. Patients on other acute care units of the medical center are also referred to the oncology nurse specialists for these services (if needed).

Patients returning from invasive procedures such as angiography, endoscopy, and biopsy frequently require professional nursing observation for limited periods of time. The Cooperative Care Unit contains a 6-bed observation room. Here patients are attended by their care partners under the direction of a third-level nurse clinician. The observation room is staffed Monday to Friday from 8:00 AM to 12:30 AM Thus, experienced nursing care is available to patients immediately postprocedure, when complications are most likely to occur. The duration of time spent in the observation room is usually 2–4 hours. In addition, patients who require continuous direct nursing observation for increased symptoms or new pathology can be cared for in the observation room until a bed on a more traditional unit becomes available. Emergency equipment, oxygen, suction, and other supplies for critical medical intervention are available in the observation room.

A small, versatile group of nursing assistants work in the cooperative care setting to provide support services. Two assistants are scheduled for the day and evening shifts and one is scheduled for the night shift. Nursing assistants take vital signs, maintain the flow of patients to the senior nurse clinicians, assist nurses and physicians with treatments as necessary, and maintain supplies and equipment.

Clerical support is provided by 11 full-time clerk typists. With a census of 104 patients and 104 care partners, keeping track of where everyone is can be difficult. Physicians frequently call the clerk typists prior to coming to the unit to request their patients report to the 14th floor. Room assignments and problems with rooms are handled by the clerk typists. Charts of all patients are maintained on the 14th floor by the clerk typists.

Patients experience an increase in satisfaction through alleviation of the anxiety and disaffection that are so often byproducts of the more traditional hospital experience. This outcome is largely due to the control patients and care partners can maintain while in the Cooperative Care Unit. Another patient outcome is the decrease in complications related to improper adherence to medical regimes. Due to the involvement of care partners and the emphasis on education, patients are discharged to a more supportive and knowledgeable environment.

An important economic outcome of cooperative care is cost savings. Comparable care for invasive procedures or medical treatments such as intermittent IV antibiotics is almost one-third more expensive on a traditional medical unit.

The most important outcome of cooperative care is that nurses have the opportunity to make use of all their skills and education. Nurses are able to assist patients and care partners to learn new skills and change those behaviors that are not effectively promoting health. The ability to truly make a difference in the lives of patients and their families provides the sense of satisfaction many nurses looked for when they decided to become nurses.

Chapter 8

A Cost Containment Model of Primary Nurses at Cedars-Sinai Medical Center

*Linda Burnes-Bolton, MaryAnn Davivier,
Margaret M. Vosburgh, Kathy Harrigan,
Lori Urbanec, and Roxane B. Spitzer-Lehmann*

The authors of this chapter present a model of primary nursing and its cost ramifications. The cost of nursing, as well as the implementation of this model, is detailed. The authors also describe a research project that examines primary nursing and its relationship to job satisfaction, performance, personnel costs, HPPD, and various types of shifts. For hospitals planning to implement primary nursing, this chapter will certainly be of great use.

The prospective reimbursement system has given nurses the unique opportunity to emerge as the vital link between cost-effectiveness and quality care. It has become increasingly evident that the successful American hospitals will be those that emphasize quality as their primary internal motivating force. Consumers, who may have no prior knowledge of health care, will be judging institutions with regard to quality care based on their perceptions of efficiency and caring. There is no one better positioned to understand the patient's concept of quality care than the nurse. Primary nursing is a model that allows meaningful relationships to develop between nurses and patients. These relationships, and the communication which develops, can ultimately reduce fragmented care, enhance collaboration with the medical staff, foster the patients' feelings of trust, and decrease the patients' length of stay.

The primary nursing philosophy underlies the Cedars-Sinai Medical Center (CSMC) professional practice model. This model puts responsibility and authority into the hands of nurses, each of whom has 24-hour accountability for the quality of care administered to a given group of patients. It is a system that allows decision making and resource mobilization to occur at the bedside and without costly delays. This professional nursing practice model has a positive impact on the quality of care, and it can positively influence the hospital's revenue base.

A recent cover story in *Hospitals* (Powills, 1988) described nursing turn-over as a major factor examined in determining credit worthiness. It suggests that poor quality of care can eventually weaken a hospital's credit rating.

It has been recognized for some time that turnover rates and low job satisfaction are attributable to a perceived inability of nurses to control their practice, provide quality care, and achieve positive patient outcomes.

In this era of prospective payment, the emphasis has changed from process-focused activities to outcome criteria. Nurses' quality assurance activities, and indeed their practice, have been influenced by the need to provide quality care that will result in a decreased lengths of stay for patients. Hospitals understand that financial stability is linked to well-managed patient care, which prepares patients for timely discharges. Adequate staffing levels have been shown to reduce nosocomial complications (Flood & Diers, 1988), which directly affects patient discharges and translates into a favorable bottom line for the hospital.

Allowing nurses to practice in a milieu of control where they can exercise professional judgment and establish caring, beneficial patient relationships will increase job satisfaction, reduce turnover, and may ultimately protect an institution's financial health. A recent study done in Ontario (Blenkam, D'Amico & Virtue, 1988) analyzed job satisfaction components 1 year and 3 years after instituting primary nursing; it found statistically significant increases in job satisfiers, specifically nurse-patient relationships and autonomy.

COMPONENTS OF THE MODEL

Philosophy

The primary nursing care philosophy is based on the belief that the patient is the central focus of the nurse and that nurses should have 24-hour accountability for patients. Primary nursing provides comprehensive and continuous patient care from admission to discharge by using the same RN (primary nurse) to coordinate, evaluate, and provide direct patient care (the RN uses the nursing process in planning this care). The patient's and family's involvement in care encourages a trusting nurse-patient relationship, thereby promoting continuity and effective discharge planning. The patient's and family's individual and collective needs are met efficiently as a result of the nurse's collaborative efforts with physicians, peers, and other health team members.

Peer accountability, review, and support are integral parts of the primary nursing system and they result in a continuous evaluation of patient care. In primary nursing, the responsibility (and authority) to make decisions about patient care devolves to the individual nurse. This responsibility allows the nurse to act as a change agent and patient advocate.

Primary Nursing Concepts

Primary nursing is a method of delivery nursing care so that the total care of an individual is the responsibility of one nurse rather than several. It implies a philosophy of nursing in which the patient is the central focus of the nurse and accountability for patient care is paramount. The *primary nursing coordinator* is a registered professional nurse who assumes 24-hour, 7-day responsibility and accountability for activities of an assigned nursing unit, with the main focus on patient and nursing staff needs. The *primary nurse* is a registered professional nurse responsible and accountable for (1) the nursing process for a specified number of patients, including but not limited to assessing patient needs and planning, implementing, and evaluating all aspects of patient care; (2) the delivery of care 24 hours a day from admission to discharge; and (3) participation in a communication triad between patient and physician. The *associate nurse* is a registered professional nurse who, in the absence of the primary nurse, assumes responsibility and accountability for maintaining individualized quality nursing care for a designated number of patients for an 8-hour period.
Keystones of primary nursing are

- continuity of patient care
- centrality of the patient
- responsibility to the patient
- patient advocacy
- centrality of the patient's life style and family
- emphasis on health (in the sense of wellness)
- patient education
- accountability to peers, the patient, and the physician
- goal directedness
- job fulfillment and retainment
- nurse practitioner autonomy
- patient inclusion in planning care

Comparison of Primary and Team Nursing

Given the characteristics described earlier, certain advantages of primary nursing are clear. Nurses who are aware of their patients' diagnoses and the ramifications become more involved with their patients. Continuity of care is fostered by uninterrupted care planning—shift to shift, nurse to nurse, and hospital to home. The scope of practice of RNs widen as they use their knowledge.

Patients realize that someone knows them as individuals from certain cultural and social backgrounds. Primary patients have opportunities to express their needs and concerns, and they will usually feel confident that their nurses will integrate these needs into their care. Within the system, patient care goals become clearly defined, which leads to increased patient participation in care, creates a platform for patient teaching, and increases the probability of a shorter hospital stay. Primary nursing ("my nurse," "my patient") has a positive effect on hospitalization.

Primary nursing also improves collegial relationships between physicians and nurses, who are then more likely to communicate and coordinate goals. Lastly, primary nursing helps bridge the gap between nursing education and nursing practice.

IMPLEMENTATION OF THE MODEL

Implementation planning began at CSMC in 1984, with designated task forces established in each unit. Each task force was responsible for an implementation schedule, determining staff education preparation needs, facilitating communication during implementation, and preparing a primary nursing resource manual.

The Primary Nursing Implementation Planning Committee

The purpose of this committee was to identify the specific needs of the unit and to facilitate the successful implementation of primary nursing through careful completion of the planning guide. The methodology for meeting the unit's primary nursing needs was determined by this committee.

Committee Establishment

The staff selected three staff nurses to represent all three shifts. The chairperson was the staff nurse who received the most votes or was elected chairperson at the first meeting.

Committee Ground Rules

1. Membership in the committee is voluntary.
2. The focus is on preparation and implementation of primary nursing.
3. The flow of ideas should be free, and all ideas deserve consideration.
4. Decisions can be made by members present at meetings.
5. All staff members are welcome to all meetings.
6. All decisions, before they are finalized, are to be discussed with the nurse manager or ADN.
7. Minutes from the meetings, as well as the unit's implementation schedule, are to be available to all staff, with copies for the ADN, ADN-special projects, and primary nursing coordinator.
8. The research process must be integrated into the timetable of events.

Chairperson's Responsibilities

1. Chair the meetings.
2. Follow up on tasks, such as the distribution of minutes and agendas.
3. Meet informally with the nurse manager and the committee members to discuss progress and needs.
4. Ensure that minutes are taken and recorded.
5. Adhere to committee ground rules.
6. Communicate the schedule of meetings to the nurse manager, the staff, and the primary nursing coordinator.

Exhibit 8-1 presents the implementation steps of the neurology unit.

ROLE EXPECTATIONS

In the primary nursing handbook, the following role expectations were identified for the various positions.

Nursing Coordinator

1. Knowledge of the philosophy and objectives of primary nursing as a modality for the delivery of health care.
2. Knowledge of each nurse's capabilities and limitations.
3. Acceptance of overall accountability for the quality of nursing care on and administrative management of the unit on a 24-hour basis.
4. Coordination of the primary nursing unit with ancillary departments and other members of the interdisciplinary health team.

Exhibit 8-1 Steps to Implementation on the CSMC Neurology Unit

1. Medical staff education—presentation of principles of primary nursing to all applicable attending staff.
2. Nursing staff education—presentation of principles of primary nursing and specifics of implementation to all levels of nursing personnel; focus on staff input and contribution.
3. Interdepartmental education—presentation of principles of primary nursing; focus on impact of support services and departments.
4. Patient room assignment—mechanism to be developed in which nursing coordinator, in collaboration with bed reservations, determines patient room assignment.
5. Walking rounds—establishment of protocol for walking rounds to be conducted between individual district personnel.
6. RN buddy system—establishment of RN buddy system for the specified time schedule.
7. LVN II job description—development of LVN II job description to provide motivation for and reward excellence of performance.
8. Medication administration—procurement of third set of keys for District III RN.
9. Measurement tools—selection of data collection tools to evaluate staff performance, staff perception of role, and patient perception of care.
10. Patient communications clerk (PCC) procedures—establishment of procedures/resources (e.g., 3 kardex, labelling, color coding, etc.) needed to handle orders and other clerical tasks.
11. Neuro step-down unit—procurement of resources and administrative support for establishment and maintenance of specialized district within unit.
12. RN staff—procurement of appropriate personnel to fill present vacancies on unit (e.g., RN for 7P–?).
13. Patient-nurse assignment—development of criteria to facilitate assignment of individual patients to primary nurse.
14. Discharge planning—education of staff regarding principles and methodology; development of protocol for continuous discharge planning.
15. Documentation—revision, development, and selection of appropriate forms, flowsheets, etc., to enhance documentation.
16. Supports—selection and maintenance of system of supports to provide for personal and professional development of staff.

5. Assignment of primary nurses to patients based on nursing expertise and patient and family needs.
6. Conformity of unit management with CSMC and nursing service policies and procedures.
7. Evaluation of primary nursing as an effective modality for delivery of quality patient care.
8. Accessibility as a resource for primary and associate nurses, patients, physicians, and other members of the interdisciplinary health team.

Clinical Nurse Specialist

1. Knowledge of the philosophy and objectives of primary nursing as a modality for the delivery of health care.
2. Facilitation of staff development through the identification of learning needs and provision of inservice education related to patient care.
3. Accessibility as a resource for the primary and associate nurses, patients, physicians and other members of the interdisciplinary health team.
4. Demonstration of excellence in theoretical and clinical aspects of patient care through role modeling for the primary and associate nurses.
5. Evaluation of primary nursing as an effective modality for the delivery of quality patient care.

Primary Nurse (RN, LVN II)

1. Accountability for the nursing care delivered to two to six patients.
2. Identification of the primary nurse's role with respect to patients, families, physicians, and interdisciplinary health team members.
3. Initiation and completion of a comprehensive assessment within 24 hours of the admission of a patient.
4. Development of a 24-hour patient care plan that prioritizes patient problems, identifies patient outcomes in behavioral terms, and delineates nursing interventions clearly and specifically.
5. Evaluation of nursing care based on patients' responses to interventions or progress toward desired outcomes.
6. Documentation of all pertinent aspects of the nursing process as it relates to the individual patient.
7. Administration of skilled, comprehensive, and individualized patient care.
8. Maintenance of open and effective channels of communication between the physician, patient and primary nurse.
9. Initiation of discharge planning upon admission.
10. Initiation of patient-centered conferences.
11. Utilization and coordination of various members of the interdisciplinary health team in the provision of care to individual patients.
12. Verification of physician's orders for those patients within the district.

Associate Nurse (RN, LVN I and II, NA)

1. Administration of skilled, comprehensive and individualized patient care as directed by the primary nurse.
2. Identification of the associate nurse's role with respect to patients, families, physicians, and interdisciplinary health team members.
3. Documentation of all pertinent aspects of the nursing process as it relates to the individual patient.
4. Participation in the communication triad of physician, patient, and primary nurse.
5. Participation in and, when indicated, initiation of patient-centered conferences.
6. Participation in discharge planning as directed by the primary nurse.
7. Participation in the development of 24-hour patient care plans.
8. Verification of physician's orders for those patients within the district (RN and LVN II only).

STAFF DEVELOPMENT

1. Inservice education (weekly): theoretical and practical information related to assessment, disease processes, and intervention techniques.
2. Psychiatry rounds (weekly): staff interaction with psychiatrists concerning personnel and patient issues.
3. Journal club (weekly): staff presentation of nursing or medical literature relevant to patient care on the unit.
4. Discharge planning conferences (weekly): interdisciplinary team review of each patient's status in relation to discharge.
5. Patient care rounds: patient case presentations for the purpose of problem solving and dissemination of information.

SUPPORT STAFF

Key to the implementation and effective operation of primary nursing at CSMC is the establishment of nontechnical support staff positions. In particular, the nursing services technician and the patient communications clerk are unitwide (one per unit) support personnel who can assume a number of nonnursing tasks and help increase the primary nurses' efficiency. The duties of a nursing services technician include

- ordering supplies and restocking unit cabinets
- checking patient rooms for cleanliness and safety

- transporting equipment to decontamination areas
- responding to code situations and gathering emergency supplies

Patient communications clerks handle much of the clerical work, maintain log books, answer phones, and enter data on computer terminals.

The LVN II is a clinical ladder upgrade of the standard LVN position. An LVN II, who requires more advanced medical and surgical concepts than an LVN, enters and verifies medication orders in the computer and performs other tasks in collaboration with the primary RN. LVN IIs not only enhance the productivity of primary RNs, but the position helps motivate many who desire upward mobility.

Others who support the primary nurses are the clinical instructors, who report to the nursing manager, and the clinical nurse specialists, who report to the clinical director but are available as resource persons throughout the department. Clinical instructors and nurse specialists are responsible for maintaining and developing the clinical competence of the nursing staff.

ORGANIZATION

As Figure 8-1 shows, the staff nurses, patient communications clerks, and nursing services technicians report to the assistant nurse manager, who

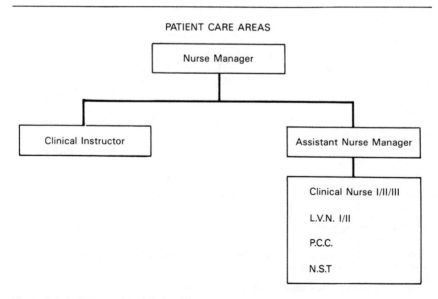

Figure 8-1 Staff Reporting Relationships

in turn, along with the clinical instructor, reports to the nurse manager. In many areas today, the nurse manager's position has evolved into a senior nurse manager position, with several assistant nurse managers and clinical instructors reporting to that position.

As many as six to eight nurse managers report to a clinical director, as does the clinical specialist for that nursing specialty (see Figure 8-2). Figure 8-3 shows the overall structure of patient care services, including medical social work and home care.

Supporting this structure, and in keeping with CSMC's decentralization, is an extensive committee structure, including unit-based quality assurance and joint practice committees and a staff nurse advisory board that brings input to the top executive level and coordinates efforts at the staff level. The Nursing Operations Committee is responsible for coordinating and overseeing clinical practice, and the Patient Care Executive Committee reviews and approves policies and procedures and new programs and services throughout the patient services area.

Thus, the autonomy and accountability of the primary nurse at the bedside is supported and coordinated by an extensive communication matrix (for more information on this structure, see Spitzer, 1986).

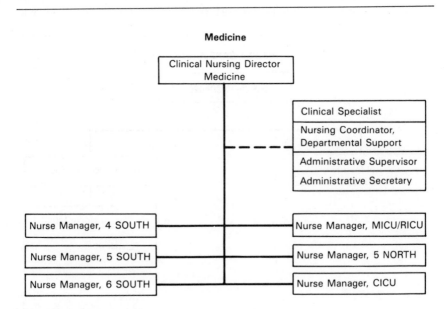

Figure 8-2 Organizational Chart for a Nursing Specialty

Patient Care Services

Vice President
Patient Care Services

Assistant to the VP

ADN, Special Projects
Staff Specialist

Director,
Nursing Operations

Director, Nursing
Research and Development

Director,
Medical Social Work

Assistant Administrator,
Nursing Finance

Medical

Surgical

Diversified Services

Operating Room Services

Parent-Child Health

Nursing Recruitment and
Marketing

Nursing Resources

Home Care Program

Palliative Care

Figure 8-3 Patient Care Services Organizational Chart

THE MODEL AS IMPLEMENTED AT CSMC

Advantages of the Model

1. The plan of care is designed and implemented by one nurse with an associate backup.
2. There is increased consistency.
3. Staff demonstrate increased collaboration with the nurse who has knowledge of the case.
4. There is increased communication with physicians and other health care team members.
5. The model increases continuity of care, with the primary nurse and associate nurse interchanging the same patients.
6. Follow up and problem solving is easier with lab, diagnostic studies, meds, and new orders.
7. Satisfaction among patients and nursing staff is increased.

Disadvantages of the Model

1. The decrease in RNs and the increase in LVNs creates an added burden for the RNs, who have to manage their own primary patients as well as cover the LVN's patients.
2. It is very difficult for the charge nurse (primary resource nurse) to lead staff on a shift basis and carry a full load of primary patients.
3. With 12-hour shifts, a primary nurse may admit a patient, yet the patient may be discharged during the 3 days the primary nurse is off duty.

Career Ladders

Primary nursing increases the motivation of staff to excel within the clinical ladder. The clinical ladder was developed at CSMC by staff nurses and includes four vertical levels (CNI–IV), with five steps in each. The criteria were written generically so as to be applicable to all units and specialties. Eight ladders were established for RNs, including Medical/Surgical, Operating Room, Labor and Delivery, Emergency Room, Thalians (Psychiatry)/Chemical Dependency, Pediatrics, Critical Care, and Ambulatory Care.

An RN may transfer from one specialty to another without affecting the clinical ladder. All applicants are evaluated by a credentialing board based on forms completed by the nurse manager, the clinical instructor or specialist, and one or more peers. Reevaluation occurs annually on the nurse's anniversary. The clinical level determines the nature and number of patients and responsibilities assigned but does not affect the nursing style. Primary nursing is used throughout the institution.

By taking full responsibility for total patient care, nurses are able to develop and promote themselves. Primary nursing has given clinical staff nurses an added incentive to use the clinical ladder. One requirement for clinical ladder promotion is the presentation of a patient case study. Primary nursing allows for the total patient care and acquisition of knowledge necessary to present the case in conference. Clinical nurses continue to utilize their role as primary nurses to move upward within the clinical ladder system.

Physical Structure

The patient rooms at CSMC are arranged in quads (groups of four). This is beneficial to primary nursing if assignments are based on location rather than order of admission. By grouping a primary nurse's patients together, call lights and patient needs can be handled promptly. However, in an area where assignments are made according to order of admission, this structure presents a problem. If patients are assigned at both ends of the hall and either side, the call lights cannot be seen by the same nurse. It is therefore considered best to have patients assigned to a primary nurse based on location insofar as this is possible.

CASE STUDY

Mrs. Brown was admitted on 10/10/88 to room 4802 with lung cancer. She was to receive her second course of chemotherapy. Nurse Tucker, RN, is assigned as Mrs. Brown's primary nurse. She admits the patient and explains that she will be Mrs. Brown's primary nurse from admission to discharge. She then formulates the plan of care based on Mrs. Brown's nursing diagnosis for this admission. Nurse Tucker will be responsible for her patient's care 24 hours a day. An associate nurse is assigned to Mrs. Brown on Nurse Tucker's days off. The plan of care is monitored and modified by the primary nurse throughout the hospitalization, based on short-term and long-term goals set initially in the care plan. Mrs. Brown is discharged on 10/15/88, having completed her second course of chemotherapy.

On 11/24/88 Mrs. Brown is readmitted to room 4815 for her third course of chemotherapy. Nurse Tucker is again assigned as Mrs. Brown's primary nurse, because she has acquired a knowledge base of the patient's disease process and can best formulate a plan of care pertinent to this admission. The patient-nurse relationship is already established, which will facilitate implementation of the plan of care and achievement of goals set by Nurse Tucker.

THE COST OF IMPLEMENTATION

The length of time necessary to institute primary nursing will vary from institution to institution. The first part of this chapter describes one hospital's approach to implementation. The following should serve as a general guideline for anyone considering the implementation cost of primary nursing.

Because primary nursing involves the application of a particular philosophy, the majority of resources go into communication and implementation design. If a nursing unit is to implement primary nursing, it must budget the time and resources to allow staff to learn the concepts embodied in the philosophy, discuss how the concepts relate to their particular area, design and implement their model, and make necessary readjustments. There has to be an understanding that primary nursing is an evolving, individual process and requires careful budget planning and administrative commitment.

Using the implementation schedule from CSMC, it was estimated that approximately 33 hours of nursing time per participant were utilized to meet the implementation schedule guidelines. An institution's total hours and cost can be calculated based on the total number of individuals involved at each stage in the process. Costs can be controlled and time saved if the primary task force leader is skilled in group dynamics. Once the task force members have a clear understanding of the principles and have agreed on how they will be applied in their unit, the momentum picks up and each task force member becomes both an advocate and resource person. A skillful task force leader makes use of open communication and consensus building and directs the group toward a common goal. Clinical nurse specialists now serve as task force leaders, but at the outset of the project, CSMC engaged a project leader whose sole responsibility was the institution of primary nursing.

Table 8-1 summarizes the time investment necessary for each activity listed in the primary nursing implementation schedule. Table 8-2 gives the approximate total time for each of four broad categories of implementation activities. Education was defined as formal instruction. Communication included any activity that involved information sharing or the creative application of formal principles.

The time variables change from unit to unit, and economies of scale are realized as the staff become familiar with the process and proceed along the learning curve. Some peaks and troughs in efficiency should be expected as individuals progress through the stages. In the final analysis, expending resources to educate staff to exercise their full charge as professionals is wiser than embarking on an expensive recruitment campaign. CSMC's nurses and patients also profit from its utilization of a delivery system that enhances professional practice.

EVALUATION STUDY

In 1987 the CSMC Nursing Research and Development Department conducted a formal evaluation of the professional practice model based on primary nursing from its inception. The objectives of the evaluative study were to

1. determine if nursing job satisfaction would increase as a result of primary nursing
2. determine if nursing performance would improve as a result of primary nursing
3. determine if nursing hours per patient days could be decreased under primary nursing
4. determine if personnel costs would remain constant under primary nursing
5. determine the effect of primary nursing on patient and physician satisfaction

Goals

The central question investigated in this study was, When given an opportunity to practice primary nursing (with support provided during evenings, nights, and weekends), will nursing personnel perform better? The goals of the project were to determine if

1. primary nursing affects job satisfaction, performance, personnel costs, and hours per patient day

Table 8-1 Primary Nursing Implementation Schedule Guidelines

1st Meeting	2nd Meeting (All Staff)	3rd Meeting	4th Meeting	5th Meeting	6th Meeting
1. Inservice all staff to primary nursing. 1.0	1. Complete planning guide questionnaire. .30	1. Complete planning guide questionnaire. .30	1. Complete planning guide questionnaire. .25	1. Complete planning guide questionnaire. .25	1. Complete planning guide questionnaire. .20
2. Update staff on nursing process. .30	2. Establish goals and measurable objectives for primary nursing practice. 3.0 1.0	2. Have task forces from previous meetings present completed tasks. .45	2. Have task forces present completed tasks. .45	2. Have task forces present completed tasks. .45	2. Have task forces present completed tasks. 1.00
3. Select Primary Nursing Implementation Planning Committee. .15	3. Identify staff educational needs. 1.30	3. Delegate tasks. .40	3. Delegate tasks. .40	3. Delegate tasks. .10	3. Delegate tasks. .10
4. Outline behavioral objectives consistent with clinical ladder criteria for PN and APN. Development 3.5 Communication 1.0	4. Delegate tasks. .20			4. Inservice house staff, other disciplines, and departments. 1.30	4. Set target date. a. Day of week with good staffing and high census. .10 b. All patients to be assigned. .50
5. Review timetable with staff. .15					
6. Contact primary nursing coordinator. .20					

Table 8-1 continued

7th Meeting	8th Meeting	9th Meeting	10th Meeting	11th Meeting	12th Meeting
1. Complete planning guide questionnaire. .20	1. Complete planning guide questionnaire. .20	1. Complete planning guide questionnaire. .15	1. Complete planning guide instructions. .15	1. Complete planning guide instructions. .15	1. Complete planning guide instructions. 1.0
2. Outline comprehensive roles of nurse manager, clinical instructor, assistant nurse manager, clinical nurse specialist, PN, APN. Development 4.0 Communication 1.0	2. Delegate tasks. .10	2. Delegate tasks and research summary and data collection responsibilities. .20	2. Review and revise research summary. 1.0	2. Review decisions with staff and committee. 1.0	2. Distribute questionnaire .30
3. Have task forces present completed tasks. .20	3. Have task forces completed present tasks. .40	3. Contact quality assurance coordinator regarding quality assurance studies. 1.0	3. Submit summary to Nursing Research. .15	3. Schedule feedback sessions. .15	3. Complete quality assurance audit. .40
4. Delegate tasks. 1.0	4. Contact Nursing Research. .25				4. Set dates for quarterly questionnaire and quality assurance audits. .20

Table 8-2 Time Investment by Category

Category	Percentage of Total
Educational Time	15%
Communication Time	25
Implementation Time	53
Evaluation Time	7

2. a Monday–Friday 8-hour work schedule affects job satisfaction, performance, personnel costs, and hours per patient day
3. a Saturday–Sunday 12-hour work schedule affects job satisfaction, performance, personnel costs, and hours per patient day
4. significant differences in job satisfaction, job performance, hours per patient day, sick time, and overtime exist among
   - primary nurses working Monday–Friday, 0700–1530
   - associate primary nurses working Monday–Friday, 1500–2330
   - associate primary nurses working Monday–Friday, 2300–0700
   - associate primary nurses working Saturday and Sunday, 1900–0700

Methodology

A multiple indicator evaluative design was employed to monitor the effect of the staffing model on nursing, patient, and institutional outcomes. This design has proven effective in measuring change in personnel delivering care and in recipients of nursing care by examining outcome criteria. Prior to implementations of the model, cost analysis, process quality assurance audits, personnel management variables, and staff nursing and physician satisfaction were measured.

The nursing unit chosen for the study was a general 24-bed medical-surgical unit. Staff were asked to participate throughout the medical center. Those nurses who participated did so because they wanted to be involved in the demonstration project. The model was implemented and data were collected for a period of 10 months.

Data Collection

The process variables measured in the study were nursing process documents, including the patient care plan, discharge plan, and medical record data retrieval tools, which were previously tested for reliability and validity.

The outcome variables measured were nursing, patient, and institutional outcomes.

Process audits were conducted monthly by the quality assurance coordinator. Results were reviewed at regularly scheduled meetings. The nurse coordinator was responsible for collecting data on overtime, agency usage, and nursing hours per patient day. These data were also collected by comparing the budget against actual reports prepared by the department's financial analyst. Satisfaction tools were administered to physicians, staff, and patients and the results were tabulated by the research department.

Findings

The cost per unit of service (UOS) decreased gradually from $75 per UOS to $62 per UOS, a total savings of 24%. Personnel indices also drastically decreased: no turnover, 1% sick time, and no agency supplementation. Nursing hours per patient day decreased from 5.0 to 4.2 as a result of the change in the number of personnel (a mixed staff of 17 reduced to 12 full-time RNs).

The ability of the staff to implement the nurse process vastly improved. Patient care planning, nursing documentation, and patient education all improved. Nurse, physician, and patient satisfaction increased. Physicians reported that "Nursing care is vastly improved" and "Nurses are knowledgeable and assume direct responsibility for patient care." Patients reported that they received quality care and that "their" nurses spent more direct time with them and their families. Nurses stated they had more professional autonomy, collaborated more with physicians, and experienced greater satisfaction overall.

Discussion and Summary

The data from this project indicate that a supportive professional practice model based on primary nursing can positively affect patients, nurses, physicians, and institutions. The study demonstrated that nurses can provide cost-efficient, quality care that addresses various needs of the health care system. Exhibit 8-2 illustrates cost savings inherent in the model. CSMC will continue to conduct research on effective and efficient practice models in an effort to improve quality and increase practitioner satisfaction and flexibility.

Exhibit 8-2 Comparison of Traditional Staffing to Professional Practice Model Staffing

---

Traditional Staffing Model
  Assume: 16 patients per day
          5 NHPPD
          RNs on 12-hour shift
          LVNs on 8-hour shift
          VHSO Factor—1.13
          17% employee benefits
          5% agency/overtime supplementation
          8:9.6 RN:LVN ratio
  Cost: $411,000 (18.6 FTEs)
Professional Practice Model
  Assume: 16 patients per day
          4 NHPPD
          RNs on 8-hour shift Monday through Friday
          RNs on 12-hour shift on Saturday and Sunday
          No LVNs Monday–Friday
          No LVNs on 12-hour shifts on Saturday and Sunday
          VHSO Factor—1.13
          17% employee benefits
          2% agency/overtime supplementation
          12:2 RN:LVN ratio
  Cost: $390,000 (12 FTEs)

Measurable patient care outcomes such as length of stay, rate of return to functional capacity, and patient and family response to nursing must also continuously be investigated. CSMC nursing believes that its primary nursing model, which can positively affect both cost and the quality of care, must be supported and validated through extensive research.

CONCLUSION

Primary nursing has provided an excellent means for improving patient satisfaction, overall quality of care, and staff job satisfaction while reducing costs and increasing productivity. It has also allowed ample opportunity for development of staff professionalism through involvement in CSMC's system of participative management (Spitzer, 1986). However, with increased economic pressures, along with the continued shortage of RNs, the institution is now exploring the feasibility of adapting a case management model with integrated patient care services. Nonetheless, primary nursing is seen as a necessary and effective intermediate step in the evolution toward a more efficient patient care delivery system.

REFERENCES

Blenkam, H., D'Amico, M., & Virtue, E. (1988). Primary nursing and job satisfaction. *Nursing Management, 19*(4), 41–42.

Flood, S.S., & Diers, D. (1988). Nurse staffing, patient outcome and cost. *Nursing Management, 19*(5), 34–43.

Powills, S. (1988, May 5). Nurses: A sound investment for financial stability. *Hospitals*, pp. 46–50.

Spitzer, R.B. (1986). *Nursing productivity: The hospital's key to survival and profit.* Chicago: S-N Publications.

BIBLIOGRAPHY

Aske, K.L. (1974). Primary nursing: Evaluation. *American Journal of Nursing, 74,* 1436.

Bakke, K. (1974). Primary nursing: Perceptions of a staff nurse. *American Journal of Nursing, 74,* 1432–1434.

Braun, B.J. (ed.). Primary nursing. (1977, Winter). *Nursing Administration Quarterly.*

Daeffler, R.J. (1975, March-April). Patient's perception of care under team and primary nursing. *Journal of Nursing Administration,* pp. 20–26.

Dahlen, A.L. (1975). With primary nursing we have it all together. *American Journal of Nursing, 75,* 426–428.

Isler, C. (1976, February). Rx for a sick hospital: Primary nursing care. *RN,* 60–66.

Logsdon, A. (1973). Why primary nursing? *Nursing Clinics of North America, 8*(2), 283–291.

Manthey, M. (1973). Primary nursing is alive and well in the hospital. *American Journal of Nursing, 73,* 83–87.

Manthey, M. (1980). *The practice of primary nursing.* Boston: Blackwell.

Manthey, M. (1980, June). A theoretical framework for primary nursing. *Journal of Nursing Administration,* pp. 11–15.

Marram, G.D. (1974). *Primary nursing.* St. Louis: C.V. Mosby.

McCarth, D. (1978, May). Primary nursing: Its implementation and six month outcome. *Journal of Nursing Administration,* pp. 29–32.

Mundinger, M.O. (1973). Primary nurse: Role evaluation, *Nursing Outlook, 21,* 642–645.

Page, M. (1974). Primary nursing: Perception of a head nurse. *American Journal of Nursing, 74,* 1435–1438.

Robinson, A.M. (1974, April). Primary nurse: Specialist in total care nursing at two teaching hospitals, Part 1. *RN, 37,* 31–33.

University of Minnesota Health Science Center, Department of Nursing Hospitals (1972). *Primary nursing: A handbook for implementation.* Minneapolis: University of Minnesota.

Wobbe, R.R. (1978, March). Primary versus team nursing. *Supervisor Nurse,* 34–37.

Wolff, K.G. (1977, December). Change: Implementation of primary nursing through advocacy. *Journal of Nursing Administration,* 24–27.

Chapter 9

Nursing Professionalization and Self-Governance: A Model from Long-Term Care

Meridean L. Maas and Janet P. Specht

Although 24-hour accountability for management of patient care units has been a part of the head nurse role in acute care settings for years, staff nurses often have not assumed 24-hour accountability for specific patients. Shared governance is new to such settings.

This chapter considers the application of both of these concepts to long-term care settings and describes some of the unique issues for long-term care. Further, the chapter describes some of the processes the Iowa Veterans Home experienced in this long-term change process. Throughout, issues are identified and the advantages and limitations of the model adopted are presented in summary.

Some nursing models described in this book are relatively recent organizational innovations. Some have evolved in response to cost-containment regulations. The responses to these regulations have exacerbated job dissatisfaction for nurses, who bear the brunt of pressures to deliver quality patient care with decreasing resources and little control over factors affecting their practice or their patients' well-being. This current crisis in health care has now increased the interest in alternative models for the delivery of nursing care, models that are cost-effective, achieve quality patient outcomes, and promote the retention of nurses by providing satisfying working conditions. Models that include structures and processes of shared governance and professional autonomy and accountability for nursing practice are the alternatives most often suggested in the literature as being able to increase nurse satisfaction and productivity (Allen, Calkin, & Peterson, 1988; Aydelotte, 1985; Ethridge, 1987; Fine, 1982; Maas & Mulford, 1989; Porter-O'Grady, 1987; Porter-O'Grady & Finnegan, 1984).

Few alternative models of nursing practice in long-term care settings have been reported. One of the first and most noteworthy models of nursing practice that emphasized professional nurse autonomy and accountability was developed in a long-term care division of Montefiore Hospital in New York (Hall, Alfano, Rifkin, & Levine, 1975). Hall et al. reported a decreased average length of stay and cost, an increased number of discharges to home, and fewer rehospitalizations for patients who convalesced at Loeb Center with professional nurse care compared with patients who convalesced in traditional hospital settings with physician-managed care and assistance by nursing staff. Although this model no longer exists at Loeb Center, it was operational for more than 15 years, demonstrating that professional nurses do make a difference in the care of convalescing patients when an environment is in place that promotes accountable practice.

The professional model of nursing at the Iowa Veterans Home in Marshalltown is another alternative model implemented in a long-term care setting in the 1970s (Maas & Jacox, 1977). A study reports the effects of this model of practice including positive changes in measures of patient welfare and nurse satisfaction (Maas & Jacox, 1977). The underlying assumptions of both this model and the Loeb Center model are (1) that registered nurses are best prepared to manage and deliver nursing care to patients, (2) that nursing care of the highest quality results when nurses have professional autonomy and accountability for patients' care over an extended period of time (24 hours, 7 days a week), (3) that registered nurses are valuable resources whose clinical skills must be reserved for patient care in order to be cost-effective, and (4) that nurses' work satisfaction is a function of the extent to which they have opportunities for professional development and control over decisions that affect their practice.

This chapter describes the model of professional nursing practice at the Iowa Veterans Home. The structures of the model and the experiences of nearly 20 years of existence can provide useful insights for nurses in all settings, which suggests that the model could be implemented in hospitals, nursing homes, and community health organizations if nurses have a common commitment to their clients through the pursuit of excellence.

THE IOWA VETERANS HOME MODEL

The Iowa Veterans Home (IVH) is a state-owned long-term care facility that provides nursing care to over 800 mostly elderly veterans and spouses. Three levels of care are provided: residential, intermediate, and skilled. Seventy registered nurses, 330 ancillary personnel, and 50 other health professionals (e.g., physicians, therapists) care for these patients. An interdisciplinary model is used to plan, implement, and evaluate health services for each patient. Core members of each interdisciplinary team are the patient's primary registered nurse, social worker, dietitian, physician, and recreation therapist.

Building on the assumptions stated above, the basic principle of the IVH model is that professional nurses must have authority and control over their practice if they are to maintain client priorities, make decisions in their clients' interests, and be held accountable for desired outcomes. The goals of the model are to provide quality, cost-effective care and to recruit and retain quality nurses. The components of the model are illustrated in Figure 9-1.

Professional Autonomy and Accountability

Professions are based on a specialized body of knowledge and a commitment to a service ideal. Professional autonomy is a precondition of self-determination and self-direction. It entails that members of the occupation govern and control their own activities. Autonomy is generally required for an occupation to achieve full professional status.

Self-regulation is a time-honored privilege that society has accorded its professions. Such regulation allows professionals to function in the public interest as well as to advance the profession. To be effective, however, self-regulation must rely on voluntary individual and collective discipline and surveillance within the profession.

Professions evolve in society because the knowledge attained by professionals and the services they provide help to meet societal needs. Society grants a profession autonomy (authority to control practice) because of the specialized knowledge possessed by its members. Thus authority is given to professionals in order to get important kinds of jobs done effectively, and such professionals are in turn the most competent judges of the needed expertise. Professionals profess to know something more than other people about certain matters and to be best able to decide matters of practice based on their special knowledge (Hughes, 1963). However, society also grants this authority only when a commitment to service in the public interest is also demonstrated. That is, society trusts professionals to act in their clients' best interests because they come to see that the professionals have the needed knowledge, are committed to their clients' interests, and demonstrate accountability to their clients and to other members of the profession—who are the best judges of their competence (Maas & Jacox, 1977).

Accountability is basically answerability to authority for one's actions. An accountable profession is answerable for the services it provides society and for client outcomes. For both the individual professional and the profession, accountability for behavior is a corollary of autonomy. In fact, neither autonomy nor accountability is possible in the professional model

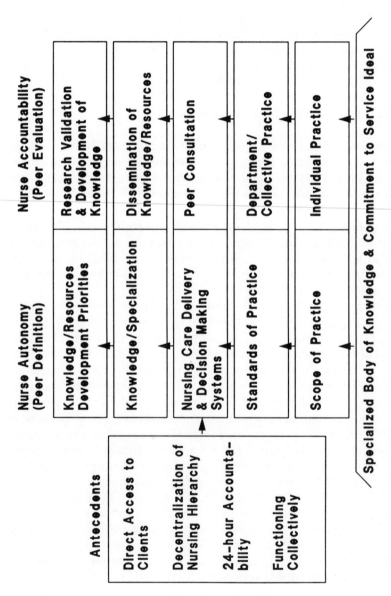

Figure 9-1 Iowa Veterans Home Model of Professional Nursing Practice. *Source:* From *Guidelines for Nurse Autonomy/Patient Welfare* (p. 25) by M. Maas and A. Jacox, 1977, E. Norwalk, CT: Appleton & Lange. Copyright 1977 by Appleton & Lange. Adapted by permission.

without the other. An occupation will not be allowed autonomy without demonstrating accountability, and true accountability in the professional model is not possible without the authority to control the services provided (Maas & Jacox, 1977).

Dimensions of Nurse Autonomy

The dimensions of nurse autonomy include peer determination and control of functions by definition of

- *scope of practice*: the parameters of practice and the phenomena that are dealt with by nurses
- *standards of practice*: the expected outcomes of nurse and patient behavior that are used to measure the quality of nursing practice
- *nursing care delivery system*: the structure and functioning of the nursing department, including procedures for collegial nursing governance (constitution and bylaws, committee structure) and caseload assignments for primary nurse case managers
- *knowledge specialization*: the knowledge needed to achieve standards of practice
- *knowledge and resource development priorities*: areas of needed research and resources

Dimensions of Nurse Accountability

The dimensions of nurse accountability include peer evaluation of

- *individual practice*: development and use of a system of peer review to compare individual practice to standards of practice
- *collective practice of nursing department*: development and use of a quality assurance program to measure the achievement of nursing department outcomes
- *peer consultation*: development and use of a mechanism of referral among nurse peers for expert assistance with care
- *dissemination of knowledge and resources*: development and use of a mechanism to distribute knowledge and other resources according to defined priorities
- *research validation and development of knowledge*: conduct of research according to defined needs

REQUIREMENTS AND PROCESS OF IMPLEMENTATION OF THE MODEL

Successful implementation of the model of practice requires (1) strong leadership within the nurse group, (2) a consensus among the nurses regarding commitment to client welfare and components of professional practice and governance, (3) consistent support from the nursing and institution administration, and (4) the enactment of the antecedent conditions (Figure 9-1). The most important requirement is that nurses individually and collectively assume accountability for decisions regarding practice and governance.

In most long-term care settings, the director of nursing would be most apt to provide the leadership and environment for changes needed to implement the model. The leadership provided will depend mainly on the professional maturity of the staff and the extent to which they have previously participated in departmental decisions. The style of leadership (e.g., directive, delegating) will need to be tailored to individual nurse characteristics as well as to the stage of development of the nurse staff as a group.

The specific governance structures and mechanisms, staffing criteria, education and training needs and programming, scheduling protocols, criteria for selection of personnel, workload measurement and management systems, and budget proposals will emerge from the decision-making process of the registered nurse peer group. Likewise, reward systems or proposals to higher administration will be defined by the peer group.

Thus, the model of practice is adaptable to a variety of circumstances, such as different staffing ratios or occupancy rates. For example, the average percentage of occupancy of the IVH over the life of the model is 95%, with nursing care hours per patient per 24 hours ranging from 4.5 to 3.8 for skilled levels of care and 1.5 to 2.5 for intermediate levels of care. Again, the model requires that nurses, individually and collectively, assume accountability for practice and governance decisions, including programming with available resources and negotiations and justifications for procurement of additional resources.

The director of nursing (or whoever assumes leadership) must believe that nurses should serve as primary case managers for clients, that nurses have the knowledge to make a difference in quality care if the appropriate conditions for professional development and practice are present, and that the circumstances in which nurses will gain authority and control over their practice can be created. Appropriate goals designed to meet the objective of improved patient welfare include

- maximum use of RNs for clinical nursing care activities
- creation of an organizational environment that fosters registered nurse growth and development as professional practitioners

- creation of an organizational environment that facilitates the participation of all nurses in decisions regarding the definition, delivery, and evaluation of nursing care

RNs must be expected and encouraged to participate collectively as peers in the development of the philosophy and objectives of the nursing department. Regular meetings of all RNs need to be held. The RNs can meet either as a committee of the whole or in unit or division groups. Issues for decision concerning administration of the program of nursing services are brought to the RN group (or groups), along with information about assets and constraints that will need to be considered. Examples of practice and conflicts with other disciplines are also reviewed by the peer group. For example, the RN group decided to separate clinical and nonclinical nursing activities (e.g., ancillary staff scheduling and hiring, clerical functions, and management of equipment and supplies) so that the activities could be divided administratively into separate divisions of the nursing department (Figure 9-2).

Such meetings develop a consensus that commitment to patient welfare is the primary concern of RNs, and they also focus attention on the constraints that prevent nurses from providing the best possible care for their patients. Thus, nurses become aware of the need to gain authority and control over their practice as professionals if they are to deliver quality nursing care. Resolutions of major constraints to assuming authority and accountability for practice are conceptualized as antecedents to the implementation of the professional practice model. Such constraints include lack of direct access to clients; lack of 24-hour accountability and authority for the care of specific clients; centralized, hierarchical authority in the nursing department; and the inability to function as a peer group (Figure 9-1).

The RNs at IVH agreed that assigning head nurses to units without giving them 24-hour accountability and authority promoted a lack of answerability and constrained the ability of nurses to pursue the care of specific clients. One year after beginning the change process, all head nurses assumed 24-hour, seven-day-a-week accountability and authority for the patients on their units. The nurses also realized that their lack of access to clients was due partly to their lack of accountability for specific patients and partly to their inaction and deference to the perceived authority of others. From that point onwards, the nurses began to assume the posture of primary advocates and case managers for patients.

The need to use as many nurses as possible for direct clinical care and a growing appreciation of the function of collegial relations among nurse peers for decision making and governance promoted discontent with the existing hierarchy of authority. Before the change, a traditional structure of authority, with supervisors and head nurses, characterized the nursing

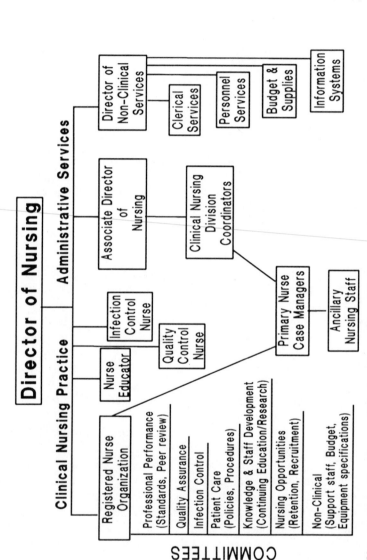

Figure 9-2 Iowa Veterans Home Department of Nursing. *Source:* From "Professional Practice for the Extended Care Environment: Learning from One Model and Its Implementation" by M. Maas, 1989, *Journal of Professional Nursing, 5(2),* p. 71. Copyright 1989 by W. B. Saunders Company. Reprinted by permission.

organization. Four years after the change process began, head nurse and supervisor positions were eliminated; staff nurses became primary nurses, each accountable for and with authority over the care of a caseload of patients. The accountability was continuous—24 hours, 7 days a week.

The change process was not linear. Rather, the process unfolded in uneven stages as the department adapted to autonomy and accountability. The first step was to define the scope of nursing practice. The IVH scope of nursing practice was defined before the American Nurses' Association (ANA) statement, *The Scope of Nursing Practice* (ANA, 1987), was published, although the two are quite similar. The ANA statement can now be used as a framework for the definition of standards of practice.

Concurrent with the decision to implement the model of professional practice, the IVH nurses negotiated the nursing role with the administration and physicians. These negotiations required the nurses to define their role and the parameters of practice more clearly. In other words, they realized that they would have difficulty negotiating authority for practice if they could not define their practice. After several months of work, the nurses' ideas were consolidated in a document entitled *Elements of Nursing Practice* (Maas & Jacox, 1977). This document was the conceptualization of the professional model of practice, and it contained each of the dimensions of autonomy and accountability that were later further defined and implemented (Figure 9-1).

For the IVH nurses, the document was analogous to the ANA statements *Social Policy* (ANA, 1985) and *The Scope of Nursing Practice* (ANA, 1987), since it outlined the nurses' contract with their clients to provide needed services and included practice parameters and processes. The focus of the document is the diagnosis, prescription, and evaluation of nursing care. The IVH nurses now use nursing diagnoses in their practice as the framework for specialization, and they view diagnoses and the interventions used to treat them as the substantive and functional scope of their practice.

Definition of standards of practice was the next step in implementing the practice model. These standards measured quality and were essential for developing evaluations. Systems for the annual peer review of each nurse and for quality assurance regarding individual and collective nursing practice were developed and implemented by the IVH nurses following the definition of standards of practice. Informal consultation among nurse peers evolved when supervisory positions were eliminated, and such consultation increased when specific procedures for referral to nurse peers were developed. Ultimately peer consultation was adopted as a means to demonstrate accountability for practice.

Self-governance became the means to translate autonomy and accountability into the organizational structure. The nurses wrote a constitution and bylaws, thus formally establishing (1) the participation of all nurses in decision making and (2) the accountability for nursing practice of each nurse to the others. The constitution gives the authority for decisions affecting nursing practice to the RN peer group, distinguishes the structures of professional decision making from the organizational structures, and defines the role of the director of nursing. It also includes a mechanism for the resolution of disagreements between organizational decisions and issues and professional ones.

Each RN on staff is a member of the Registered Nurse Organization (RNO) and is expected to participate in decision making and committee work. The constitution actually defines RNO committees and their areas of accountability and authority. Figure 9-2 depicts the professional governance and administrative structures of the Iowa Veterans Home Department of Nursing, including the RNO standing committees: Professional Performance, Patient Care, Quality Assurance, Infection Control, Knowledge, Nursing Opportunities, and Nonclinical. These committees develop recommendations to present to the RNO for adoption. The constitution also formalizes RN membership on agency planning and policy-making bodies: Administrative Planning, Clinical Planning, Infection Control, Quality Assurance, Admissions, and Information Systems.

As IVH implemented the professional practice model, nurses more clearly saw how much nursing knowledge is *not* available. This may have been the result of shifting more accountability to the case manager for both clinical and self-governance decisions. The nurses also realized that no individual nurse possesses all of the required knowledge or information. Therefore, they decided that having a database for practice would enhance care, that each nurse should specialize in the treatment of one or more of the nursing diagnoses for long-term care patients, and that the required knowledge is best organized by the nursing diagnoses of patients. As a result, nurses currently claim a diagnostic area of specialization. Each is accountable for ensuring that, in his or her area of specialization, up-to-date knowledge is available for peer consulting and there exists a current list of resources. The incidence of nursing diagnoses and interventions for the elderly and long-term care clients determine priorities for continuing education and research.

CASE STUDY

Mary P., RN, a new graduate with a Bachelor of Science in Nursing, has recently joined the IVH nursing department in a staff nurse position that requires her to work mainly day shift hours. During her interview, she carefully reviewed the performance expectations and standards for the position. At that time she was also given an explanation of the IVH model of nurse autonomy and accountability, along with a description of its components and functions. Because she was seeking a nursing staff position that would give her some autonomy, she was eager to accept the IVH position. It is now her first day of work, and she has begun the 3- to 6-month orientation that she learned she would be able to have when she interviewed for the position. She is assigned a nurse peer who will be her preceptor during the orientation period. Mary had reviewed the outline of her orientation and the numerous written materials about the IVH, the nursing department, and the model of nurse autonomy and accountability, and already she feels overwhelmed. She is grateful that she will have daily interactions with the nurse educator and her preceptor, because she has many questions for each.

After the first week of orientation, Mary is somewhat concerned about the extent to which she is expected to define her own needs for orientation and skills training and to be self-directed in arranging appointments with key members of other departments at IVH. She feels quite overwhelmed but has noted the willingness of the nurse educator and preceptor to be of assistance. She has also noticed that all the nurses she has met have been especially friendly, have welcomed her, and have offered to help her in any way they can. She feels some hesitancy to ask too many questions—in case her peers will think she is poorly prepared to be a nurse. During a review of her progress with the educator and preceptor, both assure her that her feelings are normal, that these feelings will continue for some time, but that they will eventually subside.

At the end of 1 month of orientation, Mary has a fairly good understanding of the IVH organization, but she is still a bit vague about the model of nurse autonomy and accountability. At this point she has attended one RNO meeting and has visited a meeting of the Professional Performance Committee with her preceptor, who is a member. Her preceptor suggests that she reread the written material (articles) that describe the model of practice and that she again study the diagrams of the model and the nursing department. Mary notes that the standards of practice are the measures of quality of nursing care, and she understands that they are a critical dimension of IVH nurses' authority for practice. By this time Mary has reviewed her preceptor's caseload of patients, has accompanied her perceptor during patient rounds and assessments, has discussed the nursing diagnoses and plans of care with the preceptor, and has offered some theory and research base for analysis of the patient data. Mary has also accompanied her preceptor to two interdisciplinary care conferences as an observer.

Because the preceptor is impressed with Mary's grasp of the practice environment and expectations and with her nursing diagnostic and intervention skills at the end of 6 weeks, Mary begins at her own request, to assume a caseload of patients as primary nurse case manager. At this same time Mary begins to be scheduled into her assigned unit's coverage group. She knows that she will work 1 weekend out of 3 and that she will arrange her own hours collaboratively with the other nurses assigned to the same coverage group. This idea seems really strange and a little scary, but the idea of being responsible for her own schedule appeals to her. She hopes she can work things out agreeably with her peers.

At the end of 6 months, Mary is about to have her first peer review, which marks the end of her orientation period. She is nervous and a little disgruntled. Several of her patients have diagnoses of impaired skin integrity and altered bowel elimination. She now has 10 patients in her caseload, the majority of which are new admissions. She seriously wonders if she can meet the expectations that are outlined for this stage of her employment, especially when she is to gain 5 more patients in her caseload within the next month. She is especially uncertain of her abilities regarding the skin and bowel elimination diagnoses, since she knows that these tend to be treated independently by IVH nurses. She expresses her concerns during the peer review and is relieved when the nurse educator suggests that she contact a particular nurse peer who has special expertise with treatment of both of these diagnoses and had been helpful to her in a similar circumstance.

In addition, she accepts an assignment to do the major database research for a Professional Performance Committee proposal regarding minimum staffing specifications for a specific case mix category of patient nursing diagnoses. Several nurse peers have expressed some impatience because they feel the staffing is underestimated for this category of case mix. Mary wonders if it wouldn't be better if a supervisor or the director decided the staffing specifications. She suggests this to the preceptor, who tells her that the current specifications were temporarily defined by the director of nursing so that staff could be reallocated following an emergency staff cut due to budget constraints. The preceptor adds that most nurses believe that the director's specifications do not accurately reflect the care needed by these patients relative to the needs of patients in other case mix categories.

During the 6-month peer review, Mary receives mostly positive feedback regarding her performance. However, she shares her sense of frustration and her feelings of being overwhelmed. Because of these feelings, she did not complete her self-defined goals for the coming year but did list her perceived strengths and the areas that need improvement. There is a discussion of the need to decide the staffing specifications, which Mary feels strongly about. The preceptor points out that Mary could perhaps use her time more wisely if she outlined the elements that are required in the database reports needed for developing the staffing specifications proposal. Then Mary could ask the administrative clerical staff to complete the summary reports. The preceptor offers to help her with the design of the needed reports and the proposal and suggests that Mary also add data regarding quality assurance audits of outcomes for the case mix category of patients. She also offers assistance with identification of Mary's goals for the coming year.

At the next meeting of the RNO, Mary presents her proposal, which has been approved by the Professional Performance Committee. The proposal contains specifications very close to those that were temporarily established by the director. Mary is bombarded with questions from the members of the RNO. This makes her nervous, but she is able to respond with facts drawn from workload measurement and quality assurance data. After all the facts are presented and discussed by the group, the proposal is accepted. A number of nurses compliment Mary on the proposal, the data used to support the proposal, and her poise in responding to questions.

This case study illustrates several aspects of the IVH model. First, it shows the careful attention that is given to socialization of new nurse staff members. Second, the importance of standards of nursing practice for individual and collective professional autonomy and accountability is highlighted. The mechanisms of peer review and peer consultation and their role in evaluation of practice as well as in providing collegial support are emphasized. Finally, the decision-making structures and processes for professional governance, their relationship to organizational authority, and the role of the director of nursing are depicted.

EVALUATION AND OUTCOMES OF THE IVH MODEL

Advantages

One indication of the emphasis on knowledge and continuing education is the number of nurses who have been certified by the ANA. During the 2 decades that the model has been evolving, 38 nurses have been certified by the ANA as gerontological nurses, 1 as a mental health nurse, and 1 in community health. Thirty of these certified nurses are currently employed, and 5 more are preparing for the 1989 certification test. Although travel is required, 36 nurses have continued formal education in baccalaureate and master's programs. These are impressive statistics, since less than 6% of the nurses employed in nursing homes in the United States are certified by the ANA (Aiken, 1983), and most nurses employed in nursing homes have a diploma or associate degree in nursing (Institute of Medicine, 1983). According to a 1983 national survey of 2,715 nurse administrators in long-term care institutions, only 2% were certified in gerontological nursing or nursing administration and only 8% had a bachelor's degree in nursing (Lodge, 1987).

Continued implementation of the IVH model of professional practice is the shared responsibility of the RNs and nursing administration. Much attention is given to the socialization of nurses who join the staff. Applicants are interviewed by the director and by members of the RN peer group. Criteria for the appointment of new staff are defined by the peer group and guide the interview and selection process. The model of governance is shared with each applicant so that the nurse who is hired understands the contract for accountable practice. However, every new nurse needs remediation and socialization to be able to assume individual and shared accountability according to the practice model. A flexible 6-month orientation is tailored to the needs of the new staff member and a nurse preceptor is paired with the new nurse for guidance and support. The IVH nurses are organized in coverage groups for specific patient care areas. Therefore, each new nurse begins with a support group of peers who share responsibility and authority for the nursing care of the patients, including staffing. One of the functions of the group of peers is to determine their own work schedules and maintain safe staffing. The RNs determine their own hours and schedules, within coverage groups, according to specifications defined by the RNO. Greater control of their practice and working conditions, increased tenure, opportunities for professional growth and development, peer support and feedback, and increased motivation are positive outcomes for nurses.

Clearly, the investment in socialization is large, but once nurses are employed and socialized into the IVH model of practice, they tend to stay. During the past 5 years, the average annual turnover among RNs was 5%, and the average length of employment for RNs who have been on staff for this period was 7.5 years. Further, there are 50 current RN applications on file. In contrast, an average length of employment of 1 year for RNs in nursing homes has been reported (Aiken, 1983). In view of current concerns about nurse retention and the need to restructure nursing practice organizations for professional self-governance, the IVH model has advantages for nurses and patients but also advantages for the organization.

Further, use of specialized knowledge and consensus decision making has helped nurses work more effectively in an interdisciplinary mode of care. As the IVH nurses progressed toward a consensus regarding their commitment to clients and professional accountability, they recognized the need for more depth and breadth of knowledge and also the consequent need for research to validate nursing diagnoses and test interventions and to improve diagnostic reasoning. At the IVH, the emphasis is on collaborative research involving nurse clinicians, nurse scientists, and scientists from other disciplines. Nurses at the IVH have participated as investigators, consultants, research associates, and research assistants in a variety of descriptive and experimental studies of diagnoses and interventions to improve the quality of patients' lives. Currently three funded studies are being conducted at the IVH, with IVH nurses collaborating with nurse scientists and scientists from other disciplines in the testing of nursing interventions (Hardy, 1987; Maas & Buckwalter, 1986; Frantz, 1988).

Enjoyment of a national reputation for quality care, higher productivity of nurses, low turnover and less replacement costs, reduced complaints from patients, and enhanced resources through collaborative research and education with other institutions (e.g., the University of Iowa) are other positive outcomes for the organization.

The nurses discovered that the results of interventions for nursing diagnoses included increased patient welfare and increased approval from families, administrators, and other health disciplines. There are a number of indicators of increased quality of nursing care. For example, the number of indwelling catheters and decubitus are much fewer than before the model of practice was implemented, even though the proportion of patients with complex nursing care problems has increased. The rates of monitors of poor quality care are also consistently below the average rates for other comparable long-term care institutions (Iowa Veterans Home Study Advisory Committee, 1987). Measures of the quality of the patients' lives also reflect achievement of high standards (e.g., the extent to which patients' rights to determine their care and to control other circumstances of living are respected). The model provides continuity of care and attainment of mutually established goals for all patients through primary nurse case management. Each patient has one nurse to turn to if there are problems or concerns with care or quality of life.

Disadvantages

The length of time and cost required for implementation depends on a number of factors. Clearly, the professional maturity of the nurse staff, the quality and commitment of the leadership, and the support from administration and other departmental units are important variables. The process of change must be expected to take from 2 to 5 years in most settings and it should be approached as planned instead of directed change for maximum success (Hersey & Blanchard, 1988). There are no cookbook recipes that allow "drop in" installations for the development and implementation of professional models of nursing in practice settings.

The amount of time required for socialization of nurses and for consensus decision making can also be viewed as a negative outcome for nurses, patients, and the organization. However, this cost is offset by a higher quality of care for patients, by increased job satisfaction for nurses, and by increased nurse productivity per unit of cost for the organization.

Implications

Although there was little consideration given to the professionalization of nursing in hospital settings prior to the economic crisis of the 1980s, there has been even less interest in models of professional nursing practice in long-term care settings. However, interest is increasing, because cost-containment and prospective payment mechanisms have been implemented for hospitals and because health care demographics are changing, with larger numbers of elderly and chronically ill patients demanding a higher quality of care. The shorter average length of hospital stay has resulted in more nursing home patients who required more complex care and has shifted more of the problem of cost containment to nonhospital settings, underscoring the need for RN-managed care (Institute of Medicine Report, 1986; Ash, Lodge, & Yura, 1988).

Recognition of the need for alternative models for nursing practice is not new. In 1970, Esther Lucille Brown called for models of nursing that would transfer more accountability for nursing care to the nurses providing the care. Although the cost-containment environment provides incentives to professionalize nursing, the powerbrokers in health care, who benefit most from traditional structures, are likely to continue to resist the implementation of alternative models of nursing practice. This is most probable if nurses fail to discern that professional autonomy and accountability are needed for client welfare regardless of the economic incentives that currently make them attractive to administrators and physicians. Further, nurses should realize that professional autonomy and accountability are essential to ensure quality nursing care regardless of the particular system of care delivery.

The IVH model was developed in a resource scarce environment to provide the highest-quality care at the least cost, demonstrated positive results, and was reported in the literature over a decade ago. Yet few organizations followed IVH's example until economic incentives for administrators emerged in the 1980s. Hopefully, nursing will capitalize on this opportunity and also continue to pursue professional prerogatives for the benefit of clients regardless of what happens to be expedient for those who typically hold a power advantage.

REFERENCES

Aiken, L. (1983). Nurses. In D. Mechanic (Ed.), *Handbook of healthcare and health professionals*. New York: The Free Press.

Allen, D., Calkin, J., Peterson, M. (1988). Making shared governance work: A conceptual model. *Journal of Nursing Administration, 18*(1), 37–41.

American Nurses' Association. (1985). *Social policy statement*. Kansas City, MO: Author.

American Nurses' Association. (1987). *The scope of nursing practice*. Kansas City, MO: Author.

Ash, C.R., Lodge, M.P., & Yura, H. (1988). Educating nurse administrators in long-term care in a changing environment. In *Perspectives in nursing 1988–1989* [Pub. No. 42-2199]. New York: National League for Nursing.

Aydelotte, K. (1985). Structure of nursing practice departments: Governance and professionalization. In J. McCloskey & H. Grace (Eds.), *Current issues in nursing*. Boston: Blackwell.

Brown, E.L. (1970). *Nursing reconsidered: A study of change*. Philadelphia: Lippincott.

Ethridge, P. (1987). Nurse accountability program improves satisfaction, turnover. *Health Progress, 68*(4), 44–49.

Fine, R.B. (1982). Creating a workplace for the professional nurse. In A. Marriner (Ed.), *Contemporary Nursing Management: Issues and Practice*. St. Louis: C.V. Mosby.

Frantz, R. (1988). Effects of TENS on healing of decubitus ulcers. Center for Nursing Research Grant Proposal, National Institutes of Health, Bethesda, MD.

Hall, L., Alfano, G., Rifkin, H., & Levine, H. (1975). *Longitudinal effects of an experimental nursing process*. U. S. Department of Health, Education, and Welfare, Division of Nursing Research. Grant NU-00308.

Hardy, M. (1987). Effects of selected bathing interventions on dry skin in the institutionalized elderly. Biomedical Seed Grant Proposal, University of Iowa, Iowa City.

Hersey, P., & Blanchard, K. (1988). *Management of human behavior: Utilizing human resources*, 5th ed. Englewood Cliffs, NJ: Prentice Hall.

Hughes, E. (1963). Professions. *Daedalus, 92*, 644.

Institute of Medicine. (1983). *Nursing and nursing education: Public policies and private actions*. Washington, DC: National Academy Press.

Institute of Medicine. (1986). *Improving the quality of care in nursing homes*. Washington, DC: National Academy Press.

Iowa Veterans Home Study Advisory Committee. (1987). *Iowa Veterans Home policy issues study*. Marshalltown, IA: Author.

Lodge, M. (1987). *Professional education and practice of nurse administrators/directors in long-term care: An executive summary*. Kansas City, MO: American Nurses Foundation.

Maas, M., & Buckwalter, K. (1986). Nursing evaluation: A special Alzheimer's care unit. Center for Nursing Research Grant Proposal, National Institutes of Health, Bethesda, MD.

Maas, M., & Jacox, A. (1977). *Guidelines for nurse autonomy/patient welfare.* New York: Appleton-Century-Crofts.

Maas, M., & Mulford, C. (1989). Structural adaptation of organizations. In M. Johnson & J. McCloskey (Eds.), *Series on nursing administration* [Vol. 2]. Menlo Park, CA: Addison-Wesley.

Porter-O'Grady, T. (1987). Shared governance and new organizational models. *Nursing Economics 5*(6), 281–286.

Porter-O'Grady, T., & Finnegan, S. (1984). *Shared governance for nursing: A creative approach to professional accountability.* Rockville, MD: Aspen Publishers.

Chapter 10

The Professional Nursing Network

Gerri S. Lamb and Delma Huggins

This model for nursing practice distinguishes itself by having the case manager link the patient with appropriate nursing services within a defined network of services. It takes case management and moves it into a group practice where clinicians, researchers, and administrators all manage cases. This latter feature offers one way to deal with the traditional problem of keeping administration and researchers close to the client.

The authors describe a way to meet patient needs with professional nursing and to provide continuity in multiple settings over time. The model has evolved during its existence and has been molded by the variables of cost of care, consumer wants, the value of Indian traditions, and the shift in worker values regarding shared compensation.

The authors' description of the evolutionary process points to the fact that looking within rather than imposing a model from elsewhere offers a key to change.

One of this model's strengths is the changes in organizational structure that occurred in support of the stated value of collaboration. Conflicts, which often arise from organizational structures, have a greater chance for being managed when incentives and decision making flow from the stated values.

It sounds like the organization has made the shift in thinking from acute to continuous care and that it sees health in the way Margaret Newman does–as an expansion of consciousness.

The authors recognize limitations of the model and continue to look for the evolving themes inside at the same time that they remain sensitive to outside themes.

The nursing network at Carondelet St. Mary's Hospital and Health Center (St. Mary's) in Tucson, Arizona enables nurses to fully contribute their expertise in promoting health and self-care. The various components of the network have been designed to create an integrated system of nursing care in which nurses maintain accountability for cost-effectiveness, access to care, and quality of care. The network links acute care, long-term care, and ambulatory, hospice, and home care nursing services, and it positions professional nurse case managers to move with clients throughout the network.

Within the nursing network model, clients and their families have access to a full complement of nursing services. Working in collaboration with physicians, other health care professionals, and community agencies, nurses provide comprehensive nursing services, including acute care; preventative care; health promotion and education; and ambulatory, home health, and long-term care.

Unlike traditional systems of health care, the nursing network emphasizes recovering, maintaining, and promoting health. Care is continuous rather than episodic, and it is based on a holistic nursing practice model. Eligibility for nursing care within the network depends on criteria developed by nurses. This ensures that individuals and families who can benefit from nursing services will have access to them.

The nursing network has many advantages for clients, nurses, and St. Mary's. Nurses help clients manage their health problems, increase their self-reliance, and arrange for needed support services. Health care and support services are more accessible than usual. For nurses, the network provides a practice arena where the full scope of professional nursing can be delivered over time. Recruitment and retention may be positively impacted. St. Mary's also benefits from the nursing network. Clients who find the network responsive to their needs tend to choose St. Mary's for other health care services. In addition, preliminary data indicate that individuals cared for in the network enter the hospital at lower acuity levels and contribute to a reduction in revenue loss due to capitated payment.

COMPONENTS OF THE NURSING NETWORK

The nursing network at St. Mary's has a number of components, including

- acute care inpatient nursing services
- long-term care nursing services
- home health nursing services
- hospice services
- ambulatory care services (nursing wellness centers)
- professional nurse case management services

Relationships among the components of the network are shown in Figure 10-1. The professional nurse case manager facilitates the client moving between components and consequently is a vital link in the nursing network. The nontraditional network components, professional nurse case management and the nursing wellness centers, are described below in detail.

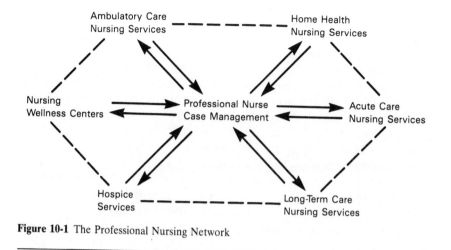

Figure 10-1 The Professional Nursing Network

Professional Nurse Case Management

Originally, the professional nurse case management program was developed in response to nursing's concern about reduced length of hospital stay and the need to coordinate nursing services in the hospital with other programs across the care continuum. At St. Mary's, nurse case management emphasizes the importance of helping people to help themselves through mutually planning, coordinating, and evaluating services designed to maximize self-care. The professional nurse case manager develops a long-term relationship with the client and family. The case manager facilitates access to the continuum of health care services, provides direct nursing care, and monitors patient and family progress toward the attainment of health goals. Professional nurse case management seeks to enhance client and family self-care skills and to promote effective and efficient use of health care resources.

The professional nurse case manager coordinates care across the service continuum for individuals at high risk for readmission or for individuals who are expected to have significant difficulty managing in the home. Individuals offered nurse case management typically have multiple and interactive nursing diagnoses, limited or inadequate support systems, and chronic, recurrent health problems. Additional high-risk criteria may include age of client, age of family caregiver, and potential for complications based on the presence of multiple health or social problems. Nurse case managers receive referrals from both the community and the acute care setting. At present, the majority of referrals are initiated in the acute care setting.

Nurse Case Management in the Network

Several features distinguish the nurse case management program at St. Mary's from other models of case management. Chief among these are the community and group practice components. Case managers in the nursing network move with the client across the care continuum. Unlike many other case management models, including the New England Medical Center Model (Zander, 1988), case management in the nursing network goes beyond the walls of the institution into the community.

A second distinguishing feature of the nurse case management program is the collaborative group practice model. The nurse case manager group practice comprises clinicians, nurse administrators, and nurse researchers. Each member of the group practice, in addition to other responsibilities, follows clients as a case manager. Caseload size is adjusted on an individual basis to maintain a balance between clinical and nonclinical responsibilities. The different roles and the different educational preparation of members of the group ensure that diverse perspectives will emerge and contribute to patient care. Members of the group practice have regular meetings to discuss practice issues and to provide clinical information and feedback to one another. Nurse-to-nurse consultation occurs often and provides an important mechanism for problem solving and sharing information and support.

Nursing Wellness Centers

The nursing wellness centers are community-based clinics in which nurse practitioners provide health promotion, health screening, and counseling services to the elderly. The 14 wellness centers are located in areas of easy access for the elderly, including mobile home parks, low-income housing projects, churches, and retirement communities. Referrals come from the community and numerous health care providers, including physicians and nurse case managers. In addition, community volunteers educate members in their neighborhood about the wellness center services and are an important source of referrals.

Care in the wellness centers focuses on health promotion, health risk appraisal, and strategies for life style change. The centers offer screening for blood pressure, blood sugar, cholesterol, and colorectal cancer; they also provide counseling on nutrition, special diets, medications, stress reduction, exercise, and community resources. Lectures and workshops on a variety of health-related topics are offered free of charge. Nurse case management is available to wellness center clients who need additional support to remain in the community.

ASSUMPTIONS OF THE NURSING NETWORK MODEL

The professional nursing network model is based on several assumptions about professional nursing practice. The assumptions underlying the model are as follows:

1. The quality of client services is directly related to professional accountability.
2. The quality of client services is directly related to the fit between the educational preparation of the nurses prescribing nursing care and their practice responsibilities.
3. The quality of client services is directly related to continuity of care and to a holistic approach to individual and family needs.

Professional accountability of nurse to the client is integral to the achievement of quality care and positive health outcomes. Within the nursing network, nurses are accountable for explaining the goals, processes, and outcomes of their care. The educational preparation of each nurse provides the framework for establishing the domain of that nurse's professional responsibility and accountability. In addition, the nursing network is based on assumptions about characteristics of nursing care that are linked to quality of care. Holistic and continuous care reduces fragmentation of services and contributes to the achievement of comprehensive nursing outcomes.

SUPPORT STRUCTURES FOR THE NETWORK

Several planned features of the nursing service structure at St. Mary's have supported the development of the professional nursing network model. These include shared governance, professional salaried status, acuity billing, and traditional Indian medicine. Each of these features was introduced to increase nursing autonomy and accountability for quality, availability, and cost-effectiveness of nursing care. Together they provide a system that encourages and rewards professional nursing practice and active participation in decisions that affect patient care.

The first support structure of the professional nursing network, shared governance, establishes the joint accountability of the nursing administration and nursing staff for the development and evaluation of systems of patient care. The nursing staff participate in the decisions that affect nursing practice through their professional staff nursing organization. The subcommittees of this organization address such topics as institutional policies and procedures, educational programs, and clinical advancement in collaboration with members of the nursing administration.

Shared governance has several major components, including the credentialing program and the joint practice committee. The credentialing program was developed to recognize clinical competence and excellence. General practice competencies are defined and operationalized on four levels. Clinical practice, leadership, and education are integrated into each of the four levels. A peer review program ensures that nursing staff receive systematic criteria-based feedback from their professional colleagues for professional growth and promotion. Professional and monetary awards are commensurate with the level of nursing practice. Currently, the credentialing program is undergoing reevaluation and revision to prepare for the implementation of an education-based clinical ladder. Job descriptions for the four levels are to be differentiated based on knowledge, skill, and ability gained through education and experience.

Another component of shared governance, the joint practice committee, promotes collegiality between the nursing staff and the medical staff. The committee, composed of representatives from nursing and medicine, focuses on the working relationship between nurses and physicians within the institution and their impact on the delivery of patient services. Collaborative problem solving among committee members has resulted in the identification of innovative strategies that enhance patient care.

The second support structure of the professional nursing network, professional salaried status, reflects a change in the traditional terms of employment for professional nurses. In this program, the salaries of professional nurses are negotiated on a contractual annual basis rather than by hourly rate. Professional salaried status was implemented to increase nursing accountability for professional practice. An additional feature of professional salaried status is the "no float" policy for unit-based professional staff.

The third support structure is acuity billing. Direct costs for nursing services are identified and patients are billed according to an acuity rating that reflects hours of nursing care. Within this variable billing system, the professional nurse is responsible for the explanation of care rendered and the daily acuity charges identified on the patient's bill.

The fourth support structure, the traditional Indian medicine program, was started at St. Mary's to provide counseling services for Native American patients and their families and to increase staff and community understanding of the holistic approach to health care and healing that is characteristic of traditional Indian medicine. Regularly scheduled workshops are available to orient staff and outside participants to the traditional Indian medicine framework for healing and self-care and to offer opportunities to examine the implications of this holistic framework for professional nursing practice.

IMPLEMENTATION PROCESS

The professional nursing network model was implemented over several years through a process that integrated and expanded available nursing services. Several of the components of the network, including acute care nursing services and hospice services, had been in place for a number of years but lacked formal linkages to other nursing services prior to model development and the implementation of the nurse case manager role. Other components became part of the network through expansion of institutional services or through the deliberate movement of nursing services into the community.

Support structures for the nursing network were introduced in stages, and all were in place prior to the implementation of the nursing case management program and the creation of wellness centers. Shared governance, for example, has existed in various forms at St. Mary's for over a decade.

Introduction of the nurse case manager role was a pivotal step in the implementation of the nursing network. As the hub of the network, the nurse case manager holds primary responsibility for coordinating care among the various components. The current professional nurse case management program evolved as a result of previous experience with a decentralized home care program. In the decentralized home care program, staff nurses followed selected clients through the acute care episode into the home in order to provide needed home care (Rusch, 1986). Although the program was discontinued for a number of reasons, it established the framework for the development of the nurse case manager role. Through their experience with decentralized home care, nursing staff and administrators identified several factors, including staff education and clinical skills, that needed to be taken into account in future efforts to move out of the hospital into home and community settings.

The professional nurse case manager program was implemented gradually and without fanfare. The decision to initiate case management was made at the unit level, and typically the person selected as case manager had been a staff nurse on the unit for some time. The first case managers were unit based and had more formal unit responsibilities than the present case managers. Over time, the nurse case manager role evolved to become more integrated with other network components and to increase its emphasis on community. More recently, the nurse case management program has moved to a group practice format and is experimenting with marketing nurse case management to other health care service organizations, including health maintenance organizations.

The ambulatory arm of the nursing network, the system of nursing wellness centers, was created in response to a community need for accessible health promotion services for the elderly. Several of the wellness centers were initiated at the request of residents or administrators of communities of the elderly. The first wellness center was developed at a low-income housing project for elderly Hispanics in collaboration with a social service agency for the Hispanic community. One of the newer wellness centers was developed at the request of the administrator of a retirement community who identified the need for wellness services and elected to incorporate the cost in the charge for rent.

COST-EFFECTIVENESS OF THE NURSING NETWORK MODEL

Nursing administrators and researchers are working together to identify appropriate methods to evaluate the cost-effectiveness of the nursing network. Analysis of cost-effectiveness, according to Prescott and Sorenson (1978), is a systematic process in which qualitative and quantitative outcomes of a program are examined relative to their costs. Current efforts are focused on identifying meaningful and sensitive outcomes and associated costs.

Preliminary studies of the professional nursing network model indicate that the model may have a substantial impact on several quality and cost outcomes of care, including quality of life, functional status, patient and nurse satisfaction, length of stay, and acuity level. These findings are discussed in greater detail in the section "Evaluation of the Nursing Network."

To date, the total costs for the nurse case management program are based on hours of care and include salaries and travel. In subsequent stages of the cost-benefit analysis, total costs will need to be broken down according to categories of nurse case manager activities, including direct patient contact activities, coordinating activities involving other components of the nursing network, referral and coordinating activities involving other services in the hospital and community, and activities needed to maintain the clinical information systems. As the nurse case manager program evolves, it will be possible to identify and track activities in greater detail. At present, case study analysis is being used to examine the component costs of case management and to create hypothetical scenarios for the purpose of determining costs with and without case management.

The costs of developing and maintaining the nurse wellness centers are also under scrutiny. Total costs for the centers include the salaries of the nurse practitioners, and funds for travel, equipment, and educational materials. Space and the indirect costs associated with each setting are covered by the setting rather than the hospital. Total costs may be broken down by categories of nurse practitioner activities, including health promotion and counseling activities, performance of screening procedures and laboratory tests, training and coordination of care with volunteers, and recordkeeping. As noted earlier, detailed cost data are not yet available.

In summary, preliminary studies support the cost-effectiveness of the nursing network model. However, definitive conclusions must await the development and implementation of a systematic evaluation process.

CASE STUDY 1

The first case study illustrates how the various components of the nursing network are integrated to provide comprehensive, community-based care for individuals with complex health problems and multiple hospital admissions.

Ms. A. is a 54-year-old woman with a history of multiple admissions for reconstructive surgery of primary joints due to arthritis. Ms. A. is divorced and lives with her parents, who are in their 80's and serve as her major caregivers.

Ms. A.'s past medical history is complex and includes osteoarthritis, rheumatoid arthritis, a seizure disorder of undetermined origin, lupus, and osteoporosis. Ms. A. has been disabled according to Medicare and Social Security criteria for over 25 years.

Nurse case management was implemented for Ms. A. during an extended hospital stay. Ms. A. entered the hospital for total hip revision following recurrent hip dislocations. At the time of surgery, osteomyelitis of the bone surface surrounding the joint was found, and a girdle stone procedure was performed. Ms. A. underwent months of antibiotic therapy and experienced numerous complications, including septic shock and intractable joint pain.

Ms. A. was referred to nurse case management by the nursing staff, who identified her as being at high risk for readmission due to her complicated recovery course and her potential for recurrent infections. The nursing staff also were concerned about Ms. A's elderly parents and their ability to care for her at home. Ms. A. and her parents had refused temporary long-term care placement for rehabilitation.

In the early discharge period, the nurse case manager visited Ms. A. and her family twice weekly to assess wound healing, pain control, and the family response to the agreed plan of care. Ms. A. received daily whirlpool treatments in the hospital burn center. When whirlpool treatments were discontinued, the nurse case manager coordinated referrals to home health nursing services for daily wound and personal care and to community agencies for respite and shopping services.

Ms. A. remained at home for 6 months without another hospital admission. Nurse case manager visits were gradually decreased in frequency, and telephone contacts enabled regular updating of plans. During this time, Ms. A. attended an outpatient rehabilitation program designed to increase her functional abilities and to reduce her dependence on pain medications.

Following this relatively stable period, Ms. A. had a series of illnesses, two requiring hospitalization. Each hospital stay lasted 5–8 days. Prior to nurse case management, Ms. A. had been hospitalized for several weeks for similar problems.

To date, Ms. A. has received 150 hours of nursing case management at an approximate cost of $22.00 per hour. In the 10 months immediately preceding case management, Ms. A.'s hospital costs exceeded a quarter of a million dollars. In the 21 months following implementation of case management, costs have been approximately one-third of this amount.

At present, Ms. A. is able to manage transfers and personal care with minimal assistance. She has been off intramuscular narcotics for 6 months and is slowly decreasing her use of oral narcotics. With encouragement from the nurse case manager, Ms. A.'s parents have sought long-needed health care for themselves that had been postponed due to their caregiving responsibilities. Without nurse case management, it seems probable that Ms. A. would have continued her previous pattern of frequent emergency room use and lengthy hospital stays. Anecdotal records indicate that the nurse case manager averted a number of unnecessary emergency room visits through systematic assessment, support measures, and collaboration with Ms. A.'s physician. The case manager's attention to the health and social needs of Ms. A.'s elderly caregivers also has substantial implications for the quality and cost of care.

CASE STUDY 2

The second case study illustrates how various components of the nursing network work for individuals who are chronically ill and require community-based ambulatory services for health maintenance as well as hospital and posthospital care for acute exacerbations of chronic illness.

Mr. and Mrs. F. were referred for nurse case management during Mr. F.'s hospitalization for gastric surgery. The request for case management came from the couple's daughter, who lived out of town and was concerned about her parents' ability to care for themselves at home.

Mr. F., 81 years old, had a medical history that included two previous heart attacks and chronic respiratory disease due to work exposure. Mrs.

F., 76 years old, also had several chronic health concerns, which were partially the result of two previous strokes and the residual effects of childhood polio. Prior to Mr. F.'s hospitalization, the couple had lived alone in an apartment and managed independently, with occasional assistance from their daughter.

The goals of nurse case management were discussed with Mr. and Mrs. F. and their daughter in the hospital, and arrangements were made for a home visit. At the time of the initial assessment, Mr. and Mrs. F. were feeling well and able to manage their daily activities independently. Mrs. F.'s major concern was her high cholesterol level. The nurse case manager developed a dietary and exercise program with the couple and then referred them to the wellness center nearest to their home for monitoring of blood pressure and cholesterol levels and for further education on diet and exercise. After 6 months of bimonthly visits to the wellness center, Mrs. F.'s cholesterol level came down and remained within the normal range. Mr. F. had no further gastric problems.

In the year following their referral for case management, Mr. and Mrs. F. remained in their home and made bimonthly visits to the wellness center. They also had monthly contact with their nurse case manager and physician. Then Mr. F. was hospitalized for angina and tachycardia and was given continuous oxygen therapy. During this hospitalization, the nurse case manager acted as a resource for Mr. F.'s primary nurse and participated in the development of his nursing care plan and discharge plan. Mr. F. remained in the hospital for 10 days.

The nurse case manager resumed home visits after Mr. F.'s discharge and instituted a plan to increase the couple's knowledge about and comfort with home oxygen therapy and to increase Mr. F.'s exercise tolerance. After 2 weeks of biweekly visits, Mr. and Mrs. F. had achieved each of the mutually negotiated short-term goals. Case management visits were reduced in frequency, and Mr. F. was again referred to the nearest wellness center for continued monitoring. Six weeks after discharge, Mr. F. was referred to a community-based respiratory fitness program. He has now resumed his daily walks and uses oxygen only when active. Mr. and Mrs. F. and the nurse case manager evaluate health status and revise goals monthly.

Through coordination of services in the nursing network, Mrs. F. reduced her cholesterol, a significant cardiovascular risk factor. Mr. F. negotiated two transitions from hospital to home with relative ease and improved his functional status. He reports that his current life style is satisfying to him. Both Mr. and Mrs. F. have remained at home and are confident of their ability to care for themselves with appropriate family and community supports. Without support for life style changes and coordination of services during and after hospitalization, both risked suffering complications from numerous chronic health problems. These complications would probably have reduced the couple's functional status and quality of life and increased their utilization of acute health services.

STRENGTHS AND WEAKNESSES OF THE NURSING NETWORK

Strengths

The nursing network has numerous strengths that recommend its implementation in other settings. One major strength is the formal structure that the network provides for integrating nursing services across the health care continuum. Although it is common to expect nurses in various settings to communicate with one another and to cooperate in the development and implementation of plans of care, it is still relatively uncommon for institutions to structure environments to maximize effective use of diverse nursing resources. In the nursing network, nurses are encouraged to cross boundaries and to link their efforts for the benefit of clients.

A second strength of the network is the shift in perspective from episodic to continuous care. Current funding mechanisms for health care reinforce a short-term episodic approach to care, and in doing so, they often ignore the potential quality and cost benefits of an ongoing nurse-client relationship. The nursing network allows for integration of short-term and long-term nursing goals. During an acute care hospital stay, the nurse case manager works with the nursing staff to individualize goals and to ensure a transition to long-term care. Often it is the ongoing relationship with the client and family that contributes to the achievement of higher levels of self-care and personal growth.

This leads to the third major advantage of the model: The shift to continuous care requires that the acute care hospital move its base of functioning into the broader community. Few institutions have fully recognized the cost savings that may be realized through enhancing community services. For example, early identification of health care complications, identification either in the home by the nurse case managers or in the wellness centers by the nurse practitioners, may result in lower admission acuity levels. A high community profile also can increase referrals to the hospital and its affiliated physicians.

Weaknesses

The nursing network does have significant weaknesses, many of which may be attributed to its early stage of development. Confusion about roles, frustrations due to lack of standardized practice protocols, and the lack of adequate information systems are to be expected in the introductory phase of any innovation in health care delivery.

Introduction of the nurse case manager program has been associated with role confusion both within nursing and across disciplines. Because the nurse case managers cross service boundaries, there has been a tendency to confuse their services with those of discharge planners, home care nurses, and social workers. In the early stages of the nurse case management program, this confusion was compounded by the nurse case managers' inability to articulate their functions and goals. As time passed and the number of nurse case managers increased, the boundaries of the role—its unique and complementary aspects—became clearer. Nurse case managers have had to take an active role in educating consumers and other health professionals about their services.

Second, group practice presents a unique set of problems for each of the participants in establishing job priorities. Clinicians in the practice often have unit-based responsibilities in addition to their community-based caseload. Administrators and researchers in the group practice have to balance numerous other responsibilities against their clinical practice responsibilities. Fluctuations in practice demands may necessitate rapid adjustments in daily schedules. Although nursing academicians have addressed similar issues with respect to faculty practice models, it is likely that group practitioners in clinical environments will require new solutions.

A third limitation of the model is the lack of computer support for integration of various components of the nursing network. Ideally, nurses participating in the nursing network would be able to track and coordinate the movement of clients by means of computerized information systems. Relevant information would be communicated to minimize duplication of efforts and to enhance continuity of care. Unfortunately, the requisite computer systems are not in place and gaps in communication and continuity do occur.

Evaluation of the Nursing Network

The nursing network evolved in an environment that had an established record of quality nursing care. In 1983, prior to the implementation of many of the current components of the nursing network, St. Mary's was recognized as one of the 41 magnet hospitals in the United States (McClure, Poulin, Sovie, & Wandelt, 1983). Its selection as a magnet hospital was based on its reputation for quality nursing care and its demonstrated success in recruiting and retaining a professional nursing staff. St. Mary's was also included in a follow-up study of 16 of the magnet hospitals conducted by

Kramer and Schmalenberg (1988). These authors found strong similarities between magnet hospitals and topnotch business corporations.

Plans for systematic evaluation of the nursing network are being developed. Pilot studies conducted over the past 5 years indicate that the nursing network may contribute to several quality and cost outcomes. In one study, Ethridge (1987) compared job stress and job satisfaction on the acute care units at three intervals prior to and during the implementation of various components of the nursing network. Job stress decreased following the implementation of professional salaried status and subsequently remained at the lower level. Job satisfaction increased following the implementation of the support structures. Job stress and job satisfaction have not been measured among nurses who work in the nonacute components of the model.

Preliminary outcome data are available for the nurse case management program and the wellness centers. In the 3 years since the development of the professional nurse case management program, nurse case managers provided care to more than 1,500 clients and their families. Results of two pilot studies show an increase in client satisfaction with case management (Sohl, 1986) and a reduction in length of stay in two diagnostic categories selected for study—chronic obstructive pulmonary disease and total hip replacement (Strong, 1986). Recent comparisons of acuity levels and length of stay between nurse case–managed patients with chronic respiratory disease and similar patients without case managers show striking trends. Nurse case–managed patients with chronic respiratory diseases entered the hospital at lower acuity levels and had shorter hospital stays than non-case-managed patients with respiratory illness (Ethridge, 1988).

Preliminary case histories and interviews with professional nurse case managers indicate that nurse case management, as part of the nursing network, may have an impact on several quality outcomes of care, including quality of life, functional status, attainment of treatment goals, and readmission rates.

Since the first wellness center opened in 1986, more than 19,000 visits have been recorded. Visit rates for the first 3 months of fiscal year 1989 are more than double the rates for the same period during fiscal year 1988. Almost half of the individuals who have used the wellness centers are seasonal visitors to the community. Thirty-nine percent of the wellness center clients have no identified physician in Tucson.

The wellness centers have helped to reduce the risk of cardiovascular events in the elderly through control of blood pressure and cholesterol and increased exercise. Center activities have contributed to early identification and treatment of common health problems among the elderly that often lead to hospitalization or institutionalization (e.g., depression). The centers have improved the elderly's access to care by providing an array of screening services and referrals to physicians and community services when appropriate. Over the past 2 years, the nurse practitioners at the centers have made 1,307 such referrals. More than 50% of physician referrals were made for individuals without an identified physician, thus helping to expand the practices of physicians affiliated with St. Mary's.

Qualitative data collected through interviews and observations at the wellness centers indicate substantial satisfaction with the services and enhanced quality of life for the elderly as a result of their increased ability to care for themselves in the community and to defend their interests in dealing with the broader health care system.

FUTURE DIRECTIONS

Each of the components of the nursing network are currently operational at St. Mary's. Participants in the network are working on strategies that will permit refinement and expansion of the model and facilitate its implementation in other settings.

Refinement of the nursing network will require a systematic evaluation of its impact on care outcomes and the strengthening of the linkages among the components. Preliminary studies suggest that the network may enhance quality of care and reduce costs through reducing admission acuity levels, for example. Scientific study is necessary to understand the impact of the network on selected outcomes such as acuity and to establish the conditions necessary for causal inference. A series of research-based investigations are being designed to evaluate the nursing network. Particular attention is being given to the selection of outcomes and measurement tools that are reflective of and sensitive to the dynamics of the network.

Implementation of the network in other settings presents a critical challenge for the future. Close collaboration across institutions will be necessary to discover how the network may be modified for successful application in different environments. As other institutions experiment with various components of the nursing network, it is anticipated that they will contribute to its refinement and to an understanding of how to improve nursing systems through restructuring.

REFERENCES

Ethridge, P. (1987). Nurse accountability program improves satisfaction, turnover. *Health Progress, 68*(4), 44–49.

Ethridge, P. (1988). Professional nurse case management reduces costs. *Arizona Nurse, 41*, 1, 7, 9.

Kramer, M., & Schmalenberg, C. (1988). Magnet hospitals: Part 1: Institutions of excellence. *Journal of Nursing Administration, 18* (1), 13–24.

McClure, M.L., Poulin, P.A., Sovie, M.D., & Wandelt, M.A. (1983). *Magnet hospitals: Attraction and retention of professional nurses.* Kansas City, MO: American Nurses' Association.

Prescott, P.A., & Sorenson, J.E. (1978). Cost-effectiveness analysis: An approach to evaluating nursing programs. *Nursing Administration Quarterly, 3,* 17–40.

Rusch, S. (1986). Continuity of care: From hospital unit into home. *Nursing Management, 17,* 38–41.

Sohl, L.M. (1986). *Nursing case management: A pilot study on patient satisfaction.* Unpublished manuscript.

Strong, B. (1986). *Nurse case management in acute care.* Unpublished manuscript.

Zander, K. (1988). Nursing case management: Strategic management of cost and quality outcomes. *Journal of Nursing Administration, 18* (5), 23–30.

Chapter 11

The Role of the Patient Care Technician at the New England Deaconess Hospital

Marjorie Splaine Wiggins, Judith M. Farias, and
Judith R. Miller

The authors first present a nurse extender program, and they then describe the curriculum and their 2 years of experience. The use of patient care technicians has alleviated patient unit pressures and shifted the professional nursing role to areas requiring a professional. The authors describe the positive acceptance of the role, which they believe is due to an initial unfreezing of the traditional system, role negotiations between the RNs and the patient care technicians, and a well-developed and articulated process for making the change. The authors suggest cost savings probably have resulted from the change, with the promise of more documentation to establish this as the role develops and more data become available.

The role of the nurse since the inception of professional nursing has been one of the most versatile and "well utilized" in all of the health care professions. Even 100 years ago, nurses were expected not only to care for patients but to provide necessary maintenance and cleaning of the wards. Although nursing has advanced in terms of its knowledge base, scientific principles, clinical expertise, and technology, health care organizations are still trying to utilize nurses to meet all service delivery needs of patients. Nurses still perform secretarial tasks when the secretarial staff are absent, run to the pharmacy for missing medications, deliver meal trays when dietary is short-handed and, yes, empty wastebaskets and clean patient rooms when housekeeping is overburdened. In addition to delivering highly complex patient care, nurses still deliver the mail, water the plants, requisition maintenance to fix broken curtain rods, and provide countless other patient comfort services. What formerly was the efficient utilization of a position has become a waste of a precious resource.

In 1978, 54% of the nursing staff at the New England Deaconess Hospital (Deaconess) were RNs. Currently, 77% of the nursing staff are RNs, and this percentage is still not sufficient if nurses continue trying to be all things to all people. The time has come to restructure the nurse's role and allow nurses to deliver the professional aspects of care they have been educated to provide. No longer can health care organizations afford to misuse the precious resource of nursing! It does not make sense in light of the nursing shortage and of nurses' salaries, which sometimes exceed $50,000. Nursing itself needs to restructure care now—before administrators, pressured by limited reimbursement, begin to replace nurses with nonnursing personnel for some patient care needs.

THE GOAL AND THE CONCEPT

The first step in restructuring the role of the RN is to perform a detailed task analysis of the procedures and tasks currently done by RNs. A careful examination of the results of this task analysis will provide the basis for making a determination of which skills and tasks require the expertise of professional nurses and which do not. This leads to the next step, which is to establish whether or not someone could be trained to perform certain technical parts of these procedures and tasks if the assessment, judgment, and observations related to their performance remained the responsibility of an RN.

These were exactly the issues the staff at the Deaconess confronted and resolved by developing the role of patient care technician (PCT). The training of a nonlicensed individual to perform repetitive technical tasks was designed to double the hands of the RN and extend his or her ability to meet patients' needs.

THE ROLE OF THE PATIENT CARE TECHNICIAN

In the generic sense, the PCT is a nurse extender. The PCT works under the direct supervision of an RN, and the two function as a team for a group of assigned patients. The PCT can perform multiple technical tasks, but the nurse is still fully responsible and accountable for the patient's care. For example, the PCT may perform simple to moderately complex dressing changes, but the nurse is required to observe and assess the status of each patient's wound and initiate appropriate interventions. The assignment of the task has the potential of saving hundreds of RN hours on a unit that has a high surgical census and numerous dressing changes. Other tasks performed by the PCT include tube feedings, ostomy care, catheterization, removal of skin staples, and basic hygiene measures. Each task delegated to the PCT by the RN is reviewed for appropriateness before the task is assigned. It would not be appropriate for a PCT to perform ostomy care for a patient with a newly established stoma, but it would be very appropriate to perform ostomy care for a patient who had a well-established stoma.

In addition to technical tasks, the PCT assists patients with activities of daily living and performs all the jobs related to patient care that were previously carried out by the nursing assistant. The addition of new skills and training at the PCT level has in essence provided the nursing assistant with an opportunity for advancement. Given today's acutely ill patient population, the PCT role has maximized the support a nonlicensed caregiver can provide to an RN. Throughout the preparation of the PCT, it is stressed that the PCT is not an independent agent and functions under the direct supervision of the nurse. The RN is also made aware that the full responsibility for the nursing care of the patient remains with him or her and may not be delegated to a nonnurse. With the exception of recording vital signs and limited flow sheet documentation of activities of daily living and tasks performed, the RN is responsible for documenting all nursing observations, care delivered, and responses to interventions in the patient's medical record.

ASSUMPTIONS OF THE MODEL

Three important assumptions are made that are key to understanding this model. The first and most important assumption is that nursing is a profession. As professionals, nurses cannot allow their time to be misused if they are to provide the best possible care for their patients. Doing repetitive tasks and trying to provide for all the needs of patients are not wise uses of professional time. This is not to say that the nurse should not perform physical care or technical tasks, but the performance of these tasks should be at the nurse's discretion. The assignment of selected physical care and technical tasks frees the nurse to collaborate with other health care team members, provides patient education, and prepares the patient for discharge. A popular argument why nurses should provide all physical care and services to patients is that they gain important information during the course of caregiving and can provide instruction during these contacts with the patients. At Deaconess, it is postulated that the information gleaned and the instruction provided in this manner tends to be haphazard and inconsistent. The belief is that patient assessment and teaching are most effective when both patients and nurses can devote their full attention to the process at hand. When nurses teach in a fragmented fashion and are distracted by trying to accomplish something else at the same time, patient care is likely to be compromised.

The second assumption is that technicians can be taught to do certain procedures proficiently and that the quality of care will not be reduced as long as nurses are responsible and accountable for the care of patients. Many of the procedures used in patient care do not require extensive training or an in-depth understanding of the sciences, yet performing such procedures usually consumes a valuable portion of any nurse's day. What makes nursing a profession is not the performance of procedures but the utilization of the nursing process, the diagnosis of the patient's need for nursing care, and intervention on the patient's behalf.

The last assumption, and the one that is key to the success of this model, is that nurses will be able to adapt their role to the new method of delivering care and assign appropriate tasks to PCTs. Such adaption requires ongoing education and development. One myth of primary nursing, that the RN has to do "everything" for the patient, discouraged the delegation of tasks to other providers. In addition, the RN's basic education does not necessarily ensure the development of leadership skills or the ability to delegate effectively. This is aptly demonstrated by the newly graduated nurse who has difficulty assigning tasks to the nursing assistant. Maximizing the utilization of the PCT role depends on the abilities of the nurse and PCT to work effectively as a team to provide care.

IMPLEMENTATION

Developing the Job Description

At Deaconess, the first step in the implementation of the model was to form a task force to develop a job description for the PCT. The task force was chaired by the director of Medical Surgical Nursing and was composed of staff nurses, staff development personnel, nurse clinicians, nurse managers, and nurse educators (one of whom was the curriculum consultant). A job description and a list of functional responsibilities that identified exactly which procedures the PCT could perform were developed by the task force. These tools not only described the role of the PCT in detail but served as the basis for development of the curriculum to prepare candidates for the position. The task force was also instrumental in deciding how to handle many of the issues associated with implementation of the role (e.g., the uniform to be worn by the PCT, reporting lines, qualifications of the candidates, the number of students in each class, etc.). It is strongly recommended that each institution develop its own task force to discuss and make decisions regarding these issues. A job description that is appropriate for one institution may not be appropriate for another. Even within Deaconess it was found that specialization among units creates the need for specialized PCTs. There may be a need for a PCT to perform certain additional specialized tasks within certain areas for best utilization of the role. For example, if a PCT was assigned to the telemetry unit, additional skills needed to assist in maintaining the monitoring equipment would be taught.

Designing the Curriculum

Once the PCT job description had been finalized, the next step was to appoint the faculty (who were Deaconess clinical nurses) and develop the curriculum for the preparation of PCTs. A curriculum guideline and format was developed and provided to assist the faculty in preparing a course outline. The depth of knowledge required by a PCT to practice safely was described as the knowledge base an informed consumer would be expected to have regarding his or her illness. The technical procedures that PCTs would be trained to perform were those patients would be required to perform after discharge. With this rule in mind—and under the guidance of the curriculum consultant—the faculty was able to determine what theoretical background was necessary to provide PCTs with a basic understanding of patient problems and of the rationales and principles related to each procedure.

Each faculty member developed unit objectives, study guide questions, a bibliography, and test questions for the unit (or units) he or she was responsible for. Utilizing the hospital's own clinical people and allowing them to develop the curriculum ensured that the content would be most relevant to the particular setting.

EDUCATIONAL PREPARATION

Curriculum

The PCT program has been developed as a 3-month educational program consisting of correlated theoretical and clinical experience. Students with no prior nursing assistant experience enter the program a week earlier and attend classes on basic hygiene, bed making, and vital signs. During this week, the students have the opportunity to practice those skills in the clinical area.

The program "officially" begins when all students enter the class, and for the first 2 weeks of the program everyone receives classroom instruction. Resources for student learning include a textbook, course outline, study guide, bibliography, procedure manual, and handouts from the faculty. Infection control, body mechanics and transfer, the patient medical record, and patient admission and discharge are some of the content areas covered at this time. From the 3rd week of the program on, the schedule consists of 2 class days and 3 clinical days. Additional class presentations include relevant anatomy, physiology, and microbiology to provide students with a basic understanding of the patient problems they will be seeing in the clinical area.

During the clinical component of the program, each PCT is assigned to work with an RN, who serves as a preceptor. A program clinical instructor assists with the supervision of the PCTs and functions as a resource for the nursing staff on the patient care units. A list of procedures is maintained for each student throughout the period of clinical education. Following successful demonstration of each procedure, the student is "checked off" by the preceptor and may then perform the procedure independently. Rationales for all activities and procedures are stressed. Students also spend a day in the operating room and, as an observational experience, attend nursing rounds with the ostomy clinician.

The curriculum plan covers 12 weeks and topics are sequenced as shown in Exhibit 11-1.

Faculty

Resource people at Deaconess were identified and selected to teach the components of the course in which they were clinically expert. The nursing content of the program is taught by a nursing faculty made up of clinical specialists, clinicians, and other nursing personnel who have expertise in a particular area. For example, the ostomy clinicians teach ostomy care, the nurse epidemiologist teaches infection control, and unit teachers on the medical-surgical units teach several modules on the care of the respiratory patient, the urological patient, and the postsurgical patient. Other faculty include clinicians from the Department of Dietetics, the Physical Therapy Department, and the Department of Radiology. Utilizing Deaconess clinical resource people and allowing them to develop curriculum content with the guidance of the curriculum consultant ensured that the content was relevant and applicable to the hospital's setting and patient population.

Exhibit 11-1 Curriculum Plan for the Patient Care Technician Program

Week	1	2	3	4	5	6	7	8	9	10	11	12
	Class	*Class*	*Class*	*Class*	*Class*	*Class*	*Class*	*Class*	*Class*	*Class*	*Class*	*Class*
			Quiz	Quiz	Quiz		Quiz	Quiz	Quiz	Quiz	Quiz	Final comprehensive exam
	Lecture, discussion, demonstration	Lecture, discussion, demonstration	Pre-op care	Post-op care	Food/ fluids	Fecal and urinary diversion	Fecal and urinary diversion	Suicide precaution	Diabetic patient	Peripheral vascular disease	Values/ rights/ responsibility	
					Enteral feedings							Course evaluation
	Basic skills	Basic skills	Wounds/ dressings	IV therapy	Rehabilitation		Radiation therapy	Cardiac patient	Exercise and activity		Ethics	Clinical evaluations
			Clinical 7–3:30 (3 days)	*Clinical* 7–3:30 (3 days)	*Clinical* 7–3:30 (3 days)	*Clinical* 7–3:30 (3 days)	*Clinical* 7–3:30 (3 days)	*Clinical* 7–3:30 (3 days)	*Clinical* 7–3:30 (3 days)	*Clinical* 7–3:30 (3 days)	*Clinical* 7–3:30 (3 days)	*Clinical* 7–3:30 (2 days)
							Midterm evaluations					

Course Requirements

To successfully meet the program objectives, the student must complete the theoretical and clinical components of the course. Clinical performance is graded as satisfactory or unsatisfactory. The theoretical component consists of weekly quizzes and a final comprehensive examination. A satisfactory clinical evaluation and a theory average of 70% is required.

Course Evaluation

A comprehensive course evaluation is completed by each student at the end of the program. Students are asked to rate their satisfaction with program structure, content presentation, and performance evaluation and to offer suggestions for improvement. One recommendation from the first class of PCTs was to have students with no prior nursing assistant experience enter the program a week earlier than those who have experience. (This is now done.) The course evaluation summary is shared with the faculty and students. Feedback from the first two classes of PCTs has been overwhelmingly positive.

Educational Preparation of Nurse Preceptors

All faculty members and nurse managers who have responsibility for supervising the students during their clinical experience attend a workshop designed to ensure that the nursing staff will be familiar with the expectations of the students. At this workshop a packet is distributed that includes the following:

- a description of the purpose and objectives of the program
- guidelines for interacting with students during the clinical experience
- a schedule that identifies course content and indicates when the student should be ready to perform certain procedures
- a procedures list that clearly identifies any restrictions on student performance of the procedures

Professional Nurse–Patient Care Technician Role Expectation Workshop

Staff development includes this additional educational offering for the RNs to whom the PCTs will be assigned once they have completed the course. Among the topics covered are the following:

- the professional nurse's role—new opportunities and new responsibilities
- the skill preparation of the PCT
- role issues and answers

The target audience for this workshop may also include nurses who have had the opportunity to work with PCTs, thereby allowing the exchange of first-hand experiences in sharing assignments. Nurse managers are also encouraged to participate.

MARKETING THE PROGRAM

There are essentially two areas of marketing to consider when implementing a program like the PCT program at Deaconess: internal marketing (which allows the concept to be seeded and grow) and external marketing (which is important for recruitment and public relations).

Internal Marketing

Programs like the PCT program can have a major effect on hospital administration, medical and nursing staffs, and support departments. Therefore, the first place to start internal marketing is at the top administrative level. Deaconess prides itself on providing an environment that encourages innovation and top administrative support. To ensure the success of a PCT program, it is imperative that the nurse executive be well informed about the program's merits and costs and its probable impact on staffing and patient care. Such information is crucial for developing a plan for internal marketing. Informing nursing management is another key to the success of the project. At Deaconess, the concept was first discussed with the nurse managers, who demonstrated strong interest in and support for the concept. When the nurse managers' support was assured and the task force had brought the job description into focus and identified PCT performance responsibilities, the concept was marketed to the nursing staff. This was accomplished by meeting with the staff of each patient care unit and discussing the concept, including what the concept's implementation was intended to achieve and how it would affect day-to-day practice. Since the nursing shortage had already begun to place a noticeable burden on the staff, a new type of skilled support person was looked upon as a welcome addition. In fact, many staff members offered suggestions for enhancing the educational process, and some were more willing to expand the PCT's job responsibilities than those in charge of implementation.

The medical staff were informed of the program through the Clinical Co-ordinating Committee and the Medical Executive Committee and through the medical staff newsletter (not to mention word of mouth). Since the medical staff were acutely aware of the impending nursing shortage and understood that nurses would retain full responsibility for the nursing care of patients, they did not find the concept of a PCT program objectionable. They were, in fact, quite positive about the fact that there would be additional support for nurses, whom they saw as already overburdened by current demands.

Department heads were informed at one of the monthly leadership meetings. They were told that the idea was to create a new position that would extend the nurse's ability to care for patients but would not in any way replace the nurse's role. The point was made that patients would continue to receive the same quality of care they always had received at Deaconess. (It was important to reiterate this message throughout the entire implementation process.) The nurse would be responsible for the patient and the PCT would be used to perform procedures and tasks that were of a technical nature. Assessment, planning, and evaluating the patient would remain within the purview of the RN.

Finally, a special meeting was held to inform the nursing assistants employed by the hospital. Since the program would entail job advancement for the nursing assistants at Deaconess, it was anticipated that they would show considerable interest. In fact, the turnout at the meeting was exceptionally high. The nursing assistants saw not only an opportunity for career advancement but also an opportunity to do more for the patients. As one nursing assistant expressed it, "Many times I have to get the nurse to do something for the patient that I know I could do but haven't had the proper training. The patient and I have to wait till the nurse is available, and sometimes that interferes with the care the patient needs. I want the best for our patients too, and I know I can be more of a help."

External Marketing

When you are confident that your hospital staff are comfortable and demonstrate understanding of the concept, then and only then should you begin to market the concept externally. This sequence is important, because your staff are your most important asset and have the right to be fully informed at all times. Second, your staff are your best recruiters. Many of Deaconess's applicants came as referrals from the hospital's own staff.

The approach used to market the program was a little different from the usual marketing approach used at Deaconess. Massachusetts "suffers" from a record low unemployment rate of approximately 2%. This is certainly good for the local economy, but it makes recruitment difficult. Many different industries are competing for the same potential employees. Hospitals in Boston aren't just competing with each other but also with local food stores and restaurants, which pay competitive wages for untrained labor and offer full benefits and flexible hours.

Very important in marketing the program was the name chosen for the role. Probably if Deaconess had advertised for nursing assistants or even advanced nursing assistants, it would have not reached the markets it did. The title "Patient Care Technician" not only aptly described the role but also struck a responsive chord in individuals who wanted to enter the health care arena in a paraprofessional role instead of as an assistant or aide.

After Deaconess identified the population it wished to recruit, it decided to segment the market. The intent was to attract individuals from two distinct categories. The first market segment consisted of nursing assistants who wanted to advance and improve their skills and financial position. The second market segment consisted of individuals who were interested in human services but were not ready or could not afford to invest 4 years in school. The role appealed not only to new high school or college graduates but also to those individuals who were considering a career change. Because the program is considered "on-the-job training," a full salary (approximately 10% less than the beginning PCT salary) is paid during the training period and the employee receives full benefits. This enables the person who is in career transition and has financial responsibilities to maintain an income while learning a new role.

The Public Relations Department was involved from the beginning and was instrumental in helping publicize the program in area newspapers and on radio stations. Several community newspapers were interested in the program, because it was seen as a way of easing the nursing shortage. For months the media had been reporting the effects of the nursing shortage and could now report on a new program designed by nurses to address the problem. The Public Relations Department also produced a short article about the program that appeared in the educational section of the major Boston newspaper. Informational mailings were sent to high school guidance counselors and to area offices of the Department of Employment Services.

Recruitment

In addition to marketing the concept of the program, advertising was done in the want ad section of the local newspaper. But instead of advertising as usual in the medical help section, a copy of the ad appeared in the nonmedical section. Also considered for advertising were community newspapers, college and high school publications, and literature directed at guidance counselors and high school teachers. These publications were not used initially because the response rate was so high that further advertising was not necessary.

A deliberate decision was made to fill the first class half from inside the hospital and half from outside. The high degree of interest mentioned earlier made the establishment of an internal application pool easy and quick. Outside applicants were screened by Human Resources and then by the director of Medical Surgical Nursing and the manager of the PCT program. It is recommended that someone from the clinical area and someone from the academic area interview candidates to get different perspectives on how each candidate would function as a student and as an employee. Both groups of candidates (internal and external) were required to have the following:

1. a high school diploma or GED (general equivalency diploma)
2. an average academic standing at the very least
3. two references, including the most recent employer
4. a satisfactory employment and attendance record

IMPLEMENTATION COSTS

The concept of a PCT program was first developed in the fall of 1986, and plans for implementation began in the spring of 1987. Because this was a new idea and the literature did not contain accounts of similar projects, every aspect of the project—from the PCT job description to the program and the curriculum—had to be designed. Initially, a significant portion of the time and energy of one individual, who also had full-time nursing management responsibilities, was devoted to implementation. Later, a second individual, who had full-time teaching and administrative responsibilities, worked on the project. Through their efforts, and with the assistance of the PCT task force, the program was in place by June 1988.

The cost of the program was minimized as a result of the way it was designed. The majority of the cost for this type of program would normally be for faculty salaries, but as indicated earlier, the majority of the faculty are Deaconess clinicians, unit teachers, and resource people who were already employees. The only new employees were the manager of the program and a part-time clinical instructor (3 days a week). The use of staff nurse preceptors to work with the PCT students on the patient care units minimized the cost of clinical supervision.

Other significant costs of the program to be considered are the salaries paid to PCTs during the 3-month training program. Salaries paid during this program are at the nursing assistant level. Although the salaries are considered a cost, it should be noted that the PCTs are on the nursing units at the beginning of the 3rd week of the program and do provide some patient care. This care is at least at the nursing assistant level, and although the PCTs are being trained, they constitute an asset that can be taken into account when planning unit staffing. Thus, it is unrealistic to consider as a cost the full salary of a PCT while in training.

PCTs are expected to provide their own uniforms during the clinical experience and upon completion of the program. In the case of Deaconess, this is a savings, since uniforms are provided to nursing assistants. The only other costs of the program are clinical supplies used in skill labs and texts and class materials, all of which do not amount to much in the way of expense.

EVALUATION OF THE PROGRAM

The main purpose of the program was to develop PCTs who can function in the role of nurse extenders, thereby freeing nurses from some technical work so that they can perform more advanced nursing tasks. Another purpose was to create an advanced level of nursing assistant to maximize a resource that was believed to be underutilized. To measure the attainment of those goals, a questionnaire was developed in conjunction with the Deaconess Center for Nursing Research.

Four months after the first class of PCTs were assigned to work with RNs, questionnaires were distributed to the RNs, the PCTs, and the nurse managers involved in the project. The questions concerned job satisfaction (for both RNs and PCTs), role expectations (for the PCTs), and the overall effect of having the nurse extenders on the unit.

Three different questionnaires were developed in order to address specific issues for each group. Ten of the 12 RNs (83%) responded, 10 of the 12 PCTs (83%), and 5 of the 6 nurse managers (83%). Among the findings were that the PCTs generally

- met or exceeded expectations
- were very strong in communicating observations and pertinent information to the RNs
- were positive additions to the health care team

Areas identified for future discussion included

- the time period for RN-PCT coassignment (should there be a system for rotating a PCT to other RNs?)
- the patient ratio for PCT-RN teams
- the effects of the program on staffing patterns

The overall response to having PCTs on the patient care unit has been very positive. Table 11-1 shows the responses from all three groups surveyed.

The survey findings were very positive. They indicate that the program is a success and a welcome addition to the Department of Nursing. Not only has the program successfully equipped Deaconess with trained health care workers to assist the nursing staff in maintaining high-quality care, but it has attracted new resources to the health care field. An informal survey of the PCTs indicate that 50% have an interest in entering a school of nursing. Hopefully, some of today's PCTs will become some of tomorrow's nurses.

PROS AND CONS OF THE MODEL

At Deaconess, nurses are viewed as vital for the success of the organization and the achievement of its goals. When a program can be established that ensures nurses are provided with the support they need to deliver care to today's higher-acuity patient population, it is well worth the investment that is required. The PCT program provides a skilled support to nurses, thus freeing them of some of the technical tasks that in the past consumed the greater part of their day. This new extender has allowed nurses to restructure their day to provide the teaching, planning, and emotional support that in the past had to be given on the run or not at all due to the more pressing physiological needs of the patients.

In addition to meeting today's patient care needs, the PCT program provides many individuals with a career track into health care, individuals who may later pursue education in the field of nursing or in allied health care professions.

Table 11-1 Overall Response to Having or Being a PCT

	Negative	Not Sure	Positive
RN responses to being assigned a PCT	10%	20%	70%
Nurse manager responses to having a PCT on the unit	0	20	80
PCT responses to PCT role	10	10	80

Ongoing patient satisfaction surveys show that Deaconess patients are very positive about having PCTs assist in their care. Comments from patients indicate a high level of satisfaction regarding the quality of care, concern, and support provided by the PCTs during their hospitalizations. Because the nurses and PCTs make it very clear to patients that both will be providing care, patients end up satisfied that they received an optimal level of professional nursing care.

Three major benefits to the hospital have resulted from implementation of the PCT program. First, the addition of the PCTs to the work force has helped maintain adquate nursing care hours, thus alleviating the threat of having to close beds due to inadequate nurse staffing—a growing concern to all hospital administrators in the face of the nursing shortage.

The second major benefit is the increase in employee satisfaction due to greater job mobility within the hospital. Many of the employees have worked at Deaconess for many years, and the addition of the PCT program has allowed interdepartmental transfers at a higher level than was previously possible. The program has had applicants from a number of departments, including the clerical pool, admitting, and building services.

The third major benefit is an increase in the recognition and development of staff potential. For years, the nursing assistant population was known to be an excellent resource, but the hospital did little to advance the role or upgrade the position. Intuitively and from years of experience, many of the nursing assistants were knowledgeable about more tasks and procedures than their job description permitted them to do. With the introduction of the PCT program, Deaconess was able to tap into and develop this potential. The classes not only taught the nursing assistants the rationale for certain aspects of care but also gave them skills that dramatically increased their job satisfaction and productivity.

The negative aspects of the model hardly constitute an argument against it. At best they indicate that certain adjustments need to be made. Nurses are continuing to adapt to the model but are still learning how best to rearrange their day. It is clear that RNs need additional education and discussion about the utilization of PCTs. Providing support positions is only one step of a two-step process. The second step is helping nurses utilize these support positions more effectively and efficiently. Theories about the art of delegation and leadership may be learned in a 1-day workshop, but internalizing theoretical concepts and skillfully leading and delegating on a daily basis involves a long-term learning process.

SUMMARY

The implications of the addition of PCTs are numerous and widespread. The PCT role allows nurses to address and develop solutions to the nursing shortage within the profession and to prevent outside sources from determining the fate of the profession. The nurse extender model can enhance the profession by allowing nurses to provide professional nursing care that is consistent with the concept of total patient care, thereby preventing fragmentation of care, which has been a problem with other solutions (e.g., team nursing). Nurses have difficulty giving up any component of total patient care, but the physical demands made by acute patients reduce the amount of nursing time that can be given to more cognitive tasks. Once nurses learn they can control the quality of physical care without necessarily doing everything themselves, they will feel more comfortable assigning technical tasks to their extenders. Nurses will then be freed to concentrate on the higher-level aspects of nursing care. But if the idea persists that nurses must actually do everything for patients, then these higher-level aspects will continue to receive less than their due as a result of the growing acuity of patient needs. As the science of nursing grows, nurses must continue to grow with it by assessing and restructuring what they do and how they do it.

Chapter 12

Definitions and Basic Elements of a Patient Care Delivery System with an Emphasis on Primary Nursing

Marie Manthey

Marie Manthey provides definitions of common terminology used in discussing primary nursing. She then describes the four basic organizational elements of a patient care delivery system using primary nursing as an example.

Manthey also presents her new staffing system, called Partners-In-Practice, *and provides a brief summary of this new system, which involves partnerships between professional nurses and auxiliary workers. The financial implications of this system are only briefly mentioned, and we look forward to reading more about the details of this new and interesting concept.*

DEFINITIONS

JARGON. 1. Confused, unintelligible talk or language; gabble; gibberish. 2. The specialized vocabulary and idioms of those in the same line of work, such as journalism or social work or nursing. Somewhat derogatory term, implying unintelligibility.

SYSTEM. 1. A set or arrangement of things so related or connected as to form a unity or organic whole, such as a solar system, irrigation system, supply system, or delivery system. 2. A set of facts, principles, rules, and so on, classified to show the links between the various parts.

MODEL. 1. Anything of a particular form, shape, size, quality, or construction intended for imitation. 2. A person or thing considered as a standard of excellence to be imitated.

THEORY. 1. Originally a mental viewing; contemplation. 2. That branch of an art or science consisting of knowledge of its principles and methods (as opposed to practical application of the art or science); pure as opposed to applied science.

ROLE. 1. A part or character represented by an actor. 2. A function or office assumed by someone, such as a counselor's or nurse's role.

PROFESSIONAL. One who engages in autonomous decision making based on an identifiable body of knowledge acquired in a formal education program.

In the delivery system of *primary nursing,* a person can fulfill the role of a *professional nurse,* performing care activities chosen using Orem's theory of nursing and managing the care in the context of the patient's progress and compliance with the predetermined critical pathways, which is called *case management.* In this example, case management is an expanded role concept.

In primary nursing, an RN can also function (simultaneously) as an *associate nurse,* following the care instructions of another RN who is off-duty at the time. Therefore, it is possible to function in two *roles* in the same *delivery system,* using a particular *theoretical framework.* Whether the role configuration is "classical" primary nursing or case management depends in part on the level of collaboration between nurses and physicians hospitalwide.

Conversely, it is possible to use primary nursing with role differentiation determined by basic job descriptions, in which case one nurse would always function as an associate nurse. Strict definition of *levels of practice* does not result in a new delivery system but does require specific staffing levels for each role and careful scheduling practices. Again, whether the role of the professional nurse is broadly scoped as defined in case management is largely a function of the degree of collaboration between the medical staff and the nursing department as a whole.

Another example of term use: A case manager is a professional nurse who has continuous responsibility for decisions about the care of a particular set of patients. The nurse's theoretical framework may be Roy's or Orem's and his or her practice is based on the nursing process and uses nursing diagnosis and nursing orders to achieve independence. So far, the description (which contains pure jargon) could apply to the job of primary nurse. What makes the case manager different are two components of role expansion:

1. The case manager's span of control over a patient's care crosses unit lines.

2. The case manager has authority to manage the overall hospital care, especially when the patient is not experiencing outcomes consistent with preset standards.

Thus, case management is an example of role expansion, not a new delivery system.

DELIVERY SYSTEMS DEFINED

A nursing delivery system is a set of concepts defining four basic organizational elements. The definitions of these elements are based on principles that are in turn based on fundamental values. These fundamental values will ultimately determine the quality of the product. If the workers are not valued as independent decision makers by the definers of the principles of work organization, independent decision making will not be characteristic of their practice. If the definers do not believe the average staff nurse has the ability to manage a patient's care (to be distinguished from clinical ability), the system will not give decision-making authority to staff nurses.

The four fundamental elements are

1. clinical decision making
2. work allocation
3. communication
4. management

SYSTEM IMPACT

These four elements—decision making, work allocation, communication, and management—are the cornerstones upon which a delivery system is built. The more clearly they are articulated, the better they will be.

Roles are developed to function within the framework of the delivery system, and that framework impacts the functions in such a way as to support or prohibit various behaviors. For example, imagine a well-qualified, competent nurse functioning one day as a primary nurse, the next as a team leader, and the third day as the medication nurse. The knowledge contained in his or her brain and the skill reflected in his or her hands-on practice and verbal interactions will differ dramatically depending on the *role* created to fulfill the functions assigned in the context of the expectations inherent in the delivery system.

There is another major way the delivery system impacts work performed and the worker's experience of it. When work is allocated according to tasks rather than patients, a body of knowledge about the patients is simply not accumulated by the staff. This absence of knowledge has a negative impact on the clinical decisions that need to be made. In addition, the absence of patient information severely impacts the quality of data communicated. Data communication is one of the major sources of evidence available after the fact to judge the quality of performance. If little nursing data are available, nursing practice is judged to require only a low level of intelligence. (Thus, charting that is routine and noninformative substantiates the belief of physicians and administrators that nursing can be taught at the diploma and practical nurse levels.) In this way, task-based work allocation methods completely sabotage nursing's claim to professionhood. Delivery system design is the framework within which roles are developed and clinical knowledge is required and formulated.

An intellectual understanding of system design is a prerequisite for the successful implementation of any system, but by itself it gives no assurance of success.

Managing a successful implementation is one of the trickiest challenges confronting nurse administrators. Every bit of the change theory and knowledge in RosaBeth Moss-Kanter's book *Changemaster* and a lot of luck and good will are essential to success. The reason the change process is so complex is that, in a complex, hierarchical bureaucracy, it must embody a very sophisticated development process within itself.

FUNDAMENTALS OF PRIMARY NURSING

The philosophical cornerstone of primary nursing is decentralized decision making, which is defined as decision making at the level of action. The level of action in caring for patients in hospitals is the bedside. Thus, decentralization means decision-making responsibility and authority is allocated to (and must be accepted by) staff nurses at the bedside. The resulting care is not something new. It is the kind of care society has always believed the sick should receive—care given by someone with a consistent relationship with the patient. However, the process of returning to this kind of care is revolutionary, in that it represents a reallocation of power from a faceless, anonymous, hierarchical, authoritarian bureaucracy to the staff nurse who is responsible for the care of a patient. In order for this reallocation of power to occur, a major change is required in the structure and operation of nursing departments.

DESIGN OF PRIMARY NURSING

In a primary nursing system, patients are divided among the eligible nurses in such a way that each nurse is responsible for the care of a small group of patients. Each nurse makes decisions about how that care will be administered and leaves instructions to be followed by those who care for the patients in the nurse's absence. The care instructions need not be elaborate or comprehensive. The main thing is that each patient is under the responsible care of the nurse.

In addition to deciding how care shall be administered, the nurse personally administers the care whenever possible. This design element is in recognition of the fact that the person performing an activity is the person best able to decide how it should be done.

In deciding how much hands-on care should be administered by the primary nurse, several factors are taken into account. Staffing levels, the nature of the patient's condition, and the need to update the nurse's knowledge base are the most important. Of these, the first two are self-explanatory. However, special attention needs to be focused on the third factor.

"Nursing is a knowledge-based practice profession" is a principle that guides nurses in deciding how much direct care a primary nurse should administer personally. As previously stated, a professional is "one who engages in autonomous decision making based on an identifiable body of knowledge acquired in a formal education program." The first decision to be made is the amount and kind of actual care a particular patient will receive and how that care will be administered by the staff of that unit. In order to make this decision, the primary nurse must acquire information about the patient through hands-on care at the bedside. This knowledge is combined with the knowledge acquired during the nurse's formal education.

In some cases, the primary nurse may decide merely to give the patient a bath. In other cases, the decision may be to change a dressing, accompany the doctor on rounds, attend a team conference, or provide assistance during the patient's first walk down the corridor. The decision as to which activities of care to perform is one of the more seminal autonomous decisions the nurse makes.

In order for responsibility to be truly accepted, others need to know that a responsibility relationship exists. Thus, the patient, the patient's friends and relatives, the physicians, the other nurses, and the other members of the health care team must know the name of the primary nurse and the type of care decided upon.

There are three major areas of responsibility. First, the primary nurse is responsible for making available the necessary clinical information others need for the intelligent care of the patient in the nurse's absence. This means the nurse not only must be knowledgeable but also must be able to recognize what information is essential for the others to have. The areas of significant information are not defined in advance, and so it is up to each nurse to determine what they are on a patient-by-patient basis. In some cases, the important information may be the etiology or prognosis of the disease; in others, the fact that the disease is a familial one. Sometimes it may be important to describe symptoms to watch for or a new form of treatment that is being used. In some cases, the primary nurse may even decide there is no clinical information that needs to be shared with colleagues.

Second, the primary nurse is responsible for deciding how nursing care shall be administered and for making available to other nurses the instructions for care. The nursing process may be useful in fulfilling this responsibility.

The primary nurse collects information using whatever sources are available, such as the patient, the chart, the physician, the patient's relatives, and so on. Then, on the basis of the data thus collected, the nurse develops a preliminary plan of care. Different hospitals provide different tools for use in data collection and in writing the plan of care (e.g., nursing history forms, kardex care plans, nursing order sheets, admission guides, etc.). Any of these tools can be helpful in the planning process, but their design should in no way restrict the quality or quantity of data collection or the clarity of information used in the decision-making process. Decisions about how nursing care should be administered are of a much higher quality when the patient and his family participate in them. Deciding how and when a treatment procedure should be performed, when hygienic care is most important, or what time of day physical therapy is well tolerated can best be done with the full cooperation of a knowledgeable patient. Since quality-of-care decisions are vastly superior in cases where the patient is an informed participant, it is incumbent upon the primary nurse to educate patients so their contributions can be meaningful.

Instructions left by the primary nurse are to be followed by others caring for the nurse's patients in his or her absence unless an alteration is dictated by a change in a patient's condition. When that happens, the nurse's instructions may be modified to deal with the new situation. Otherwise, they are to be followed by the staff members who care for the patient on the other shifts. Thus, if a primary nurse has written a comprehensive plan of instruction for a new diabetic that requires the patient to inject an orange for the first time when the primary nurse is off duty, the nurse caring for the patient on that shift should provide supervision and assistance or teach the patient how to do the procedure.

A disagreement about how a patient should be treated or instructed must be openly negotiated and resolved but must not be fought out on the battleground of the patient's care plan. Simple differences of opinion should be easily resolved in an adult fashion by the individuals involved; serious conflicts regarding patient care may require the use of conflict resolution skills by the head nurse.

The third major area of responsibility is discharge planning. The primary nurse is responsible for seeing to it that the patient and family (if the family will be caring for the patient after the hospitalization) have been prepared to provide safe and effective care. If the patient is being transferred to an agency that employs nurses, the primary nurse is responsible for communicating any information needed for a smooth transition. The nurse should tailor the discharge to the individual patient. For example, nurses in an agency or institution to which the patient is being transferred should be given relevant information in a fashion and degree of detail appropriate to the circumstances. A routine referral form may be all that is needed in one case, whereas for another patient a supplemental discharge summary letter may be indicated. Quite often, certain information will be best supplemented by a personal phone call from the primary nurse to the nurses in the nursing home or visiting nurses association. Occasionally it may be necessary to arrange for a nurse to accompany a patient to the other institution. Hospital policies should be constructed to allow for the design of individualized discharge plans.

The role described above defines the general responsibilities that must be met if nurses are to qualify for the term *professional*. It centers attention on expectations focused on the patient and the activities that occur at and around the bedside. Environmental changes, especially the change to DRGs and the nursing shortage, have stimulated expansion of this role in two interesting directions, case management and the use of nurse extenders.

WORK ALLOCATION

The remaining element of the system that needs definition is work allocation.

The work of nursing can be divided among the available staff according to two fundamentally different approaches: assigning tasks and assigning patients. There is a somewhat widely held belief that assigning tasks is the only way to use a skill-mixed staff and that the way work is assigned defines the totality of a delivery system. Thus, one frequently hears comments like this: "We used to do primary nursing, but when the RN shortage hit and we had to hire   LPNs and aides, we went back to team nursing." However, what is often meant is merely that there was a return to using a task-assignment work allocation technique. That decision (unsatisfactory as it may be from all angles) need not determine the whole delivery system.

The decision to use a task-based assignment system or a patient-centered one ultimately rests on beliefs and values. Task-based assignments are a direct descendent of industrial mass production ideas about work allocation, and as such they are completely antithetical to a professional concept of nursing. This method of work assignment (RNs pass meds, LPNs do treatments, and aides perform hygienic care) generally reflects (1) a major concern with differentiating between RNs and LPNs, (2) a scarcity of managerial tools for dealing with the issue of differentiation in more sophisticated ways, or (3) acceptance of the primitive notion that nursing care is the sum total of nursing tasks.

In a patient-centered assignment system, one person performs all the care tasks for a particular patient regardless of the skill level of the task—within the limits set by that person's job description, of course.

The underlying rationale for daily patient assignments determining which caregiver shall care for which patient on any given day is that this results in the best possible matching of the needs of patients with the abilities of available caregivers. Assignments should reflect the use of common sense!

Each person so assigned has the responsibility to administer care without frequent reminders. If the person's job description prohibits the performance of certain needed tasks, that person becomes responsible for seeing that someone else, who has the required preparation, carries out those tasks. For example, an LPN who is caring for a patient receiving intravenous fluids observes the rate of flow, informs an RN when fluids must be added, and sees that this is done at the appropriate time.

Care activities can be grouped and performed during one visit to a patient's room, and the hurry that results from doing isolated technical tasks for a large number of patients is eliminated. There is more time to talk with patients, find out what they need or would like, or learn things about them that could affect care plans or discharge plans. In several situations where, for one reason or another, it was not feasible to implement primary nursing in its entirety, switching from team nursing to total patient care still brought about a considerable improvement. Almost immediately, the hectic, harried atmosphere characteristic of busy team nursing stations became less frantic and the pace of activities became more measured.

CRITERIA FOR PATIENT ASSIGNMENTS

As noted above, the most important factors in deciding who should provide care to which patients are (1) the unique needs of each patient and (2) the skills and strengths of the available staff members. Team nursing requires the use of the most extensively prepared caregiver (the RN) as an overseer of less-skilled, less-expensive labor. It is not uncommon in team nursing for team leaders to assign themselves no patients. In situations where serious staffing deficiencies leave no choice, team leaders often take on those patients who are least in need of their advanced skills. In the case method of assignment, nurses and patients are matched according to needs and abilities. Thus, the most acutely ill patients are cared for by RNs, patients with intermediate degrees of illness are cared for by LPNs, and the least acutely ill patients are cared for by nurses' aides (assuming they are used to provide direct care).

Geography—the arrangement of patient rooms—should have little, if any, effect on assignment decisions. Admittedly, the head nurse will be challenged by the task of getting to know the staff's abilities well enough to match these optimally to patients' needs. Geographically based assignments are much easier. However, it is part of the head nurse's job to know the staff. Assignments based on patient room locations would make sense only if the top priority were to reduce the number of steps the staff nurses have to take on a given shift. Further, although assigning a nurse patients in rooms next to each other seems like it would save walking time, the fact is that the clustering of care activities for each patient made possible by the case method reduces the number of steps and the amount of time spent walking from one patient's room to another most effectively.

Nonetheless, zones, districts, or modules are enjoying a certain amount of popularity as determinants of daily assignments, despite the fact that they ultimately restrict freedom in decision making and often have a negative impact on unit morale. Geographical assignments result in territorial attention spans. They can also result in less continuity of care on units where patients are frequently transferred from one room to another. Continuity of care is best maintained by having the primary nurse administer care personally when on duty and by having all other staff members follow the care plan when he or she is off duty.

As originally defined, the delivery system of primary nursing is quite flexible and tolerates a wide variety of staffing levels and mixes. In fact, it was originally developed on a unit that was underbudgeted and had an inappropriate mix for the acuity of the patients! In that context, maximum flexibility was required and was achieved. Unfortunately, since then the rigidity of hospital structures has impacted the original design and certain myths have been accepted as truisms, among them that primary nursing requires an all-RN staff. The problem with that myth is that when RNs began to be in short supply, primary nursing was sacrificed. A second myth that surrounds primary nursing is that it must result in perfect nursing. People sometimes say, "We're using modified primary nursing . . . it isn't pure." Further exploration usually leads to finding out that the nursing care plans are not being completed to everyone's satisfaction.

Because primary nursing is the one delivery system with a conceptual design that supports professional practice (decentralized decision making clearly accepted by an individual), problems with implementation and with the complex challenge that the system presents administrators of nursing cannot be allowed to compromise the system.

PARTNERS-IN-PRACTICE

The shortage of RNs, coupled with the failure to integrate mixed ratio staffs into professional practice delivery systems, created an openness to exploring new ways to incorporate auxiliary personnel into the staff of a nursing unit. Some of these are referred to as *nurse extender systems*. The idea is that the auxiliary personnel are assigned to be "extenders" of the nurses. Rather than taking care of patients by themselves, they work as nurse helpers, and it is the nurses who are responsible for the daily care of a larger caseload of patients. Of particular interest in this regard is the possibility of forming partnerships.

The *partnership system* is a new organizational concept for delivery of care. In this system, a relationship is forged that has a powerful impact on assignment techniques. Partners work together on the same shift, same schedule, and so on, thus creating a new dynamic at the unit level. Although experience with the concept is limited at this time, evidence is mounting that the whole is greater than the sum of the parts. In other words, a well-developed two-person partnership seems to be able to handle more tasks than two people working in an unpartnered relationship.

The partnership system is not a new delivery system. It is a new staffing system based on a new relationship. This new relationship is the key to its ultimate value in furthering the professional status of nursing.

In a partnership, a bond is formed between a professional nurse and an auxiliary worker. In this relationship, an experienced RN and an auxiliary worker (who needs to have a fairly high level of technical competence) work together using a decision process for dividing the work (i.e., the division of work is not task-based). New criteria are used (instead of just the job description of the practice partners), because the senior partner (the RN) has the authority to teach the junior partner additional skills on the job and thus expand that partner's capabilities and usefulness. A system of documenting on-the-job training and of "credentialing" junior practice partners provides the hospital with assurance that appropriate steps have been taken to prepare the junior partners to perform new tasks. Of course, the expansion of tasks must respect the constraints set by each state's individual nurse practice act.

The relationship between the senior and junior partner is what is new. A partnership is not merely a matter of scheduling two people to work together frequently, nor is it a basis for dividing patients among workers. It is a new relationship that has never before existed at the unit level in an organized, systematic fashion. The development of this new relationship requires thoughtfulness and care. The bonding must be taken seriously. It is recommended that the partners "hire" each other and sign a partnership agreement (a legally nonbinding agreement) that defines the terms of the relationship and the procedure to follow to terminate it if that becomes desirable.

Partners-In-Practice is the package developed to implement this concept. One of the keys for any implementation is to determine how much of the work on any given unit can be done by non-RN staff members. A new technique for assessing competency levels required for the care of a given group of patients using nurse exemplars from the unit has been developed.

Another key element is the training of senior partners to be care managers. This training is similar to the training head nurses require. It involves a form of thinking and planning many staff nurses are totally unfamiliar with.

As experience with the concept grows, financial implications will soon become apparent. Senior partners who are able to use their professional expertise to provide care to a larger number of patients should be given a substantial salary increase (in the range of $5,000 to $6,000). This takes into account that there would still be a major dollar saving in regular FTE costs, to say nothing of the reduction in the use of agency nurses.

Chapter 13

Professional Nursing Practice Model

Kathy J. Horvath

The author describes a professional nursing practice model that has developed over the past 15 years, based on values and relationships, with the patient-family-nurse relationship being central to all other clinical and administrative activities. All elements of this model are described in detail, and an in-depth case study is included that demonstrates how the philosophy of the model is actualized.

Beth Israel Hospital, a 545-bed tertiary care and teaching hospital of the Harvard Medical School, has earned a reputation for combining scholarship with sensitivity to the clinical, emotional, and personal needs of patients. The hospital's statement on the rights of patients was the first of its kind to be published, and it has served as a model for other similar statements issued by hospitals and for legislation enacted in many states. Beth Israel's development and publication of a policy for Do Not Resuscitate orders was also considered to be in the forefront of hospital practices and demonstrates once again the institution's sensitivity to the human elements involved in hospitalization and illness. Thus, its development of a professional practice model using primary nursing as the framework for patient care can be viewed as a natural extension of the overall commitment demonstrated by this hospital to a humanistic approach to patient care.

The success currently accorded the hospital's nursing division is the culmination of a period of growth and development that has lasted a number of years. Primary nursing was gradually implemented and continuously refined in order to broaden the interpretation of improved nursing care and nurse satisfaction. The initial focus on nurse-patient assignment relationships and on direct communication between the primary nurse and other health care providers has grown into an advanced model of professional practice with multiple components. Although clinical practice is

Material in this chapter is taken, in part, from *Nursing Management and the Development of Professional Practice*, Joyce C. Clifford and Kathy J. Horvath (Eds.), with permission by Springer Publishing Company, in press.

considered central, leadership, teaching, consultation, and research are all considered essential behaviors to be supported and expected in a professional model of practice. At Beth Israel, these professional behaviors are integrated into all aspects of the clinical practice model.

The nursing practice system is value driven. Among the most important values are continuity in patient care and accountability for that care by an identifiable nurse professional. One fundamental belief is that nurses want to use their knowledge and skill to provide direct care to patients and families and that patient care is improved when the system provides for continuity in the care provider. Another fundamental belief is that nurses have an important contribution to make in determining patient care outcomes and the organization of management and support services should take this into account. Thus, the development of the professional practice model involves the development of many other hospital services.

PROFESSIONAL NURSING PRACTICE MODEL

The professional nursing practice model at Beth Israel is a conceptual model that represents the principles and relationships that are central to the nursing practice system. As such, it provides a framework for Beth Israel nurses to view the world from one perspective and to communicate that perspective to others. Being derived from Beth Israel's philosophy, the practice model focuses attention, both clinically and administratively, on the activities that are most highly valued.

The central phenomenon of the practice model is the caring relationship that exists between the patient and the nurse (this relationship inherently includes the patient's family). Thus, the focus of the model and the fulcrum on which all other concepts are balanced is this interrelationship (Figure 13-1). "Patient/family-nurse interrelationships provide all activities, behaviors, and processes occurring among the nurse, patient and family" (Rempusheski et al., 1988, p. 44). Patient-nurse interrelationships are influenced by the three constructs of the model: (1) the nursing practice system, comprising three concepts (accountability, continuity, and collaboration); (2) the organizational/administrative health care environment, comprising five concepts (decentralization, coherence, advancement, recognition, and compensation); and (3) developmental support services, comprising three concepts (evaluation, learning, and inquiry). For discussion purposes, each of the three constructs is discussed separately to describe how the components are operationalized on a day-to-day basis. In practice, however, the components of the model are closely interrelated.

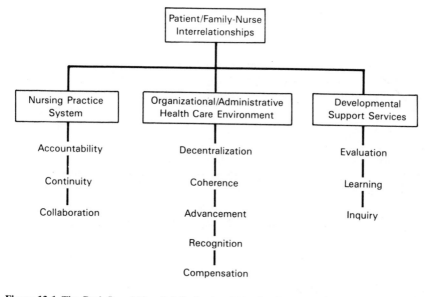

Figure 13-1 The Beth Israel Hospital Professional Nursing Practice Model

Nursing Practice

Primary nursing as defined by Manthey (1980) forms the foundation of Beth Israel's professional model of nursing practice. The system of care is designed to provide each patient with a special relationship with an identifiable RN, who is known to the patient as the primary nurse. This relationship continues throughout the patient's hospitalization, except in rare cases. Such cases usually involve a change in a patient's clinical condition requiring the patient to transfer to another patient care unit where the special expertise of the care providers—medical or nursing—are deemed more essential to the patient's care than the relationship developed in the initial primary nurse–patient assignment. Whenever this change becomes necessary, the transfer to another unit and primary nurse always includes the patient and family members in the decision and provides for ongoing contact with the original primary nurse.

However, a change in the primary nurse during hospitalization is the exception rather than the rule. Most patients are cared for by the same primary nurse and associates from the time of admission through the time of discharge. Direct care is provided by the RN staff and is supported by the use of nursing assistants/coworkers as well as other unit support personnel described later in this chapter. The primary nurse fulfills his or her responsibility as case manager for the patient by assuring that continuity of care will occur throughout hospitalization and beyond. This is accomplished through the use of written nursing care plans that incorporate the care of physicians and other health professionals and through direct communication with the other care providers involved in the patient's care. Clinical nurses function both as primary nurses and as associate nurses for nurse colleagues who are not present. The associate nurses are critical to the success of this practice model. The associate serves not only as an "extension" of the primary nurse, but also as a peer reviewer and a colleague providing support, particularly during difficult situations.

In this system, the primary nurse becomes extremely well informed about all aspects of a patient's care requirements and responses to the medical and nursing treatment regimes. Consequently, the patient and family develop strong, trusting ties with the nurse, and other health care providers accept the nurse as a partner in care. In particular, strong collaborative relationships often develop between primary nurses and primary physicians. The work of the nurse is valued, respected and recognized in this professional system of care.

Organizational Environment

Beth Israel believes its goals of improving patient care and increasing job satisfaction for RNs have been achieved. The success of this practice model required changes in the work environment as well as the practice system. In a professional practice system, nursing can no longer be viewed as part of hotel or support services. Nursing must be recognized as a full clinical discipline, with the same rights and obligations as other professional disciplines in the hospital. Recognition of the central role of nursing in the provision of patient care begins at the top of the organizational structure. Organizational placement of the chief nurse executive on the hospital's executive management team and at the head of a clinical service gives nursing control of its own practice and increases its ability to influence future policy decisions (Figure 13-2).

One of the most critical elements of the practice environment is the organization of decision-making authority, which at Beth Israel is decentralized and is located at the patient and unit level. Just as the clinical nurse is accountable for all nursing decisions affecting primary patients, the clinical nurse manager (head nurse) is fully accountable for patient care, personnel, and unit management on the nursing unit. Patient care management involves setting standards of patient care and evaluating cur-

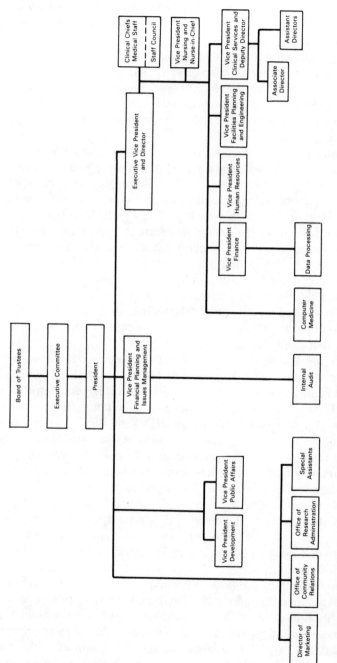

Figure 13-2 Beth Israel Hospital Corporate Organization Chart

rent practice and is not to be confused with the clinical nurse's decision-making rights for individual patient care. Other management responsibilities include interviewing and hiring all staff for the unit, managing a cost center, and participating in all planning activities for clinical and nonclinical programs on the unit. At Beth Israel, the position of clinical nurse manager is at the department head level. This gives nurses an onsite administrator who has the authority to take action, seek information and resources, and establish expectations for other departments in relation to the services provided to a patient care unit.

Experienced nurse managers identify staff development as the most important part of their management responsibilities, beginning with the selection of staff to work on their units. Of the many activities that nurse managers might choose to delegate to senior clinical nurses, the one that they always retain is the interviewing of new staff. Nurse managers view the initial interview as critical for matching the applicant's interests and characteristics with a patient population and a group of nursing peers. This interview can also help establish a working relationship based on trust and mutual respect. The process treats clinical nurses in an individualized manner—similar to the manner in which they will be expected to care for patients. This initial investment of time by the nurse manager pays off with a stronger commitment by the nurse after employment and begins a relationship that facilitates staff retention.

The clinical nurse manager position is perhaps the single most important position in determining the success or failure of a professional practice system. It is also one of the most important management positions in the hospital. Through this role, the philosophy, standards, and policies of the total institution are translated into action (Clifford, 1980). Nurse managers, as department heads in the hospital organizational structure, accept the associated responsibility for achieving overall hospital goals. This integration of nursing administration and hospital administration in the achievement of excellent patient care is an important feature of Beth Israel's organizational environment.

The full development of a nursing department depends on leadership and participation at all levels. Committee participation is often the form that this involvement takes (Figure 13-3). Clinical nurses are members of all committees of the nursing service, and nurses sit on all hospital and medical executive subcommittees. The committee structure of the hospital enables it to utilize the talents of all staff and the resources of all departments to establish the policies, procedures, and standards needed to achieve excellence in patient care. Clinical nurses are given an opportunity to influence their working environment and to collaborate with others to create a preferred future for nursing practice. Nurses are involved in all

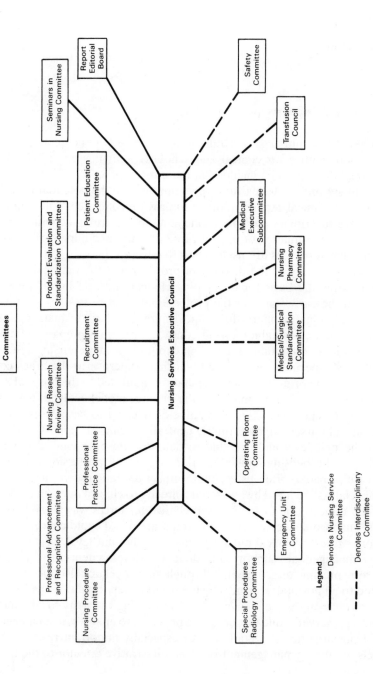

Figure 13-3 Committee Structure of Beth Israel Hospital Nursing Services

Committees

Nursing Services Executive Council

Seminars in Nursing Committee

Report Editorial Board

Safety Committee

Transfusion Council

Patient Education Committee

Medical Executive Subcommittee

Product Evaluation and Standardization Committee

Nursing Pharmacy Committee

Recruitment Committee

Medical/Surgical Standardization Committee

Nursing Research Review Committee

Professional Practice Committee

Operating Room Committee

Professional Advancement and Recognition Committee

Emergency Unit Committee

Nursing Procedure Committee

Special Procedures Radiology Committee

Legend

—— Denotes Nursing Service Committee

- - - Denotes Interdisciplinary Committee

activities that are relevant to them as professionals, and they are given opportunities to grow and to succeed in what they want to do most—take care of patients.

Developmental Supports

Recognition of nursing as a full professional discipline requires that similar opportunities for clinical and scholarly activities accorded other professional disciplines be included in the nursing practice system as well. Clinical nurses must have learning opportunities and the potential for consultation with clinical experts in order to provide competent and comprehensive care to primary patients. Concomitantly, learning activities must be driven by an evaluation of patient care outcomes and nursing processes to ensure that resources are used most effectively.

The accountability of the direct care provider and the unit level nurse manager forms the basis for developing clinical and nonclinical support services. In the early stages of the professional practice system, the focus was on educational supports for clinical nurses and nurse managers. A comprehensive and credible nursing education program prepared clinical nurses for full accountability for patient care in a primary nursing system. Clinical nurse specialists were hired who had expertise in the areas corresponding to the primary patient populations admitted to the hospital and in educational program planning. As the practice model evolved, many of the routine teaching activities for competency came to be performed by senior clinical nurses. Many formerly centralized clinical support staff are now at the unit level and are able to demonstrate both clinical nursing expertise at the bedside and integration of the full professional role as direct care providers. Because of their impact on patient care, unit-based nurse specialists are hired by and report directly to clinical nurse managers. However, the evolution to unit-based clinical resources was possible only as nurse managers received graduate preparation and could conceptualize the proper roles of clinical nurse specialists at the unit level.

Nurse managers are supported in their role development through guidance from nursing directors and through the educational opportunities provided to all hospital managers by the training department in the human resources division. Nurse manager decision-making authority for the nursing unit is preserved while resources are provided to enable nurse managers to meet performance expectations. An especially important resource for all levels of nursing management is the administrative director of the nursing administration. As an expert in business administration, the director has helped to bring the fiscal services, human resource data, and information technology to the same level of excellence achieved by the clinical programs for patient care. Nurse managers and the administrative director work closely together to translate clinical goals into budgetary realities and to develop budgets that support clinical programs.

The quality assurance program supports patient care by developing mechanisms to monitor practice standards and patient outcomes. Through the professional practice committee, clinical nurse specialists participate in standards development and work collaboratively with unit-based quality assurance representatives to monitor practice on nursing units.

Recently, the Director for Quality Assurance and Development spearheaded a pilot project to study the practice of expert nurses. The goal was to describe examples of excellent nursing practice to provide a more positive approach to quality assurance. Utilizing the interpretive approach, the group members of the expert practice project examined 17 exemplars of nursing practice. They discovered that expert nurses change patient outcomes in extraordinary ways. This approach is now being used to investigate clinical issues, such as communication breakdowns and decisions not to resuscitate.

The development supports component of the practice model is concerned primarily with professional role development. There is the need also for other clinical and nonclinical support services. Clinical nurses are assisted with patient care activities by coworkers or nursing assistants that are assigned to the nurse, not to the patient. Coworkers are used to enable RNs to provide direct care to patients—to literally stay at the bedside. All program planning includes asking what tasks take nurses away from the care of patients and who else can do those tasks.

Other departments, such as dietary, environmental services, and transportation, are needed to perform nonclinical activities that support patient care. Collaboration with those departments has enabled ongoing evaluation of the traditional systems for providing those services to occur. For example, environmental services participated with nursing in a pilot project to relieve nurses of the task of bed making and to broaden the involvement of the environmental services worker on the unit. Nurses found the service provided by the worker to be very helpful, since it left them more time for more highly valued activities, such as ambulating patients, teaching patients, planning for patient discharge, and planning care with other members of the health care team. The increased cost for environmental services was minimal and the bed-making service is now being implemented on other units.

CASE STUDY

The following case study demonstrates how Beth Israel's professional nursing practice model works on a day-to-day basis. The case presented is intended to illustrate how this practice model fosters the kind of nurse-patient relationships that result in both improved patient care and nurse satisfaction. Mrs. T., a 73-year-old widowed woman has had 10 hospitalizations at Beth Israel. Despite her frail health, she has been adamant about remaining in her own apartment. There is a serious doubt whether she would be able to if it were not for the relationship between Mrs. T. and her primary nurse, Ms. M.

Because of the continuous relationship that the professional practice model supports, the primary nurse has become intimately knowledgeable about Mrs. T., the physical and behavioral manifestations of her illness, her emotional needs, and her social and physical support systems. The therapeutic advantage of a relationship like the one between Ms. M. and Mrs. T. was demonstrated most dramatically when Mrs. T. was admitted to the hospital with an acute confusional state. The primary nurse gives this firsthand account.

Mrs. T., one of my favorite primary patients, was readmitted to the hospital with acute confusional state. I was surprised for two reasons. First, she was discharged from the hospital only 2 weeks before. She had had a long, complicated hospital course, but she was sent home with maximum community supports (VNA, a homemaker, Meals on Wheels, etc.). Also, I had known Mrs. T. for 5 years, and it was hard to picture her as confused, combative, and uncooperative. It was decided that her confusion would be worked up, but her daughter-in-law also decided to get custody of Mrs. T. and have her placed in a nursing home.

I was having difficulty in this situation, because Mrs. T. kept asking me to "save" her from going to a nursing home. I felt awkward, because if placing her in a nursing home would be in her best interest, I would advocate it. Fortunately the neuropsychological testing showed that Mrs. T.'s judgment was intact and that she could function safely. Her daughter-in-law continued to pursue the guardianship process. Mrs. T.'s mental status cleared and she was back to her baseline.

I decided to ask her attending if we could try to get her back home again. I didn't approach the intern or residents because they didn't seem very interested. They didn't stop in to see Mrs. T. on rounds. She was another "placement problem." Dr. C.,

Mrs. T.'s attending, was very receptive to the idea of giving Mrs. T. another chance. (I don't think he wanted to face the guardianship issue either!) We decided that Mrs. T. would take care of herself as though she were at home. She was to be responsible for getting her own towels, soap, and so on, for her daily shower. We placed a clock and a detailed medication administration plan in her room, along with a 2-day supply of her medications (precounted); she was to be responsible for medicating herself. She was able to properly care for herself and went home with VNA, Meals on Wheels, and a homemaker.

This was a very difficult case for me. I learned how difficult it can be to be an advocate for a patient. I also learned that one doesn't have to accept the "status quo" and that sometimes you have to change the system (like getting pharmacy to send up a patient's meds in bottles).

One and one-half years later, Mrs. T. is still living at home, despite continued major and minor health problems. In December 1988, at the patient's invitation, the primary nurse had lunch with Mrs. T. at her apartment, where, true to her character, she adamantly refused any assistance.

The primary nurse states that the organizational environment within which she practices was critical in her efforts to prevent nursing home placement for Mrs. T. The most important element of administrative support was the nurse manager's openness to having Ms. M. develop the kind of caring relationship Mrs. T. needed—a relationship that was the pivotal factor in the final outcome of the hospitalization. The primacy of the patient-nurse relationship in the professional nursing practice model is clearly demonstrated in this case study. Because the primary nurse "knew" Mrs. T., she was able to change patient outcomes. Her knowledge of the patient derived from her understanding of Mrs. T.'s response to her illness and differed from the kind of knowledge possessed by friends and family and other health care providers.

Other relationships were instrumental in achieving a positive outcome for the patient. The primary nurse and attending physician had developed a collaborative relationship based on mutual trust and respect, and together they had a continuous relationship with Mrs. T. that was substantially different from the relationships that patients typically have with house staff. The shared perspective and the alliance between the primary nurse and attending physician were of benefit to the patient long after her active medical problems were resolved.

Relationships between nursing and other departments are critical for achieving good patient outcomes. For example, the pharmacy department operates satellites on nursing units, and clinical nurses can thus work with satellite pharmacists on a daily basis. When the primary nurse needed an unconventional medication administration plan for Mrs. T., the trust that the nurse and pharmacist had in each other ensured the development of a unified treatment plan that benefited all concerned.

Lastly, this case study demonstrates the administrative and developmental supports that enable clinical nurses to provide the leadership and clinical expertise that improves patient care. Just prior to completing 1 year of employment, the nurse manager counseled the primary nurse on selecting an area of concentration in nursing practice. The nurse manager also gave Ms. M. professional days (staffing permitting) to develop her skills in her resource area: care of the elderly.

Concomitantly, Ms. M. worked collaboratively with a unit-based clinical nurse specialist who is an expert in geriatric nursing care. Now recognized as a clinical resource in her own right, Ms. M. is advanced to Level III Clinical Practice (the first optional level in the levels-of-practice program). As a CN III, Ms. M. is part of the leadership group on her unit that participates with the nurse manager in planning and problem solving. This combination of administrative support and learning opportunities has enabled Ms. M. to develop the knowledge and confidence necessary to create a highly personalized collaborative treatment plan for Mrs. T. When nurses are supported in their efforts to make a difference in patient outcomes, patient care is improved and nurse satisfaction increases.

EVALUATION OF THE MODEL

Advantages

The positive features of Beth Israel's professional nursing practice model are many, not least of which is the increased satisfaction experienced by both nurses and patients. Retention statistics give some indication of nurse satisfaction. At the time of the implementation of the practice model (1973–1974), nurses stayed in their position for approximately 3–6 months! Currently, new graduates remain 2.5–5 years. In the period 1980–1988, turnover among RNs decreased from 23.0% to 13.5%, and, during a time of nursing shortages, the vacancy rate consistently averaged 2%. The levels-of-practice program (the Professional Nurse Advancement and Recognition Program) was implemented in 1983 and advances 75–80 nurses each year, most of whom have remained within Beth Israel, another indication of nurse satisfaction.

These data indicate that nurses are attracted to the practice environment created by the professional nursing model. Nurses have also expressed their satisfaction through the exit interview process. All nurses leaving Beth Israel are provided the opportunity to have an exit interview. An analysis of exit interviews from 1985 to 1987 indicates that nurses' reasons for coming to Beth Israel are overwhelmingly related to its philosophy and practice model. Nurses report positive experiences with each of the system components of the model: the practice system; the organizational, administrative, and health care environment; and the developmental support systems. Sample statements from exit interviews follow:

Primary nursing fosters interaction, not only with the patient, but with family as well. There is recognition by them to the nurses that they make a contribution and a difference.

You know that if the clinical decisions you make as a nurse were in the best interest of the patient, they would be supported right up to [top], no matter whose toes were stepped on.

The learning environment and nursing supports are what make BI better for nurses. Continuing education at BI is outstanding and well supported by nurse managers.

Of those nurses who gave an exit interview, 42% left Beth Israel for personal reasons, such as marriage or relocation. Nurses who chose a position in another hospital often did so because a particular specialty area or management position was not available at Beth Israel.

Exit interview data also indicate that nurses at Beth Israel are representative of the nursing population as a whole in their dislike for evening, night, and weekend work schedules. The practice model, which instills professional role expectations in both clinical nurses and nurse managers, enabled the hospital to establish a salary program for RNs. In this program, RNs are considered exempt professional staff and are allowed greater scheduling flexibility. Coverage for unscheduled absences is arranged by the staff, resulting in self-contained units. The salary program for 1988 also includes different salary categories to compensate nurses proportionately for working the less desirable hours. Although an evaluation of the salary program is in progress, anecdotal reports by nurse managers indicate that it has been well received and in fact may have contributed to a decrease in turnover in 1988.

Early evaluative studies provided the first indications that patient care outcomes were positively affected by the practice model. Hegedus used

Volicer's Hospital Stress Rating Scale to measure patients' experiences of stress-producing events on primary nursing units compared with units with a team-nursing delivery system (Hegedus, 1980, 1981). Patients on the primary nursing units had significantly lower stress scores than patients on the conventional team-nursing units.

Patient satisfaction with nursing care is also expressed in the many unsolicited letters written to the hospital. Patients and families often identify primary nurses by name and indicate the central role that nursing played in their hospital experience. A former patient who encountered several setbacks following coronary angioplasty wrote the following:

> Despite the (apparent) angioplasty failure, the cardiac arrest, the kidney stone attack; no one told me (1) not to worry, (2) everything was going to be OK, or (3) these things always happen—they're very minor . . . As I look back, I marvel at the insight these BI nurses have. For what they were doing was assessing my anxiety level, my probable comprehension level, and then giving me enough information so there would be as few unknowns to worry about as possible, but at the same time presenting a situation I could accept as plausible and realistic. If I suffered a temporary loss of composure, which was often, they never averted their gaze or offered patronizing expressions of sympathy. They simply waited for *me* to gain control, allowing *me* to get myself back on track. Psychologically, very strengthening, but requiring a keen assessment of character. I don't know how I would have made out without their help. Especially from Theresa P., who was personally responsible for my care, and who always seemed to be there at critical times . . . My deepest gratitude goes out to these professionals.

A family member describes the terminal care her sister received:

> I am writing to tell you what a superb job the nursing staff did in caring for my sister during her last week of life, in particular Fran B., who was with my sister when she died. My sister fought her unavoidable death until the very end and Fran did everything possible to make her comfortable, treating her with competence, respect, and compassion. I was particularly heartened when Fran gave her a warm bath and changed her bedding and gown, even though she was very near death. I am certain that my sister was appreciative. I could tell by the expression on her face that she

was more comfortable, and grateful that she was cared for until the very end.

As a conceptual model, Beth Israel's professional practice system provides a frame of reference for understanding patient satisfaction in a more systematic way, utilizing the unsolicited letters as data. In an effort to maintain quality nursing care in a cost-conscious environment, Rempusheski et al. (1988) did a qualitative study to answer the research question, What are the perceptions of hospitalized individuals about care expected and care received, as communicated in letters sent to the hospital after discharge? Two concepts central to Beth Israel's philosophy and practice model (care and the patient/family-nurse interrelationships) were explored in order to identify the care perceptions of patients in a primary nursing environment. This research contributed to an understanding of patient satisfaction and generated hypotheses that warrant further testing. The work of Rempusheski et al. illustrates how the practice model links Beth Israel's philosophy with actual practice and how it provides a continuous feedback loop that contributes to the evolution of the model and the advancement of practice.

The practice model guides Beth Israel's approach to the unknown. It provides direction for change processes that might otherwise cause fragmentation in either service delivery or relationships essential for quality patient care. Because of nursing's central role in patient care, nurses will be key players in the restructuring of clinical practice for the future. Using the model's conceptual framework for guidance, nursing will approach change processes in ways that preserve its most cherished values. Nurses will continue to focus on clinical nursing, unit-level nursing management, and the supports that enable them to use the full range of their talents and skills on behalf of patients. For example, a new collaborative care unit will explore results of changing practice patterns of nurses and physicians. Issues of accountability, continuity, and collaboration will be evaluated as nurses become responsible for broader aspects of patient care and develop different relationships with patients and physicians.

There are many beneficial outcomes for the organization as a whole when professional nursing practice is implemented. Patient satisfaction with nursing care enhances the care delivery of other disciplines, and there are now few, if any, physicians at Beth Israel who would prefer to return to anything less than professional nursing practice. Further, the excellent nursing care has contributed to the overall image of the hospital in the community, enhancing the hospital's competitive edge. The quality of nursing care made a significant contribution to Beth Israel's reputation as one of the best hospitals in America (Sunshine & Wright, 1987).

Disadvantages

As successful as the practice model has been, it has some requirements that might be limiting factors for implementation in other systems. A dynamic practice model that often precipitates change is desirable, but the resulting constant evolution of ideas is very demanding on individuals and institutions. Values remain the same, but organizational structures may change frequently. In addition to the frequency of changes, some are accompanied by a degree of ambiguity that requires above-average levels of trust and flexibility. The nursing leadership must have an effective means of communication and a commitment to expend the time and energy needed to manage change processes successfully. Not everyone can work in this kind of environment.

The accountability of clinical nurses for patient care in a professional nursing practice system is demanding—and nurses will occasionally say it is exhausting. Continuity of care and 24-hour accountability for care planning means nurses deal with certain issues—often intense and painful ones—day after day. In addition to supportive relationships with associate nurses, clinical nurses need developmental opportunities to replenish and extend their skills. Nurse managers must be committed to professional nursing practice in order to create a staffing plan that will allow for professional career development. Furthermore, all positions in the nursing service must recognize and respect the supports needed by primary nurses to meet patient care demands.

Decentralized decision making creates an organizational structure that is very flat. Decisions for patient care are made at the closest point to care delivery, the patient-nurse interface. Managerial decision making occurs at the unit level. This structure enables creativity and flexibility to thrive, but decentralization can result in fragmentation if there is not adequate and effective central coordination. Successful nursing management requires the ability to determine which functions should be centralized and when and to thus provide some coherence for the entire nursing system without undermining the authority of the primary nurse or nurse manager. As a counterpoint, there is also a need for some of the nursing leadership to be able to conceptualize issues beyond one unit or one department—to see the "big picture," the relationship of the nursing service to the hospital and to its professional and public constituencies.

A model for nursing practice like the one that has evolved at Beth Israel requires a total institutional commitment. Other disciplines and departments change their own expectations and some of their ways of doing things in response to individual clinical nurses, who now have increased patient information and authority for decision making and planning. Other departments learn to respect the authority of the unit nurse manager for problem solving and conflict resolution. Although the change in practice is in one hospital division, the mere size of a nursing service and its central position in nursing entails that the change impacts almost every other area of the hospital.

COSTS

Primary nursing and an all-RN staff may seem intimidating to cost-conscious nurse and hospital administrators, especially in the current health care environment of shrinking resources. Both the literature and Beth Israel's experience in implementing a professional practice model indicate that fears about high costs are unwarranted. Studies show that primary nursing is not necessarily more costly than team nursing, and in fact it may reduce costs (Marram et al., 1976). Most recently, costs were shown not to increase when primary nursing was implemented in a psychiatric setting (McCausland et al., 1988).

The basic staffing plan at Beth Israel was developed in 1974 before the implementation of primary nursing. The staffing methodology has remained constant until the present, with increases in FTEs related to programmatic and organizational changes and the addition of new beds. More importantly, as a result of the current health care environment, the nursing division has deleted positions since 1985, while discharges per inpatient FTE increased from 43.37 in 1985 to 54.47 in 1987 (Beth Israel Hospital, 1988). When these discharge figures are adjusted for case mix, they are significantly higher (case mix–adjusted discharges per inpatient RN FTE equaled 64.84 in 1985 and 81.43 in 1987). These measures of productivity and acuity reflect both the challenge of maintaining quality in a cost-conscious environment and the ability of the professional practice model to meet the challenge.

The costs of Beth Israel's practice model seem reasonable when one considers surveys of nurse utilization conducted by local, regional, and national groups. Statistics compiled by the Conference of Boston Teaching Hospitals, a consortium of 18 hospitals in the Boston metropolitan area, show that the hospitalwide implementation of primary nursing, as well as the continued evolution of the practice model, has not changed the relative position of Beth Israel in comparisons of paid nursing hours per patient day (Figure 13-4). Beth Israel also does well in regional and national rankings (Table 13-1).

In a professional practice model with decentralized decision making, the need for layers of supervisory personnel is eliminated. As nurses become

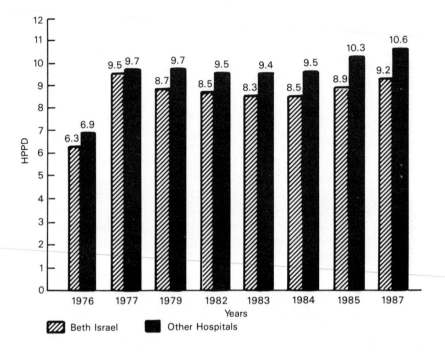

Figure 13-4 Comparison of Total Paid Hours per Patient Day Among Boston Area Hospitals

individually accountable for patient care, resources are funneled to activities that directly serve patients. This organizational change is one way in which costs have been contained.

Other indications of the cost-effectiveness of Beth Israel's practice model have been reported (Clifford, 1980). A nursing intensity study conducted in 1979 and 1980 revealed that personal time as a percentage of total time worked was significantly less for staff nurses than for nursing assistants and coworkers (7% and 13% respectively). Additionally, significant cost savings are realized through eliminating the use of private duty nurses and supplemental staffing agencies. The use of temporary nurses is antithetical to the practice model, since it undermines the principles of continuity and accountability on which professional practice depends.

No discussion of the costs of patient care would be complete without some comment about the relationship to quality. Beth Israel believes, first, that reducing costs does not necessarily mean lowering standards and, second, that lowering expectations to a realistic level does not necessarily mean less quality. One answer to the cost versus quality dilemma lies in increasing the involvement of clinicians in institutional planning. An en-

Table 13-1 Comparison of Total Paid Nursing Hours per Patient Day

	1985	1987
Beth Israel	8.9	9.2
COBTH[a]	10.3	10.6
COTH[b]	7.06–8.98	——
UHEC[c]	8.28–13.19	8.04–13.39

[a]Conference of Boston Teaching Hospitals, which comprises 18 hospitals in the Boston metropolitan area. The mean for the conference is given.
[b]Council of Teaching Hospitals, which comprises 6 Ivy League teaching hospitals.
[c]University Hospital Executive Council, which comprises 9 midwestern university hospitals.

vironment for creativity and risk taking needs to be encouraged, an environment in which care providers and the executive management team can influence each other. Further, relationships between care providers, in particular, nurses and physicians, need to be reexamined in order to understand the implications of changing practice patterns and to discover ways to improve collaboration. As a result, all members of the health care team will be able to renew their allegiance to the goals of quality patient care and fiscal responsibility.

IMPLEMENTATION

Planning for the implementation of a professional practice model begins with an assessment of staffing levels in the institution. Inadequate or unstable staffing patterns are unacceptable for any practice model. Basic standards for patient safety and minimum expectations for care must be established through analyzing multiple variables, such as acuity, age of patient population, clinical programs, and so on. In addition to ensuring adequate numbers, staffing must be stabilized, which generally means decreasing the use of float pools and agency nurses. This is a sometimes difficult and intimidating process, but a department of clinical nursing can begin by identifying one or two units at a time that will become self-contained. Some previously centralized staffing resources can be distributed to units, and many former "float" nurses will appreciate the consistency and mutual commitment that are outgrowths of unit-based staffing.

Once adequate and stable staffing patterns are established, the next step is to institute continuity in patient care, which can be achieved by the assignment of nurses to specific patients. In order to plan comprehensive patient care and collaborate with other members of the health care team, nurses must have in-depth and updated knowledge of the patient's hospital course. In order to develop the kind of caring relationships that improve patient satisfaction and clinical outcomes, nurses must become intimately knowledgeable about patients and their illness response. Interruptions in patient care assignments will prevent the development of such relationships.

One of the first objectives for a reorganization for professional practice is to increase the use of RNs in the provision of direct care to patients and to concurrently decrease the utilization of nonprofessionals. As nursing assistants/coworkers provide assistance to nurses, and nurses provide the direct care to patients, there will be opportunities to convert nonprofessional positions to professional positions on a dollar-for-dollar basis.

Clarification of roles and decision-making authority forms the basis for job descriptions and performance evaluation tools. Professional practice expectations are established first for clinical nurses and unit-level nurse managers. Once areas of accountability and authority are delineated for clinical nurses and nurse managers, the administrative and clinical supports needed for professional role development are implemented. It is this process of clarifying the roles and resources needed for professional role development that will determine the design of the organizational structure. The organizational chart for Beth Israel's nursing services has changed many times in the past 15 years. No doubt, the future will necessitate changes in the current chart (Figure 13-5).

At the same time that changes are being made in the nursing division, other departments and disciplines must be apprised of the implications of implementing a professional practice system for nursing. Decentralized decision making and increased authority in all professional nursing roles will have a considerable impact on the institution as a whole (Clifford, 1980).

A reasonable way to initiate the change processes required by a professional practice system is to select demonstration units where professional practice concepts are operationalized. Role clarification and support systems can be tested and evaluated in microcosm before general implementation begins. Concrete examples of successful professional nursing practice will provide motivation and role models for implementation in other areas. Of course, the demonstration units must be selected carefully—the nurse manager needs to be well prepared and there has to be critical mass of clinical nurses—to ensure the success of a change process of this magnitude. In 1973 and 1974, Beth Israel began the implementation of primary nursing on two units that then served as prototypes for the eventual full implementation of primary nursing.

The designation of the nurse managers as the full managers of the patient care units was a significant change for Beth Israel. With 24-hour account-

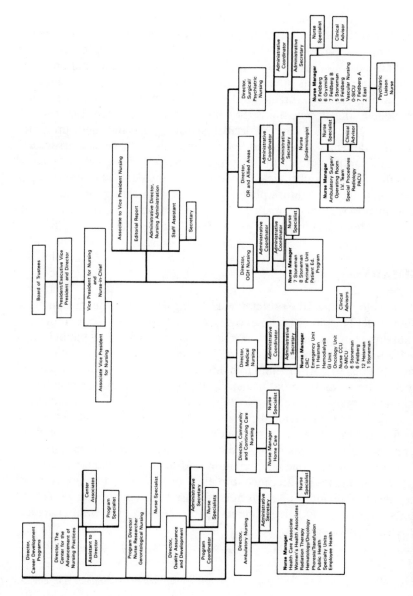

Figure 13-5 Beth Israel Hospital Nursing Services Organizational Chart

ability for the nursing unit, the nurse managers now exercise authority over a variety of activities formerly considered only marginally within their area of responsibility. As nurse managers assume responsibility for activities such as interviewing and selecting staff and establishing staffing patterns, the proper role and authority of the traditional nursing supervisor needs redefinition. At Beth Israel, the nursing supervisor role has evolved to a clinical advisor role, with a new focus and new practice expectations. The clinical advisor serves as the onsite clinical and administrative resource for nurses during evenings, nights, and weekends. Incumbent nursing supervisors needed developmental opportunities to prepare them for this role change. Now the role is an important part of the advancement program, and it offers an entry into various leadership roles. Nurse managers inform clinical advisors of potential problems and their overall goals and expectations for the unit, and clinical advisors report incidents and observations to nurse managers for future planning. In this way, clinical advisors work collaboratively with nurse managers and are instrumental in operationalizing the 24-hour accountability of the latter.

SUMMARY

The development of the professional nursing practice model now in place at Beth Israel Hospital began nearly 15 years ago with the commitment of the nursing staff to "improve the nursing care provided to patients and increase the job satisfaction of the registered nurse." The long process of change that began in 1973—and in many ways continues today—respected the centrality of these initial goals, although they are now articulated in an expanded manner in the nursing division's statement of philosophy.

Essentially, the professional nursing practice model is based on values and relationships, with the patient-nurse relationship at the center of all other clinical and administrative activities. As nurses develop in this practice environment, they become well informed and their influence on patient care planning makes a difference in patient outcomes. Professional collegiality develops on many levels as nurses consult and collaborate with other nurses, disciplines, and departments in the pursuit of a common goal: excellence in patient care.

REFERENCES

Beth Israel Hospital, Nursing Division. *Retrospective analysis of key variables.* December, 1988.

Christman, L. (1980). Accountability with an all-RN nursing staff. In G. Alfano (Ed.), *All-RN nursing staff.* Wakefield, MA: Nursing Resources.

Clifford, J.C. (1982). Professional nursing practice in a hospital setting. In L.H. Aiken (Ed.), *Nursing in the 1980's*. Philadelphia: J.B. Lippincott Company.

Hegedus, K.S. (1980). Primary nursing: Evaluation of professional nursing practice. *Nursing Dimensions, 7*, 85–89.

Hegedus, K.S., & Bourdon, S.M. (1981). Evaluation research: A quality assurance program. *Nursing Administration Quarterly, 5*(3), 26–30.

Manthey, M. (1980). *The practice of primary nursing*. St. Louis: The C.V. Mosby Company.

Marram, G., et al. (1976). The comparative costs of operating a team and primary nursing unit. *Journal of Nursing Administration, 6*(4), 21–24.

McCausland, M.P., et al. (1988). Primary nursing in a psychiatric setting. *Nursing Economics, 6*(6), 297–301.

Rempusheski, V.F., et al. (1988). Expected and received care: Patient perceptions. *Nursing Administration Quarterly, 12*(3), 42–50.

Sunshine, L., & Wright, J.W. (1987). *The best hospitals in America*, pp. 131–135. New York: Henry Holt and Company.

Chapter 14

The NME Caregiver System

Lawrence J. Donnelly

Donnelly presents a thought-provoking model that utilizes multiskilled caregivers who have assumed expanded roles. The traditional nursing units are subdivided into caregiver units, which consist of 2 to 14 beds. Each caregiver unit is under the direction of an RN, but additional staff, called associate caregivers, may include RNs, LVNs, respiratory therapists, physical therapists, and so on.

The implementation of the caregiver system consists of five distinct phases and takes from 9 to 18 months. In the evaluation of this system, Donnelly points out that (1) there was a reduction in overtime costs, (2) patient incidences were decreased 50% to 90%, and (3) the actual cost of staffing was significantly reduced (while still maintaining high quality).

The caregiver system, which was developed by some National Medical Enterprise hospitals, is in sharp contrast to most other systems currently being implemented in institutions. However, the system is working well in several NME hospitals across the country.

National Medical Enterprises (NME) is one of the largest health care providers in the United States. It owns, operates, and manages acute, rehabilitative, psychiatric, substance abuse, and long-term care facilities. In 1985, NME began to examine the patient care delivery system in its acute care hospitals to determine how the company's resources could be managed more efficiently and more cost-effectively. The result was the development of the NME caregiver system.

OVERVIEW

The caregiver system, which is gradually being implemented in more than 30 NME hospitals, does away with traditional nursing units. It calls for a total redesign of the patient care delivery system to meet the medical plan of care for each patient. Fragmentation of clinical services is decreased by using multiskilled caregivers who have assumed expanded roles. The organizational and management framework of the system features clearly defines roles and responsibilities. Yet it is flexible enough to accommodate the particular needs of individual hospitals or departments. As a result, the caregiver system has been well received and can be successfully implemented at a variety of NME hospitals.

The caregiver system has produced improved quality of patient care and decreased cost per patient discharge. In a typical hospital where the system has been implemented, the cost per discharge is reduced 10% to 15%. Other outcomes of the system include increased success in recruiting and retaining nurses, better bed utilization, and an overall perception of excellence as evidenced by comments from patients, physicians, and the nursing staff. Overall, the caregiver system enables these hospitals not only to survive but to thrive, despite an environment of reduced reimbursement for health care.

ASSUMPTIONS

The NME caregiver system was developed on the basis of the following assumptions. First, the physician is the primary customer of health care. Second, health care workers have been educated to provide quality patient services. Finally, the goal of any system should be to provide affordable, quality patient care based on the current reimbursement schedule.

Underlying these assumptions are beliefs about physicians, patients, and delivery systems. First, physicians are positively or negatively affected by patient satisfaction with the care they receive, the amount of time spent in the hospital managing the patient's care, and the manner in which the prescribed plan of care is carried out. Furthermore, patients (during hospitalization) are positively or negatively affected by the care received at the bedside. Finally, current patient care delivery systems must be changed to manage resources more effectively and efficiently.

PARTS OF THE MODEL

There are three components of the NME caregiver system: the organizational management systems, the clinical patient services system, and the clinical patient management system. Before the latter two components can be implemented, the organizational management systems must be installed.

The organizational management systems are at the core of the caregiver system and have been developed with two goals in mind: increased quality of patient care and decreased cost per patient discharge. Systems that were examined and modified to meet caregiver system goals were patient care documentation, delivery of medication and patient supplies, communications, and the caregiver unit (formerly part of a nursing unit). Innovations in these systems are detailed in the case study.

Once the organizational management systems are complete, the clinical patient services are examined. The objective is to identify those services that can be consolidated or redistributed to achieve more effective and efficient care delivery. For example, didactic and clinical programs can be developed so that patient services, such as phlebotomy and selected respiratory therapies, can be transferred to the caregiver. Certification of competency assures that there is no degradation of patient service.

The third component of the caregiver system is the clinical patient management system. It utilizes standards of patient care for the most frequent diagnostic-related groups (DRGs), co-morbid conditions, and complications for each patient unit. A sample standard is given in Exhibit 14-1. Intensity of service, severity of illness, and quality assurance criteria are included in the standards of care.

Medical records are audited on a continuing basis, and patient-unit case managers are consulted whenever criteria are not met. Objectives of the clinical patient management system are decreased length of stay as a result of coordination of the medical plan of care, complete processing of the medical record within 72 hours after a patient's discharge, and completion of the billing cycle within 10 days.

PRACTICAL APPLICATION

The following simulation describes how the caregiver system would function on a medical-surgical unit.

Organizational Management Systems

The *documentation system* consists of the patient admission database, the patient care plan, and the patient care assessment record, which was developed for the caregiver system to replace the multiple forms previously kept in the patient's chart located at the nursing station. The assessment record, which is shown in Exhibit 14-2, was designed so that the intensity of service could be identified easily and the information transferred to a Scantron to calculate the severity of illness.

All documentation forms, including the assessment record for the previous 24 hours, are kept at the patient's bedside on a clipboard. Keeping documentation forms at the bedside streamlines the recording of patient data and enhances the retrieval of information when making an assessment

Exhibit 14-1 Sample Standard of Patient Care

DIAGNOSIS:	Cerebrovascular accident/hemorrhage.
NURSING DIAGNOSIS:	Communication impaired: verbal and/or written.
SUPPORTING DATA:	Depending on area of the brain involved, impairment of speech and/or understanding may occur.
DESIRED PATIENT OUTCOMES:	Communication is maintained.
MEDICAL MANAGEMENT:	As prescribed by primary physicians.
INTERVENTION: RATIONALE:	Assess degree of dysfunction. Does patient hear words, process, and respond? Determine the degree of difficulty patient has with any or all steps of the process.
INTERVENTION: RATIONALE:	Make note at nurses station about speech impairment. Provide special call bell if necessary. Will be helpful to allay anxiety related to inability to communicate. Call bell that is activated by minimal pressure is useful when patient can't use a regular bell.
INTERVENTION: RATIONALE:	Talk directly to patient, speaking slowly and distinctly. Regardless of the level of response, it is important to continue to treat the patient in a normal manner.
INTERVENTION: RATIONALE:	Anticipate and provide for patient's needs. Helpful in decreasing frustration when dependent on others and unable to communicate desires.
INTERVENTION: RATIONALE:	Provide alternative means of communication. Depending on impairment, writing or felt board, pictures, etc., may be helpful.

of the patient's progress or newly identified needs. Use of the assessment record has increased the time spent at the bedside by caregiver staff by approximately 20%.

The documentation forms may be utilized for communicating during intershift walking rounds, for identifying intensity of services to determine the staffing/skill mix, and for collecting data for utilization review and quality assurance studies.

The *patient unit,* formerly identified as a *nursing unit,* is managed by a head nurse or clinical manager. Depending on the size and complexity of the patient services, the head nurse may have management responsibility for one or more patient units. Shift management is provided by the charge nurse. The charge nurse arrives 30 minutes earlier than the rest of the staff to receive an overall report from the off-going charge nurse, to assess the patient needs, and to finalize the staffing/skill mix based on the intensity of patient services for each caregiver unit.

Thus, the charge nurses for each shift share patient and staff responsibilities, resulting in a collaborative management team comprising the head nurse and charge nurses. The charge nurses do not have patient assignments. This enables them to interact with caregiver staff, physicians, and other departments in a consultative role and to initiate effective resolutions of patient, physician, and staff problems.

The *caregiver units* are the manageable proximate divisions within the patient unit. The number of patients in each caregiver unit is based on patient bed capacity, average daily census, patient diagnosis, physician practice, intensity of services, and severity of illness. In practice, a caregiver unit in a medical-surgical unit has about 10 beds. One existing unit has only 2 beds (it's within a definitive observation unit) and another, at the other extreme, has 14 beds.

Each caregiver unit is under the direction of an RN who has been appointed as a caregiver based on clinical expertise and education. Additional staff assigned by a charge nurse to a caregiver unit are designated as *associate caregivers.* These can be RNs, LPNs, LVNs, registered respiratory therapists, registered physical therapists, and so on. For example, if a caregiver unit has respirator-dependent patients who no longer require intensive care, one associate caregiver may be a registered respiratory therapist. The caregiver may request caregiver assistants to assist in patient care (e.g., bathing, bed making, turning, ambulation, and feeding patients). Patient assignments are made following intershift walking rounds and are determined by the caregiver and the associate caregiver.

Selection of breaks and mealtimes are coordinated within the caregiver unit to assure ongoing coverage and continuity of care. In fact, at the caregiver unit level, health care workers have the flexibility of forming a unit with 12-hour shifts instead of 8-hour shifts. The charge nurse remains available to all caregiver units as a consultant should the intensity of patient service require his or her expertise. This patient assignment system is used on all shifts.

The *communication system* has three components: the intershift walking rounds discussed earlier, the patient locator board, and wall-mounted tele-

Exhibit 14-2 – Patient Care Assessment Record

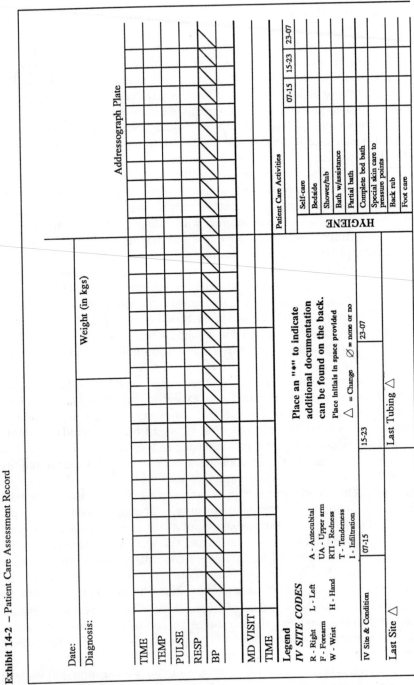

Date:

Diagnosis:

Weight (in kgs)

Addressograph Plate

TIME

TEMP

PULSE

RESP

BP

MD VISIT

TIME

Place an "*" to indicate additional documentation can be found on the back.

Place initials in space provided

△ = Change   ∅ = none or no

Legend
IV SITE CODES

R - Right	L - Left	A - Antecubital
F - Forearm		UA - Upper arm
W - Wrist	H - Hand	RTI - Redness
		T - Tenderness
		I - Infiltration

IV Site & Condition	07-15	15-23	23-07

Last Site △   Last Tubing △

Patient Care Activities

	07-15	15-23	23-07
Self-care			
Bedside			
Shower/tub			
Bath w/assistance			
Partial bath			
Complete bed bath			
Special skin care to pressure points			
Back rub			
Foot care			

HYGIENE

	INTAKE						OUTPUT					
Time	IV Up	IV Absorb	PO	Tube Feed Up	Tube Feed Absorb	Other	Other	Urine	Gastric	CT	Drains	Other

ACTIVITY
- Peri care
- Mouth care
- Sitz bath
- Unassisted
- Ambulatory w/assistance #times/shift
- Room ambulation #times/shift
- Bedpan/urinal w/assistance #times/shift
- Commode or bathroom w/assistance #times/shift
- Chair/transfer w/assistance #times/shift
- Dangle w/assistance #times/shift
- Bedrest
- Turns self
- Turn/position w/assistance #times/shift
- Range of motion

SLEEP
- Slept
- Awake at intervals
- Awake most of time

SAFETY
- Side rails up
- Call light in reach
- Restraint
- Wrist-ankle-vest
- Released q 2°

NUTRITION
- NPO
- Self-fed/assist/complete
- Tube feeding NG/gastrostomy
- Enteral pump/gravity
- Diet intake %
- Fluid restriction-amount ____

Time rows: 07, 08, 09, 10, 11, 12, 13, 14, 8° Total, 15, 16, 17, 18, 19, 20, 21, 22, 8° Total, 23, 00, 01, 02, 03, 04, 05, 06, 8° Total

Exhibit 14-2 – continued

24°
Total

Diet Type

	7-3	3-11	11-7

SOUP BOWL	150	COFFEE CUP	150	JUICE GLASS	120	MILK CARTON	240	SM. H₂O GLASS	120	STYROFOAM CUP	150
JELLO	120	7 UP	219	LG. H₂O GLASS	240	H₂O PITCHER	900	COFFEE POT	250	EMESIS BASIN	200

07-15	15-23	23-07	(Fill in treatment, time, initials)	07-15	15-23	23-07

BOWEL
Stool
Incontinent #times

BLADDER
Voided
Incontinent #times
Foley catheter

SPECIAL TREATMENTS

TREATMENTS
- USN
- ACORN
- IPPB
- Oxygen therapy
- Mask—liter
- Cannula—liter
- Tri-flow
- Ted socks
- Removed 1 time/day
- Isolation type

OBSERVATIONS/ASSESSMENT

Neurological

Genitourinary

Respiratory

Integumentary/Wound

Circulatory

Musc/Skeletal

Gastrointestinal

Psycho-Social

Signature/Date/Time

TRANSPORTATION (Time/Destination/Mode)

Time	Nursing Diagnosis/Collaborative Problem	Assessment/Intervention/Evaluation	Initials

SIGNATURE, TITLE/INITIALS

/
/
/

/
/
/

11/86

DM 8360/2504/0

Source: Courtesy of National Medical Enterprises, Inc., Santa Monica, CA.

phones. The patient locator board identifies each patient, the room number (or the location if the patient is off the patient unit), the caregiver staff responsible, and the severity of illness. Wall-mounted telephones are strategically placed in each caregiver unit to increase efficiency and bedside time. They allow the caregiver staff to communicate directly with physicians, other departments, or the central nurses station.

Clinical Patient Services System

As discussed earlier, this system decreases fragmentation of services to the patient by certifying the caregiver staff to perform EKGs, phlebotomies, selected respiratory therapies, and so on. For example, a STAT blood sugar may be ordered for a patient. The caregiver, who has been certified as a phlebotomist, could draw the blood specimen and send it directly to the laboratory using a unit volunteer or caregiver assistant. As another example, the respiratory therapist, who has been certified to perform activities of daily living, might work with respirator-dependent patients in a caregiver unit.

The Clinical Patient Management System

This system is used to provide immediate input to the case manager whenever utilization review criteria or quality assurance screens are not met. For example, while performing concurrent coding of a patient's chart, the medical record coder might also discover that the patient does not meet IS/SI criteria for continued stay in the hospital. The coder would notify the case manager, who would then review the chart and initiate the approved and established intervention. This intervention may involve contacting the physician first, then the UR coordinator (if necessary).

INSTALLING THE CAREGIVER SYSTEM AT MULTIPLE LOCATIONS

Initial Steps

Installing the NME caregiver system at each hospital required a significant commitment of time and energy. Individuals at all levels had to agree to participate in what would prove to be a sweeping change. Although the philosophy and general framework of the caregiver system remained constant, the organizational details varied from hospital to hospital. The time between initiation and completion of the change was anywhere from 9 to 18 months. NME supplied consultants from within the company to oversee and coordinate each installation. The cost for consultation, facility staff time, and expenses was approximately $42,000 per site.

The process of implementing the caregiver system has five phases. The first phase is intended to educate hospital management and enlist their cooperation. It includes a general orientation to the system and emphasizes the necessary commitment of time, people, and energy for a successful program. The process of developing, implementing, and evaluating each component of the caregiver system in relation to its goals and objectives is explained.

Phase 2 starts once a hospital has decided to proceed with the program. Central to this phase is an onsite hospital planning session to operationalize the development, implementation, and evaluation process of the system. Hospital administration and department management are involved during the planning process to identify hospital personnel at all levels to participate on the caregiver system core committee and subcommittees. Members include administrators, physicians, department heads, and staff.

Individualizing the System

Phase 3 of the development process is the formation of fhe core committee and subcommittees. The responsibility of the core committee is the development of the goals, objectives, mission statement, and philosophy for the system to be implemented at that particular hospital. Based on the goals and objectives, the committee identifies one or more demonstration nursing units on which to implement the system. At the same time, the committee sets up five subcommittees: services, management, education, evaluation, and implementation.

The services subcommittee analyzes, for each demonstration patient unit, the intensity of services for the most frequent diagnoses admitted to the unit (based on 10 charts for each of the top 10 DRGs). The intensity of services and the frequency of services is determined for each 24-hour period for each of 245 specific patient services. The services subcommittee then identifies the minimum skill level necessary to perform each service (in terms of knowledge, skill, experience, and education level).

Installation

The management subcommittee is responsible for the development and implementation of the organizational management systems. These include the documentation system, communication system, and caregiver units discussed in detail earlier. The education subcommittee prepares orientation and education programs that are intended to help achieve the goals and objectives developed for the caregiver system by the hospital.

The evaluation subcommittee analyzes the impact of the system in terms of cost, quality, and perceived changes in attitude. Financial analysis is performed on data regarding nine measures: (1) nursing agency utilization, (2) cost per discharge based on skill mix changes, (3) nonscheduled overtime, (4) transfer of patients to higher levels of care, (5) length of stay, (6) staff retention and recruitment, (7) unusual occurrences, (8) admissions, and (9) resource utilization. Quality assurance criteria are developed for the documentation system, communication system, and caregiver units.

Finally, the implementation subcommittee is responsible for developing time lines and monitoring systems to assure completion of the requirements of the caregiver system prior to its implementations. In addition, this subcommittee develops time lines for the expansion of the system to other patient units based on directions from the core committee.

Phase 4 involves development of the clinical patient services system. As indicated earlier, the transfer of specific clinical patient services to a multiskilled caregiver is based on an analysis of the particular hospital's resources, traditional roles, and frequency of services and the licensure or state health codes.

Phase 5 involves development of the clinical patient management system, which was described above.

For the demonstration unit, it usually takes 16 weeks to put the organizational management systems into place. Once those are complete, it takes another 16 weeks to implement the clinical patient services system and the patient management system, which can proceed concurrently. At each hospital, major divisions—critical care, maternal and child care, medical-surgical, and special services—will each have a demonstration unit. Once the caregiver system has been validated on demonstration units, the remainder of each division can be converted two to four units at a time.

NURSING STAFF UTILIZATION

The two criteria of success for the caregiver system are quality and cost-effectiveness. NME saw effective utilization of nursing staff as having the potential to achieve major cost savings and quality improvement, and the results of the program bear this out. The program yields these results in the following ways.

Specific staff ratios are developed for each patient unit based on the number of caregiver units per shift, patient diagnoses, physician practice, intensity of services, and severity of illness. Other factors include the number of admissions, discharges and transfers per shift, AM admits, and 24-hour Medicare holds.

Once developed, the staffing matrix for each shift is evaluated based on the cost per patient day and patient discharge. Evaluation of planned versus actual staffing can occur as needed.

The other aspect of staffing is the skill mix necessary to support the NME caregiver system. It will vary from patient unit to patient unit and hospital to hospital. The cost per patient day is developed based on criteria such as projected daily census, intensity of patient services, severity of illness, principal and secondary diagnoses, physician practice patterns and protocols, standards of patient care, and risk management.

In one example, financial analysis of a 25-bed medical-surgical unit compared the budget skill mix and the caregiver system skill mix. The latter was 15% less in the cost per patient day, or $79,000 in annual salary, wage, and benefit savings.

It should be noted that the traditional method of evaluating cost-effectiveness (hours per patient day) has been found to be inadequate as a measurement tool, because it does not discriminate between direct and indirect patient services and the cost of each. For example, suppose a unit has a low nursing hours per patient day with an all-RN staff. As a result, valuable professional time might be spent performing indirect activities that could be provided by nonlicensed staff. The caregiver system has demonstrated that although nursing hours per patient day are higher (since nonlicensed staff are utilized), the cost per patient day actually decreases. Planning the right skill mix—licensed and nonlicensed—based on the intensity of services provided to patients is the key to both quality and cost-effectiveness.

BENEFITS OF THE CAREGIVER SYSTEM

The benefits of the program are both tangible and intangible. They are listed below:

- improved quality of service to the physician
- increased quality of service to the patient
- increased job satisfaction for caregiver staff
- increased retention of RN, LPN, and LVN staff
- increased recruitment of RN, LPN, and LVN staff
- increased marketability of the hospital in the community
- increased admissions

- improved utilization of professional licensed staff
- improved resource utilization (lab tests, etc.)
- increased collaboration between physicians and nurses
- increased commitment of caregiver staff to patients
- decreased cost per patient discharge
- decreased fragmentation of clinical patient services
- decreased agency utilization
- decreased nonscheduled overtime
- decreased transfer of patients to higher levels of care
- decreased length of stay
- decreased unusual occurrences

Of course, there are also some disadvantages:

- the long period of time needed for planning, development, implementation, and evaluation
- the need to overcome management, physician, and staff resistance to change
- the need for additional educational preparation of staff for the expanded roles
- the need for research and resources for the expanded roles

The cost benefits are easy to measure. In addition to the more effective use of nursing staff, financial analysis of the organizational management systems has demonstrated a reduction in operating costs. Nonscheduled overtime was reduced by 80% on one patient unit with the introduction of the new documentation system and intershift walking rounds. Printing costs were reduced when five forms previously used were removed from the storeroom inventory. Decreased utilization of supplemental agency staffing resulted in a 50% reduction in staffing costs. Unusual occurrences were reduced by 50% to 90% as a result of the introduction of the organizational management systems.

Equally noteworthy are the benefits to patients, staff, and the hospital, but these cannot be measured as easily. For instance, the caregiver units enable the professional nurses to utilize the nursing process more effectively and reduce the transfer of patients to higher levels of care. The benefit realized from early assessment and intervention by a professional nurse is the difference in cost between a medical unit and intensive care.

In addition, the system supports the professional role of the nurse, as evidenced by the participative, decentralized management approach in assessing the current system of patient care. Nursing management and staff collaborate in the planning, development, and implementation of the new system. And nurses who have participated in this change report increased satisfaction, self-esteem, and self-actualization. In fact, hospitals in which the caregiver system has been implemented have experienced increased recruitment and retention of the "best and brightest" professional nurses.

CONCLUSION

Health care has become more complex and requires synergism between departments assigned to provide or monitor clinical services concurrently or retrospectively. Fragmentation of services must be decreased if the goal of the health care system is to be achieved. This goal, which is the same goal as will exist in the 21st century, is to provide quality services in a cost-effective manner. The NME caregiver system has been designed to achieve this goal utilizing a systems approach.

BIBLIOGRAPHY

Califano, J.A., Jr. (1986). *America's health care revolution.* New York: Random House.

Campbell, C. (1984). *Nursing diagnosis and intervention in nursing practice* [2nd ed.]. New York: Wiley.

Doenges, M.E., Jeffries, M.F., & Moorhouse, M.F. (1984). *Nursing care plans.* Philadelphia: F.A. Davis.

Kraegil, J.M., Mousseau, V.S., Goldsmith, C., & Arora, R. (1974). *Patient care systems.* Philadelphia: Lippincott.

Lenburg, C. (1984). *The clinical performance examination, development and implementation.* New York: Appleton-Century-Crofts.

Meisenheimer, C.G. (1985). *Quality assurance.* Rockville, MD: Aspen Publishers.

Nichols, M.E., & Wessels, V.G. (1977). *Nursing standards and nursing process.* Rockville, MD: Aspen Publishers.

Phibbs, W.J., Long, B.C., & Woods, N.F., *Medical-surgical nursing* [3rd ed.]. St. Louis: C.V. Mosby.

Chapter 15

Team Nursing for the Nineties

Linda K. Jackson and Sandy Alderman

The authors present a model of team nursing that brings to life the true meaning of team. *Too often, team nursing has been equated with functional nursing, a model that denies professional practice. The authors illuminate the essence of team nursing. They do not create new titles but redefine roles and concepts.*

The authors describe a change process that is organizationally and structurally sound as well as politically astute, as demonstrated by its success in bringing about salary increases.

In order to meet the staffing challenges facing Friendly Hills Regional Medical Center, a plan for changing from modified primary care to team nursing was developed. A number of goals were incorporated into the new model. First, RNs had to be allowed to focus on those aspects of patient care in which they have expertise in virtue of their education and licensure. Second, the model needed to have the flexibility to allow staffing patterns to adjust to census fluctuations, even to the point of returning to modified primary care. Finally, the model needed to respect budgetary constraints, including a reduction in supplemental service staffing.

Situated in North Orange County, California, Friendly Hills Regional Medical Center was recently purchased by Friendly Hills Medical Group. At the time of the ownership change, the 299-bed hospital faced a low inpatient census, had been unable to recruit nursing staff for over 6 months due to presale budgetary cutbacks, and was consequently utilizing increasing numbers of supplemental service nurses. In addition, the full impact of the nursing shortage was being felt in the county. Neighboring hospitals were addressing staff nurse shortages by making significant salary adjustments.

With the sale of the hospital, there was an immediate increase in inpatient census. Although the patient census continued to fluctuate significantly, the overall result was more patient days. Having had no opportunity to prepare for these changes, the use of registry personnel quickly climbed beyond what the budget could endure.

It was in this turbulent environment that the nursing management team began to focus on effectively managing its scarce human resource, the RN. Fortunately, a core of qualified, experienced RNs remained with the organization throughout this period.

The circumstances and the goals described above led to the development of a team nursing model. The foundation of the model is a nursing team that consists of an RN, who functions as the team leader; a licensed vocational nurse, who is responsible for medication administration, completion of prescribed treatments, and bedside care assistance; and two nurse's aides, who are responsible for basic bedside care. The team is utilized on the day and the evening shifts. On the night shift, the team is reduced by one nurse's aide.

In constructing the team, a number of assumptions were made regarding the model's ability to meet the defined goals. The first goal was to make certain that the RNs would be able to focus on the coordination and management of the care given to all patients. Placing the RNs in the role of team leaders ensured that patient care delivery would be based on the nursing process. Through practice and inservice education, the areas of their professional responsibility would be expanded. Support would be provided to the RNs as they gained confidence in directing the care given to patients by their team members, collaborating with the physicians and other health care disciplines, and applying the nursing process. The model was designed to relieve the RNs of nonprofessional duties by the addition of other levels of staff to the team.

The second goal was to make certain that the model allowed for flexibility in staffing as patient census fluctuated. It was determined that a basic team would be responsible for a maximum of 14 patients, which translates into 2.28 nursing hours on the 7–3 and 3–11 shifts and 1.70 nursing hours on the night shift.

Operating from the framework of the basic team, a patient census of 28 on a given unit would require two teams (see Unit 1 in Exhibit 15-1). Additional flexibility is demonstrated in the example Unit 2 (Exhibit 15-1). In this example, a census of 19 patients is staffed with one team and an additional RN, who provides modified primary care. Yet another option shown in the example of Unit 3 (Exhibit 15-1), which has a census of 25 patients. In this example, two teams are formed by the RN and licensed vocational nurse. The patients are divided among the nurse's aides to even the workload. Notice that in all three cases, the nursing hours defined for the maximum team are met or lowered. Note also that each unit has a station secretary who is not counted in determining the hours.

Built into the model is flexibility to accommodate staff availability on a given day, as well as patient population and high patient acuity. An added feature is that the staff on each unit can make final patient care assignments by adjusting the makeup of the teams to efficiently utilize the staff assigned to the unit by the staffing office. Each of the options shown in Exhibit 15-2 for the same unit maintains the integrity of the team concept. The RN

Exhibit 15-1 Team Nursing Model

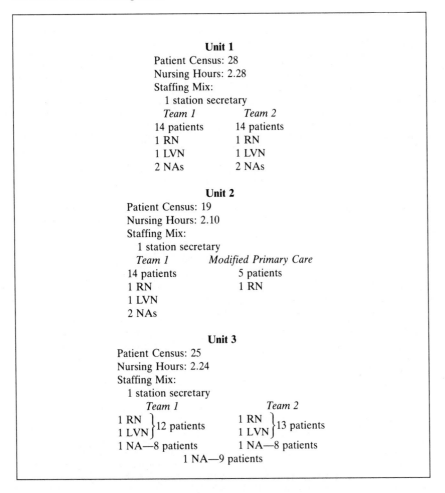

Unit 1
Patient Census: 28
Nursing Hours: 2.28
Staffing Mix:
  1 station secretary

Team 1	*Team 2*
14 patients	14 patients
1 RN	1 RN
1 LVN	1 LVN
2 NAs	2 NAs

Unit 2
Patient Census: 19
Nursing Hours: 2.10
Staffing Mix:
  1 station secretary

Team 1	*Modified Primary Care*
14 patients	5 patients
1 RN	1 RN
1 LVN	
2 NAs	

Unit 3
Patient Census: 25
Nursing Hours: 2.24
Staffing Mix:
  1 station secretary

Team 1	*Team 2*
1 RN ⎱ 12 patients	1 RN ⎱ 13 patients
1 LVN ⎰	1 LVN ⎰
1 NA—8 patients	1 NA—8 patients

1 NA—9 patients

is clearly in the role of team leader and thus the manager and coordinator of patient care.

The third goal was to reduce the use of supplementary agency nurses and thus comply with budgetary constraints. In the months preceding the implementation of the team nursing model, 40% of the dollars spent per patient day were going to agencies. Not only was this budgetarily unacceptable, but it also meant that in many cases patient care was not being managed by the hospital staff. Patient safety was compromised, since care was delivered by agency nurses who lacked thorough familiarity with the hospital's policies and procedures. Efforts by the hospital staff to monitor

Exhibit 15-2 Staffing Options for a Sample Unit

Option 1

Patient Census: 21
Nursing Hours: 2.28
Staffing Mix:
1 station secretary

Team 1	Team 2	Team 3
7 patients	7 patients	7 patients
1 RN	1 RN	1 RN
1 LVN	1 NA	1 NA

Option 2

Patient Census: 21
Nursing Hours: 2.28
Staffing Mix:
1 station secretary

Team 1	Team 2
14 patients	7 patients
1 RN	1 RN
1 LVN	1 NA
2 NAs	

Option 3

Patient Census: 21
Nursing Hours: 2.28
Staffing Mix:
1 station secretary

Team 1	Team 2
10 patients	11 patients
1 RN	1 RN
1 LVN	1 LVN
1 NA	1 NA

Option 4

Patient Census: 21 (3 patients are below the age of 5
and are thus staffed separately)
Nursing Hours: 2.28 (overall)
  3 ped patients: 2.67
  18 med-surg patients: 2.22
Staffing mix
  1 station secretary

Team 1	Modified Primary Care	Modified Primary Care
13 patients	5 patients	3 ped patients
1 RN	1 RN	1 RN
1 LVN		
2 NAs		

the agency nurses proved difficult because of their responsibility for their own patient assignments. With the critical shortage of RNs, the assumption was made that the addition of licensed vocational nurses and nurse's aides to the staff would (1) reduce the number of agency nurses utilized, (2) allow the core RN staff to supervise the care of a larger number of patients, and (3) provide the opportunity to use licensed vocational nurses and nurse's aides from agencies rather than agency RNs when supplementary staff was needed.

The team nursing model was to be implemented on both of the medical-surgical units and in subsequent units to be opened in the future. Basic guidelines for staffing were established in order to assure consistency. One basic rule was that RNs would always function as team leaders. Licensed vocational nurses would not be allowed to lead teams or do modified primary care. Licensed vocational nurses would be intravenous-certified, having passed a 30-hour vocational nurse IV class (approved by the Board of Licenses) at the time of hire or within 6 months. Nurse's aides would be required to have completed a nurse's aide certification course that included a minimum of 100 clinical hours. Station secretaries would not be included in calculating the nursing hours, as they do not provide direct bedside care. The station secretaries were also placed on 12-hour shifts to provide coverage during peak hours on the units as well as weekend support. Finally, all nursing hours were to be calculated on 8-hour shifts, even though 4-, 8-, and 12-hour shifts were available to staff.

Moving from a primarily RN staff to a model that incorporated licensed vocational nurses and nurse's aides required a review of the role of each caregiver. Registered nurses, through education and licensure, are accountable for ensuring that the nursing process is applied to the care of all patients. The role of RNs in the model would allow them to assess all patients, develop plans for patient care, ensure the implementation of all plans, and evaluate the outcomes.

Licensed vocational nurses, on the other hand, would focus on providing direct patient care under the direction of RNs and within their scope of practice. They would be expected to help obtain and record baseline data that could then be incorporated into the plans of care by the RNs. The licensed vocational nurses would also report patient responses that could be interpreted by the RN in the evaluation of patient outcomes.

The nurse's aides would be limited to those tasks for which they had been prepared. In all situations, they would be expected to function under the direct supervision of the RNs. Among the tasks performed by nurse's aides would be direct hygienic care activities, the taking and recording of vital signs, the recording of intake and output, and general activities of daily living. Nurse's aides would further be expected to assist in maintaining a safe and clean environment in patient care areas. The nurse's aides would also provide data about patients that would be utilized by the RNs in applying the nursing process.

Prior to the implementation of the model, guidelines for the optimal functioning of teams were developed. Although much of the actual management of each team would be left to the RN's discretion, it seemed important to address the question of the shift report, which in the past had tended to prevent total efficiency on the units. It was determined that the RN would continue to receive the change of shift report from the off-going shift. The on-coming licensed vocational nurses, rather than listening to the report, would count narcotics with the off-going licensed vocational nurses, receive a status report on patient medication regimes, check IVs, and begin preparations for administration of medications and treatments. The nurse's aides would begin the shift by taking vital signs, providing hygienic care, and preparing patients for meals (as appropriate). Following the change of shift report, the RN would make necessary assignment adjustments, meet with team members to delegate specific aspects of patient care, and receive from team members interim reports on the current status of patients. The RN would proceed to make an initial assessment of all assigned patients and make additional assessments (as necessary) throughout the shift. The RN would also make necessary adjustments in the activities of the team to meet the needs of patients. The RN would of course be responsible for ensuring that, for each patient, the nursing process was reflected in the documentation of the patient's status.

Once the goals of the team nursing model were described, the model developed, and the guidelines for its use outlined, the next step was to implement the model. The process was begun at the nursing management level in order to elicit their support and to familiarize them with the team concept. The nursing managers were introduced to the plan in a classroom setting through the use of lectures and simulated staffing exercises. The master staffing plan for the medical-surgical units was reworked to incorporate positions for the licensed vocational nurses and nurse's aides. The revised team model was subjected to budgetary review. It was estimated, utilizing existing salaries and agency fees, that the hospital would realize a reduction in dollars for employee hours per patient day of approximately 48%.

The staffing secretary was introduced to the system, and the supplemental staffing agencies were notified that the patient care delivery system would be changing. Each agency was given information about the qualifications required in order for their licensed vocational nurses and nurse's aides to work in the hospital.

The first step in preparing the staff for the team model took place at a general staff meeting. The team model was briefly outlined by the Director of Nursing Services, and the plans for implementing the changes were reviewed. Key to obtaining staff acceptance was the high visibility of the nursing managers at this meeting and at subsequent training classes for staff.

All medical-surgical RNs attended two mandatory classes designed to provide them with the knowledge needed to function within the scope of the team model. The first class concentrated on increasing the staff's awareness of the impact of the critical nursing shortage and its effect on the nursing department budget. The team model was reviewed in depth, and the roles of the nurse's aides, licensed vocational nurses, and RNs were touched upon. Simulated exercises involved converting staffing from the previous week into staffing consistent with the new model. Additional patient census scenarios were presented, and in workshop format staffing alternatives utilizing the team model were illustrated. Each group of nurses was assisted in these exercises by a nurse manager. Through group discussion, various alternatives to each scenario were considered.

Within 2 weeks, the second class was presented. This class dealt with the nursing practice act and the RN's role. The licensed vocational nurse practice act was discussed, and the criteria-based job description was reviewed. The nurse's aide role and job description were also examined. Throughout this portion of the class, emphasis was placed on a comparative analysis of the roles and job descriptions of the team members. The nursing process was reviewed, and a segment titled "Quick Step to Assessment" allowed the nurses to refresh themselves on the key aspects of their individual roles within the team. Since the staff previously had consisted only of RNs, special attention was given to the principles of delegation. Theories on how groups are formed and on team cohesiveness were reviewed.

Hiring nurse's aides proved to be easier than hiring licensed vocational nurses, so that within 2 months of implementation all nurse's aide positions were filled. At this point the nurse's aides attended a workshop on their scope of practice within the hospital. Patient service issues were covered in the workshop.

During the phase-in of team nursing, additional staff meetings were held to allow the staff to discuss concerns and to seek solutions. The nursing managers were available during this period to provide support. An immediate reduction in supplemental staff utilization was experienced, especially at the RN level, and this had a positive impact on the nursing department budget. As a result, the hospital board approved a 14% pay increase for all members of the nursing department, which also helped to improve the hospital's position in the employment market.

Approximately $10,000 in salaries was spent to implement the team nursing model. This figure includes expenses for class instructor preparation, restructuring, master staff, job description preparation, management team education, and staff education. Two-thirds of the implementation budget went to nurse salaries for class participation. Evaluation of the team model after 6 months reveals that the initial goals are being realized. There has been a reduction of 58% in dollars for employee hours per patient day, which is 10% greater than the original projection of 48%. Several factors have contributed to the reduction. By quickly filling nurse's aide positions, the hospital reduced the volume of dependency on agency staff. The team model allowed more efficient utilization of RNs. This, in turn, made it possible to use licensed vocational nurses and nurse's aides from agencies, thus reducing costs. The increased nursing salaries improved the hospital's position in the employment market so that more RN positions have been filled, resulting in further cost reductions. Although the hiring of qualified licensed vocational nurses has progressed more slowly, the ratio of non-RNs to RNs is 4:6, which is felt to be acceptable.

The goal of developing a model that allows for flexibility has been realized. Since the nurse's aide positions were quickly filled, team modification options have been extensively utilized, with a high degree of success and staff satisfaction. In each of these staffing options, the RNs have demonstrated steady growth in their roles. They are realizing their full potential as team leaders who are responsible for coordinating and managing patient care. Ongoing support for the RNs included a 6-hour medical-surgical RN workshop. This allowed the nurses to refresh and refine their technical skills, and it also introduced more advanced concepts in patient care.

Efforts to fill the remainder of the licensed vocational nurse positions continue. Although state approval for the 30-hour IV certification course was obtained, the number of licensed vocational nurses hired has not justified the expenditure of time and money for the class. Licensed vocational nurses have been sent to IV certification courses at other agencies or have been qualified upon hire. Plans for the development of licensed vocational nurses are centered on presenting a workshop designed to improve their skills and performance within the team model.

The overall consensus is that the team nursing model is proving a success. With the continuing rapid growth of the hospital, the team nursing model will allow the nursing department to position itself to meet the health care challenges and changes expected in the coming decade.

Chapter 16

Differentiated Practice in an Acute Care Setting

Judy Blauwet and Patty Bolger

The authors of this chapter describe the South Dakota Statewide Project for Nursing and Nursing Education, which differentiates between the BSN and ADN practitioner. Although formal education was not used as the basis for the differentiation, competencies were defined and a factoring tool formulated to derive levels of practice.

The implementation of this model at a 407-bed hospital is presented. Case management is the delivery system utilized, and differentiation of practice levels occurs between the case manager and associate case manager. Although many of the concepts presented here sound similar to other patient care delivery systems, the attempt to differentiate the BSN and ADN is applauded. We look forward to seeing the application of this concept to nurses on the basis of formal education.

Although differentiated practice is not a patient care delivery model per se, it affects the nursing process and patient outcomes and therefore is a major factor in deciding upon a delivery system for any acute care setting. The South Dakota Statewide Project for Nursing and Nursing Education was sponsored by the Midwest Alliance in Nursing and funded by the W. K. Kellogg Foundation. It was charged with defining the educational preparation for entry into practice and differentiating between the baccalaureate and associate degree nurse. Under the direction of Peggy L. Primm, the project director, a 2-year study was undertaken to plan for two levels of practice, two related levels of education, and the appropriate levels of licensure.

As part of the study, several demonstration sites were selected to implement the differentiated practice concept in the clinical area. McKennan Hospital, a 407-bed tertiary care facility, was one of the pilot hospitals. This chapter will describe the concept of differentiated practice and how it was operationalized at McKennan Hospital.

DESCRIPTION OF DIFFERENTIATED PRACTICE

The *differentiated practice model* is a system designed to provide distinct levels of nursing practice based on defined competencies that are incorporated into job descriptions. General guidelines for the concept are as follows:

1. Current RN practice will be the minimum level at which differentiation of RN competencies will be established.
2. Competencies will be consistent with the minimum expectations for the associate degree (ADN) and baccalaureate degree (BSN) levels in the education sector.
3. Client satisfaction will improve due to the comprehensiveness and continuity of care.
4. Nurse satisfaction will improve, and thus so will retention, due to placing the authority, responsibility, and accountability for the planning and provision of high-quality, cost-effective nursing care at the staff nurse level.
5. Differentiated competencies will be time- and setting-free and will be applicable to nursing practice in any setting.
6. Differentiated levels of practice will, in the future, be supported by separate licensure laws and regulatory requirements.

The differentiated competencies for the RN (ADN and BSN) were developed based on the principles of differentiated educational preparation and are described for this project as follows:

> The BSN cares for focal clients who are identified as individuals, families, aggregate, and community groups. The level of responsibility of the BSN is from admission to postdischarge. The unstructured setting is a geographical and/or situational environment which may not have established policies, procedures, and protocols, and has the potential for variation requiring independent nursing decisions. The ADN cares for focal clients who are identified as individuals and members of a family. The level of responsibility of the ADN is for a specified work period and is consistent with the identified goals of care. The ADN is prepared to function in a structured health care setting. The structured setting is a geographical and/or situational environment where the policies, procedures, and protocols for the provision of health care are established and there is recourse to assistance and support from the full scope of nursing expertise. (Primm, 1988)

The practice of nursing must be perceived as a range of functions from the more simple, observable, and technical tasks to tasks involving complex critical thinking, planning, acting, and evaluating. Within the differentiated practice model, the complexity of decision making and accountability increases in proportion to the complexity of the client, time line, and setting. As an example, the focal client for the ADN is an individual, whereas the BSN focuses on the person as a family member or a member of a family system, group, or community. The BSN is expected to have all the competencies of the ADN role while expanding to fulfill all of the needs of the professional role. In contrast, the ADN cannot be expected to "fill in" as a BSN.

The differentiated practice model displayed in Figure 16-1 shows the three major and three minor role components of nursing practice. The three major components—provision of direct care, communication, and management of care—make up the model, and their intersections form the three subcomponents. Direct client care intersects with communication to form patient teaching. Communication intersects with management of care to form coordination with other disciplines. Management of care intersects with direct care to form delegation of care. As shown by the placement of the ADN and BSN circles, the complexity of decision making in the nursing process is the basis for the differentiated levels of practice.

In Exhibit 16-1, the competencies that describe the parameters of ADN and BSN practice are organized into the three major components of the model. Within each category, the subcomponents (teaching, coordination with other disciplines, and delegation of care) are addressed. Levels of practice, as differentiated by complexity of client, time lines, and structure of the setting in reference to the nursing actions described in the competencies, can then be quantified and documented in the form of competency-based job descriptions specific to each institution or agency.

Since the differentiated practice model is futuristic in terms of educational preparation and scope of practice, a general statement directed to LPNs was developed:

The LPN cares for individual clients and interacts with individual members of the clients' families. The level of responsibility of the LPN is for a specified work period. The LPN is responsible to deliver the overall comprehensive plan of care documented by the BSN/ADN. The LPN is prepared to function in the structural health care setting where there are established policies, procedures and protocols regarding all routine and emergency nursing interventions the LPN is expected to deliver. The structural setting provides immediate and direct supervision of the LPN care in unstable to complex client situations and ready access to assistance

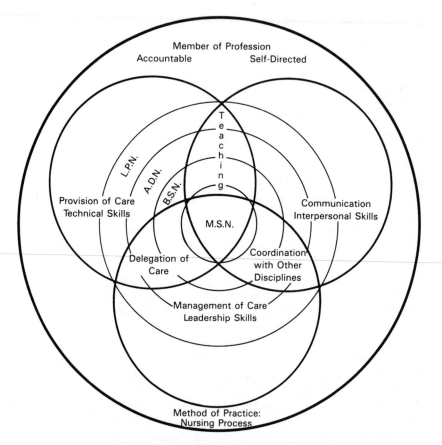

Figure 16-1 The Differentiated Practice Role of Nurse. *Source: Associate Degree Nursing: Facilitating Competency Development.* Copyright by Midwest Alliance in Nursing and W.K. Kellogg Foundation. Reprinted with permission.

and guidance from the full scope of nursing expertise in stable client situations. (Primm, 1988, p. 1)

The competencies of the currently practicing LPN (Exhibit 16-2) were also defined and are presented in the same format as the ADN and BSN competencies. Master's-prepared clinical specialists, nursing assistants, or technicians, if a part of a care delivery system, can be incorporated using a similar format. Whereas LPNs and nursing assistants would require the addition of a circle to the diagram of the model, clinical specialists would be represented within the small inner circle.

DIFFERENTIATED PRACTICE AT McKENNAN HOSPITAL

At McKennan Hospital, the differentiated practice model was implemented using case management as a delivery system. Patients are admitted and assigned to a baccalaureate RN, who functions as the case manager. Within 24 hours of a patient's admission to the hospital, the patient's case manager is expected to collaborate with appropriate members of the health care team, the patient, and the family or significant other to formulate a comprehensive plan of care. Also, the case manager identifies the potential need for further care after discharge.

The case manager may provide some direct care but also delegates aspects of care to the ADN when not on duty. The case manager also updates the plan of care as necessary and begins the discharge planning. The ADN provides care within the framework of the comprehensive plan of care. Upon discharge, the case manager is responsible for arranging referrals for any nursing diagnosis that was not resolved.

McKennan Hospital implemented the nurse roles to be consistent with proposed future minimum levels of ADN and BSN educational preparation. The RNs filling the ADN role were titled *case associates* and those filling the BSN role were titled *case managers*. As noted earlier, LPN competencies were described and incorporated into a separate job description, which outlined the competencies needed for the currently licensed scope of practice. Therefore, in actuality there existed three levels of nursing practice, plus current nursing technician positions already in place.

The differentiated practice model provided a common understanding of nursing practice in terms of the technical skills needed for the provision of care, the interpersonal skills needed for the communication aspect of care, and the leadership skills needed for the management of care. The staff at McKennan Hospital was well acquainted with and educated about the differences between the roles and the expectations for each one.

The key to success was having the staff understand that each role is different, not better; that each role contributes a different component of care, not a more important component; and that the delivery of quality patient care requires that everyone work together to provide total patient care, not just the case manager or case associate. The staff developed the ability to function as a nursing team and to provide care as directed by the plan of care defined by the case manager for each of the individual clients.

For purposes of participation in the statewide project, the actual educational preparation of RNs was not used in determining which roles nurses were given. Each staff member was placed by ability and desire in either

Exhibit 16-1 ADN and BSN Practice Competencies

DIRECT CARE COMPETENCIES	
The ADN provides direct care for the focal client with common, well-defined nursing diagnoses by:	The BSN provides direct care for the focal client with complex interactions of nursing diagnoses by:
A. Collecting health pattern data from able resources using an established assessment format to identify basic health care needs. B. Organizing and analyzing health pattern data in order to select nursing diagnoses from an established list. C. Establishing goals with the focal client for a specified work period that are consistent with the overall comprehensive nursing plan of care. D. Developing and implementing an individualized nursing plan of care using established nursing diagnoses and protocols to promote, maintain, and restore health. E. Participating in the medical plan of care to promote an integrated health care plan. F. Evaluating focal client responses to nursing interventions and altering the plan of care as necessary to meet client needs.	A. Expanding the collection of data to identify complex health care needs. B. Organizing and analyzing complex health pattern data to develop nursing diagnoses. C. Establishing goals with the focal client to develop a comprehensive nursing plan of care from admission to post-discharge. D. Developing and implementing a comprehensive nursing plan of care based on nursing diagnoses for health promotion. E. Interpreting the medical plan of care into nursing activities to formulate approaches to nursing care. F. Evaluating the nursing care delivery system and promoting goal-directed change to meet individualized client needs.
COMMUNICATION COMPETENCIES	
The ADN uses basic communication skills with the focal client by:	The BSN uses complex communication skills with the focal client by:
A. Developing and maintaining goal-directed interactions to encourage expression of needs and support coping behaviors. B. Modifying and implementing a standard teaching plan in order to restore, maintain, and promote health.	A. Developing and maintaining goal-directed interactions to promote effective coping behaviors and facilitate change in behavior. B. Designing and implementing a comprehensive teaching plan for health promotion.

Exhibit 16-1 continued

The ADN coordinates focal client care with other health team members by:	The BSN collaborates with other health team members by:
A. Documenting and communicating data for clients with common, well-defined nursing diagnoses to provide continuity of care. B. Using established channels of communication to implement an effective health care plan. C. Using interpreted nursing research findings for developing nursing care.	A. Documenting and communicating comprehensive data for clients with complex interactions of nursing diagnoses to provide continuity of care. B. Using established channels of communication to modify health care delivery. C. Incorporating research findings into practice and by consulting with nurse researchers regarding identified nursing problems in order to enhance nursing practice.
MANAGEMENT COMPETENCIES	
The ADN organizes those aspects of care for focal clients for whom he or she is accountable by:	The BSN manages nursing care of focal clients by:
A. Prioritizing, planning, and organizing delivery of standard nursing care in order to use time and resources effectively and efficiently. B. Delegating aspects of care to peers, licensed practical nurses, and ancillary nursing personnel, consistent with their levels of education and expertise, in order to meet client needs. C. Maintaining accountability for own care and care delegated to others to assure adherence to ethical and legal standards. D. Recognizing the need for referral and conferring with appropriate nursing personnel for assistance to promote continuity of care. E. Working with other health care personnel within the organizational structure to manage client care.	A. Prioritizing, planning, and organizing the delivery of comprehensive nursing care in order to use time and resources effectively and efficiently. B. Delegating aspects of care to other nursing personnel, consistent with their levels of education and expertise, in order to meet clients' needs and to maximize staff performance. C. Maintaining accountability for own care and care delegated to others to assure adherence to ethical and legal standards. D. Initiating referral to appropriate departments and agencies to provide services that promote continuity of care. E. Assuming a leadership role in health care management to improve client care.

Source: Associate Degree Nursing: Facilitating Competency Development. Copyright by Midwest Alliance in Nursing and W.K. Kellogg Foundation. Reprinted with permission.

Exhibit 16-2 LPN Practice Competencies

DIRECT CARE COMPETENCIES

The LPN provides delegated aspects of direct care for individual clients with plans of nursing care documented by the RN and ADN by:

A. Collecting standard vital signs and nursing assessment data as delineated on the established assessment forms.
B. Assisting with the selection of common well-defined nursing diagnoses.
C. Providing care organized in support of established client/nurse mutual goals for care.
D. Providing delegated aspects of nursing care using established nursing policies, procedures, and protocols.
E. Providing nursing care in support of the medical plan of care.
F. Reporting client responses to nursing care provided within the specified work period.

COMMUNICATION COMPETENCIES

The LPN uses basic communication skills with the individual client to:

A. Report client expressions of need.
B. Reinforce standard teaching plans.

MANAGEMENT COMPETENCIES

The LPN organizes own care to facilitate efficient delivery of care by all health care team members by:

A. Documenting on established chart/agency forms and reporting client changes to appropriate nursing personnel or the health care team.
B. Using established channels of communication to implement delegated aspects of care.
C. Reading pertinent up-to-date nursing literature.

The LPN organizes delegated aspects of care for individual clients by:

A. Organizing care delivery for efficient use of time and supplies.
B. Delegating aspects of care to peers and ancillary personnel, consistent with their level of education and expertise, in order to meet clients' documented needs.
C. Maintaining accountability for own care and care delegated to others to assure adherence to ethical and legal standards.
D. Reporting client concerns and need for further planning to assist in continuity of care.
E. Working effectively with other health care personnel to meet client needs for nursing care.

Source: Associate Degree Nursing: Facilitating Competency Development. Copyright by Midwest Alliance in Nursing and W.K. Kellogg Foundation. Reprinted with permission.

the case associate or case manager role. A "factoring tool" to determine ability to perform in a role was used as a part of the project. This factoring tool was appropriate for the project but will be unnecessary once educational preparation begins to dictate roles.

The factoring tool was an evaluation form requiring a yes or no response to 48 statements reflecting practice patterns. Sixteen of the 48 items were identified as key indicators of role placement. If 8 or more of the 16 key indicators were answered yes, the professional role was recommended. Key indicator statements concerned areas of professional practice (e.g., the refining of care plans based on assessment data). (The factoring tool is copyrighted by Peggy Primm, Staff Development Associates, 4885 Orchard Drive, Des Moines, IA 50317.)

The factoring tool was independently completed by each RN participating in the project and by his or her immediate manager. The RN and the manager then met to discuss individual responses and to negotiate role placement. No RN was forced into either role. The choice of role made by the RN was usually identical to the choice recommended by the manager. In several instances, the RN chose the associate role despite having factored into the professional role (reasons for such a decision included the desire for part-time status or to avoid a straight night rotation). Each RN agreed to remain in the selected role for a minimum of 3 months.

Generally, if a role change was made, it was from the associate role to the professional role. Two reasons were cited. The first was that the RN wanted more responsibility. Second, the case manager role was possible on a straight night rotation.

Staff mix was dependent upon a number of factors, such as acuity, current and projected case manager:case associate ratios, individual physician practice patterns, type of unit, and patient length of stay. Of these, patient length of stay and acuity were identified as the most critical factors. In general, the higher the acuity of the patients (resulting in higher hours per patient day), the lower the number of cases a case manager could effectively handle. In the critical care units, case managers would often only carry one or two cases, whereas on medical-surgical units, case managers would carry three or four cases. Overall, the ratio of case managers to case associates needed to be either 1:1 (in higher acuity areas) or 1:2.

The implementation of differentiated practice did not cause an increase in hours per patient day or require more nurses. Patient care requirements were determined through utilization of the GRASP Patient Classification System, which uses the patient care unit as a measure of time to determine the number of nursing care hours a patient requires. The system, as established at McKennan Hospital, did not differentiate between the hours of care provided by a case manager and the hours provided by a case associate.

Differentiated practice separated the role of each RN in caring for the patient and determined who was accountable for the final outcome of care. In this context, need for a charge nurse was brought into question. Assigning one nurse to be responsible for the care of a patient negates the need for the charge nurse to manage the care. This position evolved to be more of a resource than a management position.

One of the most important operational issues faced in the implementation process was staff scheduling. Case manager scheduling depends on a number of issues: part-time versus full-time status, 8-hour versus 12-hour shifts, and shift rotations. At McKennan Hospital, it was determined that to provide for appropriate contact with patients, care planning, and continuity of care, case managers must work 12-hour shifts for a total of at least 64 hours each 2-week period. Twelve-hour shifts posed problems, particularly in units where the length of stay was short and the case manager had difficulty in achieving consistency in assignment. Staff who functioned in a straight night shift position were unable to fulfill the case manager role due to their inability to adequately plan care with the patients, families, and other health care team members.

Another operational issue related to staffing was the need to float staff in times of low census. Floating of case managers did not occur, and staff who were floated only functioned in the case associate role.

THE IMPLEMENTATION PROCESS

To ensure that staff have the ability to function in their new roles, the nursing administration must create opportunities for success. The staff should be recognized for their accomplishments and be given positive feedback as frequently as is warranted (false positives will only serve to devalue the model). Nurses also need to be allowed to engage in problem solving and to adapt the system to the changes necessitated by implementing differentiated nursing practice. The unit-based committees must be active in the formulation of policies, procedures, and so on, in order for staff to develop a sense of ownership.

Differentiated practice shifts control to the staff nurse—appropriately so. In the differentiated practice model, self-governance is not the ideal but a must. Support must be given to staff by nursing management at all levels to achieve this. For unit directors, increased emphasis is placed on the roles of facilitator, supporter, and coach. Differentiated nursing practice puts the responsibility for all aspects of nursing care on the individual nurse caring for the patient rather than on the charge nurse or head nurse. Staff become more skilled at problem solving, teaching, and sharing and demonstrate increased confidence.

Essential to the implementation of differentiated practice is the development of a business plan that details the process and identifies time frames for each step. Key components of this plan include the following:

- selection of a strong implementation coordinator
- formation of a core planning committee (with a nursing management perspective) and individual unit-based committees
- identification of educational goals:
  —change process training
  —theory development
  —explanation of and orientation in roles and competencies, job descriptions, and factoring tools
  —nursing diagnoses
  —instruction in charting system changes
  —ongoing clarification of differentiated practice
- determination of a trial ratio of BSN : ADN competencies on each unit
- identification of evaluation criteria for the model and collection of preimplementation data
- establishment of a plan for gathering information and for the evaluation of system change

McKennan Hospital found that it took approximately 6 months to get a unit fully implemented and staff comfortable in their various roles. For the model to become fully internalized and part of the nursing practice culture, 2 years is required. The size of the facility or unit may lengthen or shorten the implementation period.

The time spent on education and in meetings about the model during implementation averaged 20 hours per staff nurse. Tapered exposure to the concept of differentiated practice was found to be necessary for nurses to internalize the competencies needed, making the training more expensive than traditional inservice education. Another issue that must be resolved in the implementation process is compensation based on the complexity of the individual RN role. The potential cost incurred may be recovered by compressing the number of middle management positions, decreasing general orientation costs, and decreasing patient length of stay.

RESULTS OF DIFFERENTIATED PRACTICE

Implementation of the differentiated practice model was viewed as a very positive change for the institution. Major benefits include the following:

- *Nurse satisfaction,* particularly in the case manager role, was identified as a major strength. The BSN-prepared nurses were able to meet additional responsibilities in a job they were educationally prepared for. Satisfaction was particularly noticeable where physicians supported a collaborative approach to all aspects of care.
- Differentiated practice required *participatory management,* which allowed support staff nurses to make decisions. The staff nurses in turn were given autonomy as well as responsibility and accountability for patient care. Ongoing support for staff nurses was essential, since the added responsibilities tended to overwhelm some staff.
- *Patient satisfaction* dramatically increased when staffing patterns supported case manager responsibilities. Some patients asked for their previous case managers upon readmission, which was highly satisfying to the staff nurses. The setting of mutual goals allowed the patients to participate in care, which ultimately increased satisfaction while decreasing nursing and hospital liability for unexpected or adverse outcomes..
- *Utilization of nursing diagnoses* was essential in this system of care delivery. Further development and increased utilization of nursing diagnoses occurred.
- Overall, *improvements in documentation* of care delivered were observed. Full documentation is important not only in meeting regulatory agency requirements but also in providing an accurate picture of all care rendered should litigation occur.
- Professional practice as implemented in the project provided an avenue for *expansion of nurse responsibilities within the realm of direct patient care.* It also provided a way of potentially increasing salaries at the case management level, thus creating an opportunity to respond to the problem of nurse salary compression.
- The possibility of a *decreased length of stay,* which would positively impact the financial status of the hospital, is very real. Although the length of stay was not changed on the pilot units at McKennan Hospital, one demonstration center (an acute care agency) identified a decrease in length of stay from 5.6 days to 4.9 days. Other agencies

participating in the project had dramatic increases in home health referrals—one went from 2.5 to 16.1 referrals per month while another went from 1.0 to 53 referrals per month.

Some difficulties in implementing differentiated practice were as follows:

- The *fluctuation in census, high acuity levels of patients (especially in critical care), and short lengths of stay* caused problems. In times of high census, case managers were required to supervise float staff while simultaneously assuming a patient load. This did not allow timely completion of comprehensive patient care plans.
- The *current shortage of RNs,* particularly case managers, created dissatisfaction in times of high census, since case managers were unable to consistently complete important aspects of care in a timely manner. This led to feelings of frustration with the change process and the concept of differentiated practice.
- *Resistance to increased salaries* for case managers was shown by fiscal intermediaries. The burden of defining and demonstrating the financial implications of the model will rest on nursing.
- The *lack of technical support* in the form of computers and other support devices, as well as a general lack of knowledge on the part of staff nurses as to how to use support devices, caused nurses to become frustrated with the increase in documentation.
- The *education curriculum* needed to support differentiated practice was not fully developed or implemented.
- The *period of time for implementing the model* must be sufficient. The model incorporates a philosophical change in care delivery and is not just a quick fix. As in any change process of this magnitude, a strong project director is required to provide support and guide the change process over a prolonged period of time.
- The *current scheduling pattern of 12-hour shifts* while working 72 hours per pay period had caused a problem with case assignments, particularly in units with short lengths of stay.

SUMMARY

Differentiated practice has provided staff with the opportunity to grow and stretch beyond the current limits of clinical practice. By empowering nurses and giving them decision-making responsibilities consistent with their education and technical expertise, the hospital was able to dramatically improve the outcomes of care. This practice system compels nurses to use their education in applying the nursing process, making nursing diagnoses, and implementing strategies to accomplish mutually agreed outcomes. With care delivery systems of this nature, the professional practice of nursing has surely come of age.

BIBLIOGRAPHY

Primm, L. (1986a). Defining and differentiating ADN and BSN competencies. *Issues, 7*(1), 3–6.

Primm, L. (1986b). South Dakota Statewide Project for Nursing and Nursing Education. *Issues, 7*(1), 3–6.

Primm, L. (1987, July-August). Differentiated practice for ADN and BSN prepared nurses. *Journal of Professional Nursing,* pp. 218–224.

Primm, L. (1988, April). Differentiated nursing care management patient care delivery system. *The Kansas Nurse,* p. 2.

Primm, L., & Karpiuk, K. (1988, June 30). *Statewide project for nursing and nursing education: Final report.* pp. 1–21.

Chapter 17

Alternative Delivery System: Primary Case Management

Carol Ann Cavouras, Lynn Walts, Sue Taylor,
Anne Garner, and Pamela Bordelon

The authors present a case management model based on the principles of primary nursing linked to a clearly articulated career ladder. They have paid attention to the three evaluation components of quality, cost, and job satisfaction, and they find that the model meets the patient care demands at Hermann Hospital.

The goal of implementing an alternative patient care delivery model is to provide a dynamic work environment in which nurses are accountable for quality patient outcomes, are responsible for cost-effective practice, have the ability to build collegial relationships, and are encouraged to collaborate on the development of a shared mission.

Hermann Hospital is reaching this objective through the development of a *primary case management system* that incorporates accountability, responsibility, collegiality, and collaboration into a care delivery model based on the concepts of primary nursing. The blending of case management with primary nursing was done in recognition of the necessity for efficient care, cost containment, and appropriate allocation of resources. There was also a desire to maintain the kind of direct patient interaction and responsibility afforded by primary nursing (Zander, 1985).

Description of the primary case management model will be accomplished through a brief overview of the structure and job expectations of the nursing department at Hermann, followed by discussion of the structure, the cost of implementation, and pros and cons of the program.

DIVISION OF NURSING ORGANIZATION

Two key organizational factors that expedited the development of case management are nursing decentralization and unit-based quality assurance.

First, the decentralization of the nursing department created the nurse manager role essential to the process. Nurse managers are responsible for

275

the delivery of quality patient care and fiscal management of their units. Each manager is accountable for the development, maintenance, and evaluation of an annual budget; personnel management; liaisons with medical and house staff; a unit-based quality assurance program; support of research activities; and, in collaboration with hospital education instructors and unit education coordinators, assurance of educational opportunities for the staff. Thus, the nurse managers had the autonomy to design and refine a nursing care delivery system to meet the needs of their individual units in collaboration with the medical directors.

As noted above, each unit is responsible for its own quality assurance, which is evaluated through an ongoing unit-based monitoring program. A unit's program is organized by the nurse manager and coordinated by the unit quality assurance coordinator. The unit develops standards related to the specific patient needs and problems. Data are then collected from multiple sources by the nursing staff, evaluated, and reported on a quarterly basis to hospital quality assurance. This direct accountability for patient outcomes naturally led to the development of standard protocols that incorporated nursing standards of care into common medical treatment regimens.

The last key element for the implementation of a new care delivery system was the presence of a clinical ladder that rewarded RNs for clinical expertise in a direct patient care role. This ladder, the third prong of the PACE (Practice Alternatives for Career Expansion) program, consists of six levels, novice to expert. The first two levels are basic staff positions, with level 3 and above requiring a contribution to the organization beyond the normally expected patient care activities (Weeks & Vestal, 1983). Thus, nurses who were clinically excellent, academically prepared, and willing to accept elevated responsibility for patient care had access to both career advancement and financial reward by becoming case managers (Taylor, Walts, Amling, & Cavouras, 1988). Differentiation of practice as described by the National Commission on Nursing (1988) is also achieved by having a clinical ladder, since lack of experience, education, or willingness to accept an independent role restricts the practice of some nurses, whereas unique opportunities for advanced practice are available to qualified and willing individuals.

DESCRIPTION OF THE CASE MANAGEMENT MODEL

Primary case management is based on the premise that quality patient outcomes and cost-effective care are best achieved by having unit-based case managers direct patient care through a system in which the principles of primary nursing are applied by staff nurses and nurse extenders. Although each unit adapts the program to conform to its specific patient population, two basic elements—standard protocols and case managers—are essential.

Standard protocols are patient care blueprints that establish a day-to-day plan encompassing the activities that must occur to produce a specified outcome. As noted earlier, these protocols are the optimal method of tracking quality, since the medical and nursing staff collaborate in evaluating patient progress and resource utilization on a daily basis. This constant review immediately identifies system, patient, or provider problems that could compromise patient care.

The second requirement for primary case management is to have case managers. The exact responsibilities of a case manager is dependent on the clinical level of both the nurse and the unit staff. However, basic definitions of clinical levels are given in Exhibit 17-1.

Nurses who have obtained Level III or IV on the clinical ladder maintain a patient focus and spend the majority of their time providing or directing patient care. Their case management functions include monitoring compliance with standard protocols that outline patient care for a specific patient type and individualizing case management for their patients. Standard protocols ideally form the basis of shift reports, with particular

Exhibit 17-1 Definitions of Clinical Levels

Level III & IV (Patient Focused)	Level V (Unit Focused)	Level VI (Service Focused)
1. Provides direct patient care and monitors patient care through process.	1. Monitors direct patient care provided by nurses at Levels I–IV and provides patient care for complex patients.	1. Consults on patient care for complex patients and interacts with other QA hospital departments in patient care problem solving.
2. Monitors daily compliance with standard protocols.	2. Develops and implements standard protocols within the unit.	2. Coordinates and evaluates standard protocols throughout the service.
3. Individualizes case management plans for specific patients.	3. Monitors case management plans for all patients within a unit.	3. Develops and coordinates case management plans for entire service.

attention given to maintaining patients on their projected hospital courses. In addition, as bedside caregivers, these nurses identify variances from the standard protocols and work with other health care team members to resolve these variances.

Nurses who have unit focus (Level V on the clinical ladder) are responsible for developing standard protocols for the patient types most frequently seen on their units. Most of these clinicians provide some direct patient care and consult on a large number of patients with special needs. These nurses are responsible for monitoring case management as it is used in their units. In other words, they are given the task of ensuring that the principles of case management (i.e., proper allocation of resources, efficiency of care, and cost containment) guide the care that is delivered to all patients on their units.

Clinical nurse specialists (Level VI on the clinical ladder) have a servicewide focus. It is their charge to follow patients as they move through the health care system. Clinical nurse specialists develop and define case management, with an emphasis on the achievement of patient outcomes in a timely fashion. They also have the responsibility of coordinating all the health care team members within the services so that patient movement through the units is both efficient and effective.

There are wide variations in staff mix among units. Some units have all RNs, and the case manager directs and coordinates the care delivered by staff nurse Is and IIs assigned as primary nurses. Other units have a high

---

Exhibit 17-2 Staffing for an Orthopedic Trauma Unit

7–3 shift	*Caseload A—13 patients* 1 case manager assigned 1 patient 2 licensed associates assigned 6 patients each
	Caseload B—13 patients 1 case manager assigned 1 patient 2 licensed associates assigned 6 patients each (12 PM–8;30 PM—1 RN assessment QA coordinator)
3–11 shift	1 charge nurse assigned 2 patients 4 licensed associates assigned 6 patients each
11–7 shift	1 charge nurse assigned 8 patients 2 licensed associates assigned 9 patients each 1 nurse attendant

percentage of LVNs and patient care technicians, and the case manager then works through nurse extenders. Exhibit 17-2 presents an example of a 32-bed orthopedic trauma unit that is organized in this manner.

IMPLEMENTATION

Establishment of the case management program was achieved on a minimal basis in 12 to 18 months through the dedicated and coordinated efforts of nurse management, hospital education, and clinical nurse specialists. However, maximum utilization will require another year.

The first attempt at case management was the reorganization of an orthopedic unit to pilot a program using RNs as case managers. The success of this model prompted the promotion of these nurses on the clinical ladder in recognition of their value. Shortly thereafter, the utility of having standard protocols for these managers became apparent, and the first major steps toward program development were taken.

This push for standard protocols coincided with the budget preparation for the new fiscal year, so a task force of clinical directors was formed to monitor this process and to determine its effect on the organization. Involvement of Laboratory, Radiology, Pharmacy, Dietary, and Respiratory Therapy became a vital part of the review procedure for the protocols to ensure appropriate utilization of the resources of these departments.

The next step involved collaboration with Hospital Education to begin inservicing nursing and support services. In addition to the usual strategies, a unique format was devised to stage a "lost cost roundup." Drawing attention to the necessity of providing cost-conscious health care was the goal of this employee activity, which marked the official beginning of managed care at Hermann Hospital.

Placement of protocols on the patients' charts, with utilization monitored by the case manager, was then finally achieved. However, refinement, development, and the identification of new areas for utilization produce ongoing changes in the program.

COST OF IMPLEMENTATION

Financially, case management required a minimal investment in the form of salary increases and nursing time commitment. Since the clinical ladder was the basis for assignment of case management responsibility, the salary cost was a 5% increase per grade level for approximately 100 nurses. No additional personnel were hired. Nursing hours invested in the development of the participative case management model included (1) the time needed to develop and write the standard protocols, (2) orientation time needed to educate staff, and (3) frequent meetings for clinical nurse specialists to monitor progress.

However, this was offset in part by the savings on nursing units that introduced nurse extenders into their case management system instead of using pure primary nursing (see Tables 17-1 and 17-2).

EVALUATION

Evaluation of this model is based on three factors: (1) quality of patient care delivered, (2) cost-effectiveness of the care, and (3) satisfaction of the nursing staff with the system. The original expectations as described for the initial pilot program aptly state the evaluation criteria:

1. The patient shall receive a quality of care equal to or exceeding minimum standards of care.
2. The patient shall receive treatment, as indicated, utilizing the multidisciplinary approach.
3. The patient shall express satisfaction that individual needs were attended to and met to mutual satisfaction.
4. The patient shall express understanding of his medical condition, follow-up instructions and appropriate community resources to assist meeting psychosocial and financial needs.
5. The patient shall be assessed and his care planned by an experienced RN trained in managing patients' care from admission to discharge.
6. Documentation of the nursing process shall be incorporated into the patient's legal records.

Table 17-1 Comparison of Primary Nursing and Case Management for One Unit

	Primary Nursing	Case Management
Total beds	32	32
Average daily census	26	26
Budgeted hours of care	4.4	4.4
Total patient days	9490	9490
Caregiver FTEs	22.5	22.5
Total FTEs	22.5[a]	26

[a]Head nurse current 0.5.

Table 17-2 Comparison of Annualized Salaries on One Unit

	Primary Nursing		Case Management	
	No. of Employees	Total Amount	No. of Employees	Total Amount
Category (midpoint)				
RN VI (17.79)	1	$ 37,003.20	1	$ 37,003.20
RN IV (13.74)	3	85,737.60	6	171,475.20
RN III (12.70)	3	82,842.10	—	—
RN II (12.12)	10	252,096.00	7	176,467.20
LVN II (8.03)	6	111,446.40	7.5	139,308.00
Patient care technician (5.50)	—	—	2	22,880.00
Unit secretary (6.07)	2.5	31,564.00	2.5	31,564.99
Net salary		600,689.30		578,697.00
6% FICA		36,041.36		34,721.86
Gross salary		636,730.56		613,419.46[a]
Labor Cost per Patient Day		67.09		64.64[b]

[a]Total annualized salary savings = $21,991.70.
[b]Budget labor cost per patient day = $65.86.

7. Evaluation of implementation and subsequent revision of the plan of care shall be continuous and documented per legal guidelines and policy and procedure.

8. The nurse shall express job satisfaction as it relates to meeting patient needs in a timely fashion.

9. Associate care givers shall express job satisfaction as it relates to continuity of care through assignments and availability of clinical resource personnel.

10. The cost of meeting these objectives shall remain within budgetary restraints.

One method for determining whether these criteria have been met is to perform quality assurance audits on sample charts to monitor patient care, as described earlier.

To establish cost-effectiveness, patient charges and length of stay are examined to estimate the variance on specific patient types. The comparison is between data from the year prior to and the year following full implementation of the system. On a short-term basis, support departments (Laboratory and Pharmacy) are monitoring utilization of their services to document utilization trends.

The final evaluation measure is the satisfaction of staff—both nursing and medical—with the process. Initial reports are very positive from nursing, as shown by the following list of advantages noted by the staff.

1. The essence of the philosophy of primary nursing, where one coordinates, directs and evaluates the plan of care from admission to discharge, was upheld.
2. The case manager is always available to present a caseload for multidisciplinary discharge planning meetings.
3. The team approach encourages utilization of peers as resources and offers a system of checks and balances to assure priorities are met. There is increased interaction among the staff, creating an environment that encourages good communication.
4. These models allow for a change in staff mix while maintaining quality of care, a critical factor with the RN shortage and regulatory constraints.

Nursing staff satisfaction can be validated by the annual nursing satisfaction survey next year. Since medical staff satisfaction is more difficult to measure objectively, the continued support of physicians and their continued participation in the program will be taken to indicate their satisfaction.

SUMMARY

In a determined effort to meet the demands of today's health care industry, Hermann Hospital has implemented a case management system that affords the opportunity to provide cost-effective care while improving quality. The combination of case management and primary nursing, which yielded the new nursing care delivery system, promises to retain the benefits of direct interaction with the patient and to open a new vista of fiscal responsibility for the RN.

REFERENCES

National Commission on Nursing Implementation Project. (1988). *Features of high quality, cost-effective nursing care delivery systems of the future.* Milwaukee, WI: Author.

Taylor, S., Walts, L., Amling, J., & Cavouras, C. (1988, December). Clinical ladders: Rewarding clinical excellence. *American Nephrology Nurses Association Journal,* pp. 331–334.

Weeks, L.C., & Vestal, K.W. (1983, December). PACE: A unique career development program. *Journal of Nursing Administration,* pp. 29–32.

Zander, K. (1985). Second generation primary nursing: A new agenda. *Journal of Nursing Administration, 15*(3), 18–24.

Part II

Adjuncts to Patient Care Delivery Models

Underlying the search for effective models for delivering patient care are several questions. What can be done to better match people and their work so that organizational productivity and the quality of the work experience are enhanced? How can we achieve a better fit between what people want from work and what they get? How can we increase the congruence between what people are asked to do and what they are willing and able to do? How can we create conditions that will support professional practice?

In the first part, contributors addressed the selection and training of nurses to fit into new nursing roles. This part is concerned with individual-organization relationships and how they affect the work environment. The ideal is to make each organization a place where people grow and flourish, where they have the information and power to get things done, and where the incentive or motivation to do work augments it.

The first contribution deals with reward contingencies. It presents a way of paying nurses that enhances professionalism and aligns performance with organizational and unit goals. Employees have a piece of the action by sharing in organizational rewards and risks. The program described here is sensitive to performance changes, unlike most career ladders, where people may go up but rarely step down. This innovative program deserves serious attention by those who are making and stabilizing substantive changes in patient care delivery.

The second and third contributions look at the issue of managing the information required for clinical and management decisions. Having the necessary information is one thing, but having it in the form needed and providing it to the appropriate person at the critical time is another. What is pertinent to one person may be irrelevant to another.

We believe that work contexts play a key role in the evolution of models of professional practice. We recognize that the kind of technology that will assist nurses and change the workplace is still in early stages of development. However, the impact of such technology is potentially so great we felt it was important to discuss it in this book. We believe that an awareness of evolving technology offers new options as we design for the future.

Chapter 18

Compensation for Professional Practice: An Incentive Model

Eunice Lawrenz and Gloria Gilbert Mayer

This chapter describes a unique method for compensation that can be adapted to all patient care delivery systems. Although patient care delivery systems are modified routinely, nurses are still rewarded by traditional means. Pay-for-performance systems provide a method of creating a gain share, increasing productivity, and compensating nurses for work done rather than time.

Compensation plans are key in restructuring the workload in nursing. The voices of potential nurses choosing not to enter the profession, trusted nurses leaving the profession, and nurses maintaining their commitment to patients are being heard. Work is being redesigned and restructured and professional practice is strong. But are the compensation systems keeping pace? Are incentives to support professional practice well designed? The connection between compensation and work restructuring is critical and tricky. Connecting pay to performance offers a way to balance and optimize change in nursing and in health care organizations today.

More health care organizations are using incentive plans to motivate and reward key executives. The successful plans build on business goals and tap into the entrepreneurial spirit that wants a "piece of the action." Richard Schmidt, CEO at Kenosha Hospital, describes a pay-for-performance system that is tied to the hospital's operating margin. He states that "performance pay is tied to the hospital's success. That changes the way people think." But can incentive plans be brought to the bedside nurse? We believe they can and must.

This book describes how some organizations have restructured the workload and how some innovations in nursing look in practice. Few of the contributors address innovations in compensation practices.

This chapter looks at issues in nurse compensation, describes commonly used plans, and presents information about Enterprise Healthcare, a performance pay system in which nurses share in the business risk and are given opportunities for greater ownership and pay as the business flourishes.

ISSUES IN NURSE COMPENSATION

Nursing salaries have generally increased over the past 10 years, and some nurse executives participate in bonus or executive incentive plans. But although salaries have increased in most instances, the methods of compensation have not changed much.

One exception is a profit-sharing program that is part of the Johns Hopkins model described in Chapter 5. In this model, patient care units operate as business entities, with each unit responsible for scheduling and staff replacement regardless of census and acuity. This approach links responsibility and accountability and builds ownership among staff.

Career ladders mentioned in several of the chapters are enjoying a resurgence of interest in the face of nurse shortages and a desire to retain top performers. They range from sophisticated and measurable programs to some that function as performance review systems. In some instances, the ladder rewards knowledge, but the more sophisticated ladders reward performance. However, one of the difficulties with career ladders as currently used is that there is no assurance that patient care results will improve or that costs will be reduced. In fact, costs may actually increase, since nurses tend to move up the ladder but rarely move down. Nor are career ladders sensitive to census fluctuations.

Nursing has never been more ready than today for a significant change in compensation that would allow nurses who have shared in organizational risk and increased organizational productivity and profitability to share in the rewards. This readiness stems from the positive effects of the women's movement, the shift in worker values (from wanting to be paid for time to wanting to participate more actively), and the strengthening of professional practice.

COMPENSATION PLANS

Generally organizations pay for time. If you come to work and put in your time, you get paid. If you leave early, you get paid less; if you stay longer, you get paid more. When an organization pays for time, it gets time. This system ensures that there will be someone working, but it does not by itself foster investment in the organization or its goals. In fact, nurses who are invested in patients and families are often less committed to the overall organization.

Selecting a compensation method other than the current one requires a review of other ways to pay employees. Joseph Scanlon (Frost, 1982) is credited with the first successful innovation in employee compensation. As a union president during the Depression, he tried to get the union to work cooperatively with a failing industry by introducing a scheme for gathering worker suggestions for productivity improvement and putting them into effect. With the company's survival, employee wages increased.

Two central features of the Scanlon plan are (1) cost-reduction sharing (gain sharing) and (2) effective participation. Cost-reduction sharing is not a substitute for competitive wages but is used in addition. Douglas McGregor (1960) used Scanlon's work and pointed out that "the distinguishing feature of the Scanlon Plan is the coupling of this incentive with a second feature, a formal method providing an opportunity for every member of the organization to contribute his brains and ingenuity as well as his physical effort to the improvement of organizational effectiveness."

These two features drive most compensation plans used in addition to or instead of paying for time. In fact, a survey by the Public Agenda Foundation found no link between pay and performance. Employees paid for time often do not associate salary with productivity or profit.

Table 18-1 summarizes some of the common compensation plans that do not use salaries or hourly wages.

Effective compensation plans help align management and staff in working toward organization goals. Successful plans—those that are acceptable to management and employees and that reward individual performance and teamwork—will allow the following questions to be answered affirmatively:

- Does the plan increase or maintain quality and service while decreasing costs?
- Does the plan pay for itself?
- Are outputs measured objectively?
- Are incentive pay and base salary separated so that the individual recognizes which is pay for time and which is incentive?
- Is the incentive offered for individual performance and teamwork?
- Does the employee receive the incentive pay frequently enough to maintain momentum?
- Does the incentive do what it was intended to do, namely, maximize productivity, reward and retain top employees, and increase teamwork?

Most compensation plans are intended to allow affirmative answers to these questions. An organization with a successful plan finds that employees are invested in the organization and its goals. Employees devise new ways to restructure work, and top performers are not only retained but attracted.

Table 18-1 Alternative Compensation Plans

Type of Plan	How It Works
Profit Sharing	Employees receive a varying annual bonus. Distribution of profits are often based on total compensation each employee earns. Profit sharing is usually paid in addition to conventional compensation rather than as a substitute. The plan is used only if there are sufficient profits. Giving an annual bonus payment may lead employees to ignore long-term performance, and factors beyond the control of employees often affect profits.
Gain Sharing	Gain share payments reflect cost savings and can be paid out annually, quarterly, or monthly. Gain share plans typically occur at the unit or departmental level rather than at the organizational level, unlike profit sharing. The plans are usually computed on cost savings of some base level or on the percentage of the goal that the unit is to achieve. Each unit will have performance targets. For instance, a certain cost per patient day may be a target. When reduced, the employees would share in some of the savings. Gain share plans can enhance coordination and team work, but they often have a limited cycle, which usually forces companies to terminate them at some point. The plans may focus only on productivity and could lead employees to ignore other important objectives, such as quality.
Bonus Plans	Bonus plans differ from profit sharing and gain sharing in that the participants do not know the distribution method in advance. The plans are used at the management's discretion.
Pay for Knowledge	In a pay-for-knowledge plan, an employee's salary increases with the number of skills or the amount of knowledge learned regardless of the job performed. Career ladders sometimes fall into this category. Employees become generalists able to work in multiple areas. The organization operates with a leaner and more flexible staff, but labor costs will rise if all employees become generalists and there is no increase in business.
Incentive Plans	The employees know in advance the performance requirements and the incentive computation formula. Incentive plans are budgeted and do not require a certain percentage of profits or productivity. Usually these plans focus on performance and do not attempt to measure the entire job function. Rewards are usually paid on top of the salary.

ENTERPRISE HEALTHCARE

Enterprise Healthcare originated from an incentive plan developed for banking and other service industries by William Abernathy, President of Productivity Systems in Memphis, Tennessee (1987). He modified the plan for health care. Enterprise Healthcare combines organizational goals and employee strengths, and the results are:

- strong professional practice
- work restructuring
- entrepreneurial employees
- reduced costs
- improved patient service
- interdisciplinary collaboration
- retention of top performers

Enterprise Healthcare differs from other health care incentive plans by the fact that it is based on specific identifiable outputs related to service to patients. Each patient or work unit identifies outputs for which incentive pay is available. These vary depending on unit and organizational goals and can be adjusted on a regular basis. Outputs often are built around numbers of patients cared for, service and quality of care, mentoring and caseload management, interdisciplinary goals, and entrepreneurial activity.

Employees are on a salary first and on incentive pay second. The latter is variable and can fluctuate weekly or monthly. For example, with a high patient census and high acuity, there is more opportunity for incentive pay. Conversely, when the workload on a unit is less than usual, there are fewer opportunities for incentive pay. Employees share in the risks of the organization while maintaining a salary base.

Nurses themselves define an expected or typical workload for professional practice. Those who exceed it earn incentive pay. Nurses who choose to handle less may earn less incentive pay, but the salary remains stable. This is particularly attractive to nurses who have left the bedside because of an inability to handle the pressures or workload. Enterprise Healthcare offers a new way to bring back into nursing the seasoned nurse, the person whose strengths are often lost to bedside nursing.

Funding for Enterprise Healthcare comes from savings in budgeted expenses. This assures management that the plan will fund itself. As Enterprise Healthcare grows, the environment changes. Professional practice is enhanced, because nurses experience a direct relationship between practice and rewards. Employees align with corporate goals as they share in financial risks and benefits. Work is restructured so that what needs to be done by nurses is being done by them. Hours of care may be reduced and the ratios of caregivers may be changed while still maintaining quality. The role of the manager changes to the role of coach, and interdisciplinary teamwork becomes the norm.

Enterprise Healthcare impacts the total organization. Incentive pay when offered to all employees builds collaborative teams. News of cost savings and incentive pay in one department spreads rapidly, which results in collective efforts to share in the rewards. The plan assists the total organization to achieve five distinct benefits:

1. *Increased productivity:* When an organization pays for time, it gets time. Time-based compensation encourages employees to pace their work to fill the day. Performance pay rewards results rather than time spent on the job.

2. *Increased performance and job satisfaction:* Research finds an average 30% improvement in employee performance when individual performance pay is introduced in an organization. Restoring the lost connection between personal effort and reward revitalizes each employee's sense of personal accomplishment.

3. *Variable compensation under present systems:* Salary expense grows at a compound rate regardless of the organization's economic success. Business downturns force layoffs. Performance pay varies with opportunity and automatically adjusts compensation to the business cycle.

4. *Less supervision:* When productivity improvement is in the best interest of the employee, the need for direct supervision and staffing control is reduced.

5. *An entrepreneurial work environment:* Performance pay unleashes the personal initiative of employees, which is suppressed by hourly wages. Each employee, manager, and professional is "franchised" in his or her own business. The result is a lean, flexible, aggressive organization that can respond quickly to new challenges.

SUMMARY

Porter and Lawler (1968) suggest that managers should develop flexible compensation practices to create a favorable match between financial rewards and employee desires. It is critical that compensation for nurses and other employees supports the best patient care possible. When you pay for time, you get time; when you pay for results, you get results. Work restructuring requires new compensation systems. Nurses are changing the way they think. Instituting a well-designed incentive plan is a way of recognizing that people are an organization's best investment.

REFERENCES

Abernathy, W. (1987). *Enterprise performance manual.* Memphis: Productivity Development Systems.

Frost, C.F. (1982). The Scanlon plan at Hermann Miller Inc.: Managing an organization by innovation. In R. Zager & M.P. Rosow (Eds.), *The innovative organization: Programs in action* (pp. 63–87). New York: Pergamon.

McGregor, D. (1960). *The human side of enterprise.* New York: McGraw-Hill.

Porter, L.W., & Lawler, E.E., III. (1968). *Managerial attitudes and performance.* Homewood, IL: Irwin-Dorsey.

Chapter 19

Patient Classification and Management Information Systems as Adjuncts to Patient Care Delivery

Sandra Edwardson, James Bahr, and Mary Serote

Although patient classification systems have been around for several years, there are repeated grumblings that, instead of being accurate tools, they are systems to be manipulated—because in fact they do not manage information accurately. This chapter looks at what can be expected from a management information system. The authors describe how one system (ARIC) offers the flexibility required for varying patient situations and models of professional practice and how current trends and needs can be reflected in patient classification. The authors show how ARIC specifically fits with several of the models presented in Part I.

Management information systems have become important tools for nursing managers. When well constructed, an information system gives the manager a method for collecting, storing, retrieving, and processing raw data so that they can be transformed into information useful in making management decisions. Such information is essential for documenting and maintaining the efficiency and effectiveness of nursing care in whatever the model of care.

Among the first information systems developed for managing nursing care in the acute setting were patient classification systems for measuring nursing workload. The primary purpose of patient classification is to predict the variable demand for nursing care and thus be able to schedule and monitor the use of nursing staff. As the name implies, patient classification groups patients with respect to some characteristic—in this case, their need for nursing care. The goal is to categorize patients so that those within a group require approximately the same type and amount of care as each other and a significantly different type and amount of care than members of other groups.

Because the needs of acute care patients may change on an hourly basis, patients are classified from one to three times per day. Needless to say, this generates a large number of data that are useful to the manager only if they can be gathered, analyzed, and reported in a usable form quickly and accurately.

Although the first patient classification systems were not automated, most systems now rely on computers to save time, improve accuracy, and increase the usefulness of data gathered about patient care requirements. The first generation of these computerized systems were dedicated to patient classification only and did not interface with admission, discharge and transfer, fiscal, and staffing databases.

An important question in considering a nursing information system is the extent to which the system can be modified to adapt to evolving methods of care and organizational structures. Most patient classification systems are built on three assumptions. The first assumption is that patients are assigned to a unit and stay there for most of their stay, or at least for whole days or shifts at a time. This assumption is increasingly challengeable. The development of specialized units has led to frequent transfers of patients as their needs change. Patients are spending increasing amounts of time in diagnostic and therapeutic laboratories away from the home unit. In addition, acute care beds are now being used for same-day surgery patients and for outpatient therapies such as burn debridement and dressing. Unless these movements of patients in and out of the unit are understood and measured, they can have a major impact on the validity of the workload measurement system.

A second assumption of most patient classification systems is that all caregivers are assigned to specific patient care units and spend their working hours there. The assumption that nurses do not move has, until now, been reasonable, because most acute nursing services have been (and continue to be) organized in this way. Some of the models presented in this volume, however, raise the possibility that nurses providing direct and indirect patient care may not be based in a single unit.

In the case management models, for example, a case manager is responsible for the plan of care throughout a patient's entire hospital stay. This entails that the case manager will be involved in the care as the patient moves from unit to unit. Furthermore, although the case managers in the Hermann Hospital and ProACT models appear to be unit-based, it is perfectly possible that a hospital may want to have case managers who serve several units.

The possibility that unit-based case managers are involved with patients located on other units or that case managers are not unit-based presents two challenges for patient classification systems. The time case managers spend in providing services to patients on units to which they are not assigned should be accounted for in order to make accurate time estimates for staffing purposes and correct estimates of resource use for cost accounting purposes.

A final assumption of most patient classification systems is that unit staff members provide all of the required care. The cooperative care models of New York University Medical Center and Vanderbilt University Medical Center challenge that assumption, because patients and their families are expected to participate in both the planning and execution of care. Any patient classification system should, therefore, be designed to adapt to these and similar models of care and changes in practice.

After describing the development and characteristics of a particular patient classification and nursing information system (the ARIC system), several innovations aimed at solving common information problems in nursing are described. The chapter closes with a consideration of the ARIC system for various models and settings of care.

THE ARIC SYSTEM*

The Allocation, Resource Identification and Costing (ARIC) system combines patient classification with a nursing management information system to address some of the deficiencies of existing patient classification systems. The system grew out of the work of James Bahr and Mary Serote in the late 1970s at Catherine McAuley Health Center of the Sisters of Mercy Health Corporation.

As is usually the case when a hospital undertakes a patient classification study, the existing classification system was evaluated and found to have problems in reliability and in its ability to predict future nursing care needs. Among the purported problems were (1) the inability of the systems to reflect adequately all the care given or needed, (2) their inability to reflect the highly variable amount of education and psychosocial support needed by a patient and family, and (3) their failure to account for the fact that patients were not on the unit during the entire shift. The developers knew that the amount of care patients receive on the shift might be affected by time of admission and discharge as well as by time spent in surgery, the x-ray unit, or the laboratory. Patients who were only on the unit for short stays might not be counted at all. To address these concerns a new approach to patient classification, the age stratified method for estimating care (ASMEC), was developed (Donaho et al., 1984). Subsequently, James Bahr modified ASMEC and added its current database management features to create the ARIC system.

As a second generation system for patient classification, the ARIC system introduced several innovations to the field. It integrates patient classification with an information system that includes admission, discharge,

---

*The ARIC system is a proprietary system owned by JBA Ltd. A patent application has been filed with the U.S. Patent Office.

and transfer data as well as information about the facility and nursing staff. Run on a personal computer, the system can also be interfaced with some mainframe computers so that clinical and demographic data about patients can be linked to information about their need for and consumption of nursing care.

PATIENT CLASSIFICATION IN THE ARIC SYSTEM

The approach to patient classification used in the ARIC system recognizes that nursing care in acute care settings derives from two sources: physician orders and hospital policies (dependent activities) and the professional judgments of nurses (independent activities). These two sources of the nursing workload are evaluated separately to determine the total amount of time required to care for patients.

During the implementation phase, dependent care activities are determined using the factor-evaluation approach. The nurse classifying patients reviews a list of possible physician orders organized into eight major care components and prioritized by labor intensity. The first step in classifying a patient is to identify the dependent type that best reflects the patient's care needs. The classifier marks on a form the two most labor-intensive orders in each major component applicable to each patient. The form can be read by an optical scanning device. These data are then analyzed to identify the subset of orders that are most critical for predicting the nursing care requirements for patients on a specific unit. As illustrated in Figure 19-1, these most important predictors become the critical indicators used to develop a prototype statement describing the care requirements of up to seven types or categories of patients. Type A patients have dependent care requirements that require the least amount of time whereas those of Type G patients require the most amount of time. An example of a typical classification instrument for a medical unit is shown in Exhibit 19-1.

Once patients are classified for the dependent portion of the care needs, the second step in classification is to evaluate independent nursing care requirements. Independent care requirements are defined as those activities prescribed by nurses in direct response to their assessment of patient needs. Examples include teaching, providing support to patients and families, initiating therapeutic and comfort measures, providing coordination and referral services, and so on. The person classifying patients retrospectively estimates the time that was required for those activities during the shift and places the patient in one of five groups. These groups range from Care Code V, representing very low independent nursing needs (0–15 minutes), to Care Code X, representing extremely high needs (more than two hours).

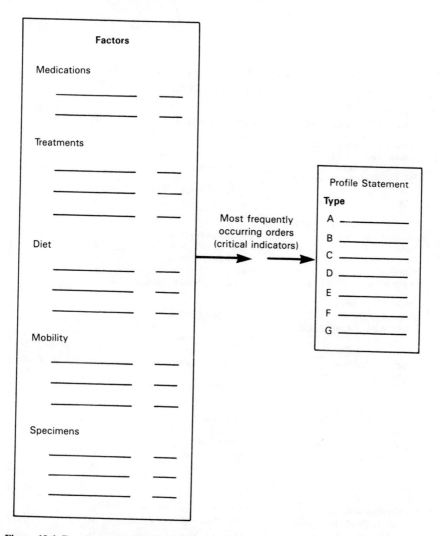

Figure 19-1 Development of the ARIC Prototype Descriptions

The dependent and independent care categories are then combined to determine each patient's classification (see Exhibit 19-2). As indicated in Exhibit 19-3, a patient with very low dependent and independent nursing care requirements will fall into Class 1, whereas a patient with very high dependent or independent requirements will fall into one of the highest categories regardless of the rating on the other component.

Exhibit 19-1 Sample Classification Instrument for a Medical Unit

ARIC CLASSIFICATION INSTRUMENT
Medicine: 6100M

STEP 1 DEPENDENT DESCRIPTION	STEP 2 INDEPENDENT NEEDS	CODE	STEP 3 CLASS
Type A 0.75 Hours (0–99 Hrs)			
Intake/Output Q 8 Hr	1. Very Low (0–15 mins)	V	1
Vital Signs Q Shift	2. Low (16–30 mins)	L	2
Routine Meds 1–3 Doses	3. Mod (31–60 mins)	M	3
	4. High (1–2 hours)	H	3
	5. Extremely High (>2 hours)	X	4
Type B 1.5 Hours (1.0–1.99 Hrs)			
Intake/Output Q 8 Hrs	1. Very Low (0–15 mins)	V	3
Vital Signs Q Shift	2. Low (16–30 mins)	L	3
Routine Meds 4–8 Doses	3. Mod (31–60 mins)	M	3
Mouth Care	4. High (1–2 hours)	H	4
Chair W/Assistance/Dangle	5. Extremely High (>2 hours)	X	4
Type C 2.5 Hours (2.0–2.99 Hrs)			
Vital Signs Q 8 Hr	1. Very Low (0–15 mins)	V	4
Routine PO, IM SubQ Meds 1–3 Doses	2. Low (16–30 mins)	L	4
Intake/Output Q 8 Hr	3. Mod (31–60 mins)	M	4
Egg Crate Mattress	4. High (1–2 hours)	H	4
IV/IV Drip/Prep/Maint. 1–4 Liters	5. Extremely High (>2 hours)	X	4
Type D 3. 5 Hours (3.0–3.99 Hrs)			
Intake/Output Q 8 Hrs	1. Very Low (0–15 mins)	V	4
Vital Signs × 2	2. Low (16–30 mins)	L	4
Routine Meds 4–8 Doses	3. Mod (31–60 mins)	M	4
Mouth Care	4. High (1–2 hours)	H	5
Flat in Bed/Log Roll	5. Extremely High (>2 hours)	X	5
Type E 4.5 Hours (4.0–4.99 Hrs)			
Vital Signs Q 1 H × 8/Shift	1. Very Low (0–15 mins)	V	5
Intake/Output Q 8 Hr	2. Low (16–30 mins)	L	5
Transfuse Blood (1–2 Units)	3. Mod (31–60 mins)	M	5
Routine Meds 4–8 Doses	4. High (1–2 hours)	H	5
Mouth Care	5. Extremely High (>2 hours)	X	5
O₂ SU per Cannula/Mask			
Flat in Bed/Log Roll			

Exhibit 19-2 Steps in Classifying Patients

Step 1	Step 2	Step 3
Determine dependent care requirements	Determine independent care requirements	Combine estimates of dependent and independent care requirements
Type	Code	Class
A	V	1
B	L	2
C	M	3
D	H	4
E	X	5
F		
G		

NURSING DATABASE MANAGEMENT SYSTEMS

The ARIC system includes a comprehensive computerized database (see Exhibit 19-4 for a complete list of data elements included in the database). In addition to the workload information derived from the patient classification component of the system, the database includes patient, staffing, performance, and cost information. Patient data such as admission, dis-

Exhibit 19-3 Patient Classification for Different Combinations of Dependent and Independent Care Categories

		Dependent Care Category						
		A	B	C	D	E	F	G
	V	1	3	4	4	5	5	6
Independent	L	2	3	4	4	5	5	6
Care	M	3	3	4	4	5	5	6
Category	H	3	4	4	5	5	6	6
	X	4	4	4	5	5	6	6

Exhibit 19-4 Key Data Elements From the ARIC Patient Classification and Nursing
Database Management System

ARIC gives the nursing department a very extensive ad hoc reporting and sorting
capability with its powerful database manager. The user can virtually build an unlimited
array of combinations using any of the following key data elements. Over forty of the
more than seventy distinct data elements stored by ARIC are listed below:

Patient ID, Location and Chronological Data:

1. Patient name
2. Patient number
3. Patient room and bed number
4. Patient age
5. Patient sex
6. Patient's admission date
7. Type of admission, i.e., ER, from ICU, elective, etc.
8. Time of admission
9. Day of stay
10. Length of stay
11. Type of day, i.e., regular care day, operative day, treatment day, or discharge
    day
12. Time of transfer
13. Destination of transfer
14. Time of discharge
15. Type of discharge
16. Destination code associated with treatment, i.e., x-ray, rehab

Clinical Data:

17. Doctor number
18. DRG number
19. ICD-9 number
20. Nursing diagnosis

Classification Data:

21. Patient classification code by day of stay
22. Patient dependent nursing care hour requirement by shift and day of stay
23. Patient independent nursing care hour requirement by shift and day of stay
24. Total patient care requirements by shift and day of stay
25. Determination of whether patient classification code was factor-based or pro-
    file (prototype) based
26. Staff (caregiver) who performed independent nursing assessment, by patient,
    by shift, and day of stay
27. Staff member who was patient classification-code rater by shift and day of
    stay

Staffing Data:

28. Worked hours by caregiver by day and shift
29. Caregiver(s) ID number(s)
30. Caregiver name
31. Caregiver(s) skill level(s)
32. Caregiver home unit
33. Unit staff function by day and shift, i.e., Head Nurse, Charge Nurse, Clinical
    Specialist, Staff RN Caregiver, etc.

Exhibit 19-4 continued

34. Nursing cost center number(s) where caregiver worked during day and shift
35. Worked hours by caregiver by day, unit(s), and shift

Service and Performance Data:

36. Accompaniment or nonaccompaniment by nursing during patient transports
37. Whether staff member worked through lunch
38. Unit service level provided to patients by day and shift
39. Amount of staff which exceeded total unit requirements for hospital specified service levels by shift and day of week
40. Worked hour to care hour ratios by unit and pay periods
41. Paid hour to care hour ratios by unit and pay period

Cost Data:

42. Unit nursing care cost by patient and day of stay
43. Department nursing care cost by patient and day of stay
44. Unit nursing care cost by patient and hospital stay
45. Department nursing care cost by patient and hospital stay

Below is an abridged list of important system files which can be maintained and updated by the nursing department on a regular or periodic basis. This open characteristic of the ARIC software insures that the nursing department is in control of maintaining and updating its classification system.

1. Cost center number
2. Bed and room numbers by cost center number
3. Standard or normal time by physician order (by dependent nursing activity), i.e., factor values
4. Expected care time by independent nursing care category
5. Forecasting coefficient by classification level, by unit and shift
6. Pay rate by skill level or job code
7. Retrospective dependent nursing care hour requirement by patient classification level by shift
8. Retrospective independent nursing care hour requirement by acuity level by shift
9. Allowance rates for fixed activities and personal, delay and fatigue periods
10. Shift starting and ending times
11. Other personnel management data files

charge, and transfer dates, times, and destinations; age; sex; physician name; diagnostic codes; and patient classification information are stored for individual patients. The name, payroll identification number, skill level, work schedule, caregiving hours, and patient and unit assignments are recorded for each person providing direct patient care. The nurse who classified patients and the average salary costs for categories of personnel are also stored in the database. These data are used to assign care hours to patients and to calculate staffing needs, unit performance indicators (e.g., service levels and targeted or actual staffing ratios), and patient-specific nursing care costs. In addition, there are several blank fields that users may define to meet their own unique needs.

Increasingly, nursing departments are interested in incorporating elements of the Nursing Minimum Data Set (NMDS) into their recordkeeping. The NMDS has been developed to allow nursing organizations to provide a set of data that is uniform in nature and content and therefore compatible with the data sets of other nursing care facilities (Devine & Werley, 1988). Similar to the Uniform Hospital Discharge Data Set, the NMDS facilitates research, education, and clinical practice by providing comparable data from a variety of settings and geographic locations (Devine, 1987; Maibusch, 1988; McCloskey, 1988).

With minor additions, the database of the ARIC system can incorporate most of the elements identified for inclusion in the NMDS (Werley & Zorn, 1988). The NMDS includes three sets of data: demographic elements, service elements, and nursing care elements. All but three of the demographic and service elements are built into the database. (These include the patient's personal identification number, date of birth, sex, unique facility number, unique patient record number, unique number of principal RN providers, admission and discharge dates, and disposition.) The three missing elements (patient residence, race and ethnicity, and payer) can be added easily if the user wishes.

The nursing care elements of the NMDS include nursing diagnosis, nursing intervention, nursing outcome, and intensity of care. The workload measure resulting from ARIC's patient classification system is an excellent measure of intensity of care. Including the other nursing care elements of the NMDS is more complex, because the discipline has yet to agree on taxonomies for those data elements. Several nursing diagnosis taxonomies have emerged. The ARIC system has built-in data fields for medical diagnoses (ICD-9 codes) and diagnosis-related groups (DRGs). Nursing diagnoses can be substituted for ICD-9 codes or can be entered as additional data in one of several reserved fields available for such purposes. As soon as taxonomies for nursing interventions and outcomes are developed, codes for these data elements could also be added.

Although discipline has not yet reached a consensus on how all of the nursing care data elements can and should be measured, the ARIC database can provide valuable information nonetheless. Because the database captures dependent and independent care requirements for each patient and each shift, the user can analyze the type and quantity of care consumed by patients with different nursing and medical diagnoses and at different times throughout patient stays.

UNIQUE FEATURES OF THE ARIC SYSTEM

Because ARIC combines patient classification and nursing information systems, it is possible to solve several common problems and address important needs in developing and maintaining patient classification systems. The system's features include precision of measurement, user maintenance of reliability and validity, staffing efficiency evaluation, patient-specific cost identification, and flexible budgeting and budget simulation. The system also has the ability to produce both standard and customized reports and to answer unique operation and research questions.

Precision of Measurement

By using statistical modeling capabilities currently available for personal computers, the system is thought to provide precise measurements. Patients are classified after care has been given based on the amount of dependent and independent care *required* rather than the amount actually received. This retrospective measurement of the patient's classification is entered into a statistical formula, along with unit-specific historical data and standard weights for the patient's care category. The product of this calculation is a prospective estimate of the time required to provide care on the next shift. As new patients are classified, the retrospective information about them is added to the historical database and is used to update the standard weights used to calculate care requirements prospectively. This results in a very low absolute error of measurement (5% to 8%).

The system also recognizes that patients are not on the unit at all times. It records the time of admission and discharge or transfer and uses this information in retrospective workload calculations and prospective estimates. It also corrects for time spent in surgery and diagnostic and therapeutic departments if a nurse is not in attendance.

Maintenance of Reliability and Validity by Users

Maintaining the reliability and validity of measurement is a necessity for all patient classification systems, because care and treatment innovations continually alter the care required. There are built-in mechanisms in ARIC to permit the user to maintain reliability and validity. Because classification data are patient- and personnel-specific, it is possible to pinpoint whether reduced reliability and validity are due to changes in patient characteristics or care practices or to inaccurate use of the instrument.

The interrater reliability of the dependent care portion of the classification instrument is estimated weekly through comparison with an alternate method. The caregiver classifies patients in the usual manner using the profile statement (classification instrument), while an expert rater completes the entire inventory of dependent nursing care activities used during the implementation phase to identify the critical indicators of dependent care. The workload estimates produced by the two methods are compared by calculating the ratio of the caregiver's estimate to the expert rater's estimate. If the ratio is not within the range from 0.90 to 1.10, then the manager investigates whether the problem is due to user error or to changes in the dependent requirements of patients. If the problem is user error, reeducation may be indicated. If the low agreement is due to changing dependent requirements, the dependent care descriptors may need to be changed using the same procedure that was employed during the installation of the system. The changes can be made by the user without outside consultation.

Reliability monitoring of the independent care portion of the instrument is based on a comparison of the classification done by nurses with the expected independent care requirements for patients in that category. These expected or normative values are established at the time the system is installed and are stored in the software. If the monitoring reveals a problem with reliability, one of the reports generated by the system (the Patient Class Assessment Average Report) can be examined to identify the unit, shift, or caregiver responsible for the variation. If all members of the unit and shift show a value outside the normal range, this usually indicates an unusual patient mix. If the unusual patient mix is temporary, nothing need be done. If the patient mix has changed permanently, the norms may need to be updated by performing a new regression analysis.

The patient classification instrument is validated during the implementation of the system using observational sampling. Two categories of time are measured: (1) variable time required per category of patient per unit and shift, and (2) fixed time per unit and shift. Variable care time is the time spent providing direct and indirect care to identifiable patients, whereas fixed time is the time spent in unit-related activities such as narcotic counts and personal activities such as meal breaks (Giovannetti, 1978).

After installation, validity of the system is measured by comparing the workload prediction made before a shift begins with the measurement of the workload that was actually required on that shift. By comparing the forecast of the number of staff required (prospective standard) to the actual number required, the predictive validity of the system is evaluated on an ongoing basis.

With the information provided, managers are able to update both the critical indicators and the staffing coefficients (time allocated to activities) as often as necessary. Given the rapid rate of change in health care, nursing departments sometimes find that, as the complexity of care increases, they must increase staffing levels to continue to meet their own quality standards. Conversely, technological changes or innovative nursing practices that reduce the time needed for nursing care may mean that staffing levels can be reduced without compromising quality.

Staffing Efficiency Evaluation

Most patient classification systems produce a measure of "productivity." Usually this measure is the ratio of the number of staff required to care for a group of patients (as estimated by the patient classification system) to the number of staff actually used (i.e., the proportion of required staff that were actually provided). Workload measurement methods used to develop patient classification systems can only quantify what actually happens on the nursing unit, not what should happen. Defined in this way, productivity is nothing more than the manager's ability to match staffing with currently accepted standards of care needs. The measure does not evaluate the adequacy of the staffing for producing satisfactory patient outcomes or the desired level of quality. It is analogous to a report that General Motors used a minimum number of workers to produce a car— without any information about whether the car will run.

There is currently considerable discussion in the nursing literature on the adequacy of evaluating only the efficiency of the delivery of nursing care (Jelinek & Dennis, 1976; Edwardson, 1986, 1988; Davis, Levine, & Sverha, 1986). Throughout the health care field there is a renewed interest in incorporating estimates of quality as well as quantity into measures of productivity. Rather than assuming that the current volume of service produces an acceptable level of quality, there is a need to demonstrate that the assumption is true.

Although many current measures of productivity are not capable of testing the assumption, information about how closely the actual staffing matched the required staffing is nonetheless important for efficient management of nursing services. Therefore, the ARIC system has introduced the term *service level* as a more accurate label for the concept. As shown in Table 19-1, the standard staffing report compares the actual and needed staffing levels and generates the service level percentage by computing the percentage of needed care that was actually provided. The system rejects the notion that more than the *required level of care* can be provided. Therefore, the service level percentage never exceeds 100%. Although in practice one could provide more *staffing* than is required according to the facility's care standards, this would represent an inefficient use of resources. Therefore, any staff provided over the number required are identified on the report as Staff Exceeding Workload.

Cost Identification

Since the introduction of prospective payment based on DRGs, nursing administrators have shown a heightened interest in identifying the cost of nursing care for specific groups of patients. According to a 1987 review of the literature, hospitals around the country have determined that the best way to do this is to use the workload data generated by patient classification systems used for staffing (Edwardson & Giovannetti, 1987). This same review discussed the importance of storing cost data on a patient-specific basis but found that most facilities were unable to do that because patient classification data were retained in aggregate form only. When information was kept on individual patients, it was typically recorded in the patients' clinical records, so that cost studies required expensive data abstracting from the charts of patients of interest (Edwardson & Giovannetti, 1987).

Because the ARIC system uses and stores patient-specific patient classification data, it permits users to calculate direct nursing costs for individual patients and for groups of patients. These groups might include patients in various DRGs, patients in specific units, or patients with various care needs. Patient-specific data are stored in the system for 4 weeks

Table 19-1 ARIC Staffing Report

	Needed	Actual	Service Level Percentage	Staff Exceeding Workload
Unit A	4.0	5.0	100%	1.0
Unit B	4.0	3.0	75	0.0
Unit C	4.0	4.0	100	0.0

following discharge and can then be transferred to a storage tape or disk for future studies.

Budget Development and Monitoring

Nursing managers long ago discovered the usefulness of patient classification data for budget development and monitoring. Historical information about the nursing care requirements of patients and how they vary from month to month provide the best clue as to what will be required in the future.

In addition to providing information on past experience, the ARIC system allows the nurse manager to simulate alternative budget hypotheses about the future. Not only can one estimate the effects of varying assumptions about expected patient days for the coming fiscal year, but historical information is used to provide a picture of how demand can be expected to vary from shift to shift and from one day of the week to the next. Furthermore, the system uses the concept of service level to estimate the effect of budget reductions on service level. In the process of simulation, the staffing levels are reduced by varying percentages to produce different service levels. With knowledge of fiscal targets and desired quality parameters for nursing services, nursing managers can select the budget configuration and related service level that best meets fiscal and quality goals.

ARIC also permits the facility to use flexible budgeting. The most common past practice has been to use fixed budgeting. In fixed budgeting, an annual budget is established using a single estimate of future census and nursing care requirements for the entire year. If the actual census or need for nursing care decreases during the budget year without commensurate reductions in the use of staff, more staffing is provided than necessary. On the other hand, if the actual census or need for care increases and the unit is staffed to meet the need, the unit will appear to be operating above its budget.

Recognizing how variable the demand for care can be in acute care hospitals, an increasing number of facilities have adopted flexible budgeting. Flexible budgeting allows the budgeted dollars to increase and decrease with demand for service. Each unit budget is divided into fixed and variable components. Fixed items, such as head nurse salaries, do not vary with census or care requirements. By contrast, flexible costs vary directly with the number of patients. They include budget items such as the salaries and fringe benefits of direct caregivers and the costs of supplies used.

The ARIC system uses flexible budgeting. At Catherine McAuley Health Center (CMHC), for example, the actual care hours provided are reported each month. They are then compared to budgeted care hours and variances are reported. If the care hour variance is positive, additional dollars are provided. If the variance is negative, budgeted dollars are reduced. Managers have a more accurate measure of how efficiently the unit is operating and how closely revenue can be expected to match expenses.

CMHC also uses a flexible staffing method in which each unit in a division has "fixed" staff. In addition, the units in the division have "flex" staff, who are unit-based personnel in a divisional float pool. The ARIC budget simulation is able to identify and use information about both the fixed and flex components of the nursing resource.

Experience has demonstrated that patient needs can fluctuate greatly among units within a division. The flex staff available on each unit are there to respond to these fluctuating needs. If service levels are low on some units and high on others, flex staff are reassigned to balance the workload among units. Since it is also known that nursing staff dislike being reassigned from their home unit to another unit, the divisional flex staff are assigned to units within the division based on the probability of each unit's use of the flex resources. In practice, this has minimized the need to move staff among units. When properly operated, this flexible staffing method allows efficient matching of nursing resources to patient needs.

Report Capabilities

A rich database is of little use unless the manager is able to retrieve information when necessary and in an understandable format. As already noted, ARIC produces reports that provide an audit trail that permits ongoing monitoring and correction of the reliability and validity of the patient classification portion of the system.

The system is also programmed to generate other standard reports that provide information for monitoring trends in patient characteristics and clinical practice. This information allows the nursing department to assess its staffing efficiency, identify its costs, and forecast future budgetary needs. In addition, the data can be used to create special reports needed to answer questions specific to that facility.

Unique Question Answering

In addition to answering staffing, efficiency, and budgeting questions common to all facilities, the ARIC system permits users to pose unique questions. For example, CMHC has recently implemented a new quality monitoring program that measures satisfaction with hospital services among patients, physicians, and nurses. The nursing staff is interested in comparing these satisfaction data with information about patient care requirements, staffing levels, and financial performance. By downloading information from the ARIC system to another program, graphs can be developed depicting financial, efficiency, and staffing adequacy indicators. These data can be used with the satisfaction data for statistical analyses and decision making about the delivery of nursing services.

Research Question Answering

The ARIC database also offers many benefits for research. Over a period of years, for example, the data can be used to track trends in clinical practice and nursing resource consumption. These trends can then be combined with data about societal, health care, and demographic trends to search for possible relationships or to test hypotheses.

At CMHC, for example, the Department of Anesthesiology conducted a pilot study on the use of epidural morphine with patients undergoing joint orthoplasty. The results were very successful in terms of pain management, but nurses on the orthopedic unit noted that these patients seemed to require significantly more nursing care. Because the ARIC system stores workload data for each patient, it is possible to test whether or not observations such as this are true.

When interfaced with a computerized clinical record system, the research possibilities increase even more. Clinical and demographic data about patients can be combined with nursing workload and staffing data to give the researcher the opportunity to study input, process, and outcome relationships. The availability of patient-specific dependent and independent nursing care data on a day-by-day and shift-by-shift basis permits unusually sophisticated studies.

RESOURCES REQUIRED TO USE ARIC

Personnel are required to enter patient and staff data on a shift-by-shift basis. In addition to data entry, the support staff maintain the database and pick up and deliver reports and forms used to classify patients. It is estimated that one FTE data entry person is required for each 250 patients.

Hardware requirements for inpatient services include a personal computer with 4 megabytes of random access memory, two 80-megabyte hard disk drives, one 350-character-per-second dot matrix printer, an 80287 math coprocessor, a 2400-baud modem, and a Scantron optical scanning device. In addition to the ARIC software, a standard operating system (PC DOS and Xenix), a relational database (Unify), and a statistical package (Systat) are needed.

Use of the ARIC system can realize significant savings. Because the system uses both ongoing classification data and stored data, such as recuperative rates and anticipated admissions, it is able to produce dynamic and significantly more accurate forecasts of personnel requirements. This precision made it possible for one midwestern hospital to realize savings of 10% to 15% (3 FTEs) for one unit.

Savings are also derived from better budgeting and better monitoring of performance. Using the service level concept to guide the allocation of budgeted staff, the nursing department can reduce the work force without compromising the targeted hours of care (service level percentage) delivered. The budget simulation feature allows the manager to identify the appropriate staff configuration and find the best possible outcome in service level that can be achieved with a given set of resources. The user can then monitor progress toward meeting this best performance goal. This can result in a 5% to 10% improvement in performance.

RANGE OF USE

As noted at the outset, most patient classification systems have been built on three assumptions: (1) patients do not move during the course of a shift; (2) nurses do not move during the course of a shift; and (3) unit staff members provide all of the required care. The ARIC system was developed to address changes in practice that may make these assumptions invalid.

The patient classification instrument specifically measures patient movement in and out of the unit and accounts for stays of less than 8 hours. Therefore, the ARIC system can easily account for patient movement.

Changes in practice that free nurses from being bound to a single unit for the entire shift can also be addressed. Case management, for example, may mean that nurses provide services to patients on units to which they are not assigned.

The amount and variability of time required for case management are empirical questions that should be answered using time studies or work sampling. If the time spent in case management is fairly constant from patient to patient, an average case management time could be calculated at the time the patient classification system is installed or when periodic studies reestablish the system's validity. Subsequently, case management can be treated as a constant staffing requirement and a fixed cost item.

If, on the other hand, the time required for case management is highly variable, it may need to be measured explicitly for each patient. Patients with multiple handicaps or medical diagnoses, for example, may require many more inpatient and discharge planning activities than other patients in the same DRG.

Although case management is clearly an independent nursing activity, the accuracy of the ARIC system is more easily maintained by treating case management and other specialized roles serving many patients as separate special functions within the database. The case manager would simply log the time spent with each patient, and this information would then be factored into the workload estimate for the relevant patients.

Cost accounting requires information about the rate of pay as well as the amount of time consumed by patient care. Presumably, case managers are paid at a somewhat higher rate than other nurses involved in providing direct service to patients. If the case manager is unit based and if the requirements for case management are constant across patients, the additional salary expense can be factored in as a constant cost item. But if the case manager is not unit based or the requirements for case management vary widely, then the additional salary costs should be allocated appropriately. This is especially important if nursing charges are billed separately and when negotiating reimbursement rates with third party payers.

Finally, the ARIC patient classification system can also be used to evaluate the amount of required care that is given by families and the patients themselves. Both the dependent and independent aspects of the caregiving role can be measured in sufficient detail to account for patient and family participation and for the extra time needed to instruct patients and families in some of the more complex care requirements.

REMAINING CHALLENGES

The preceding discussion shows that the ARIC patient classification and management information system is appropriate for or readily adapted to almost any model of care used in acute care settings. The system has been modified for ambulatory care settings, but it was not developed for, nor has it been adapted to, the needs of long-term care facilities and home nursing services. The demand for precise workload measurement in these areas has lagged behind that in acute care, but the demand is growing. Although the basic concept and principles of patient classification are readily transferable to nonacute settings, several features of these services suggest that a different set of factors are needed as critical indicators.

In long-term care facilities, the need for highly technical services is less and the demand for care varies little from day to day, making shift-by-shift measurement unnecessary. Functional ability takes on heightened importance for those requiring prolonged nursing care. In addition, because the long-term care facility is a residence as well as a nursing facility, the ongoing social and intellectual needs of residents are of far greater importance than in the short-term acute setting. Many of these needs are met in collaboration with other disciplines. It is likely that each of these differences will have an effect on staffing requirements and costs and will need to be factored into patient classification and cost accounting systems. Existing long-term care case mix systems support this hypothesis (Fries & Cooney, 1985).

In community-based services such as home health care, another set of variables becomes important. All of the differences identified for long-term care facilities are also true of the home care setting. In addition, nurses who provide service in the community do not have access to the hotel, transportation, and therapeutic services that are taken for granted in hospitals and nursing homes. Rather, the home care nurse must identify needs and then organize a package of services appropriate for meeting the needs within reimbursement limits (Edwardson & O'Grady, 1988). Furthermore, travel time to and from patients' residences is an important cost element. A workload measurement and cost accounting system for home care is likely to need data about these planning, coordination, and travel elements in order to represent the work of the home care nurse.

CONCLUSION

Current patient classification know-how and computer technology have been combined to produce a state-of-the-art nursing management information system for acute and ambulatory care. The ARIC system provides precision measurement, methods for user maintenance of reliability and validity, standard and customized reports, patient-specific cost identification, budget information, and the ability to answer unique operation and research questions.

With minor modifications, the workload measurement procedures used in the ARIC system can be adapted to all known models of care used in the acute care setting. Certain features of long-term care facilities and home care services present important challenges for those who need to obtain comprehensive data on the total cost of nursing care for episodes of illness.

REFERENCES

Davis, A.R., Levine, E., & Sverha, S. (1986). *The National Invitational Conference on Nursing Productivity: Proceedings.* Washington, DC: Georgetown University.

Devine, E.C. (1987, December). The Nursing Minimum Data Set: Benefits and implications for nurse researchers. *National League for Nursing,* pp. 115–118.

Devine, E.C., & Werley, H.H. (1988). Test of the Nursing Minimum Data Set: Availability of data and reliability. *Research in Nursing and Health, 11,* 97–104.

Donaho, B.A., Haas, J.L., Berg, H.V., Butler, M., Serote, M.E., Barr, J., Thibault, M.J., deLeon, E., Williams, C., Neff, L., Curtin, M.E., & Torres, D.D. (1984). On the scene: Sisters of Mercy Health Corporation. *Nursing Administration Quarterly, 8*(2) 12–44.

Edwardson, S.R. (1986). Measuring nursing productivity. *Nursing Economics 3,* 9–14.

Edwardson, S.R. (1988). Productivity. In E.J. Sullivan & P.J. Decker (Eds.), *Effective management in nursing* (2nd ed.). Menlo Park, CA: Addison-Wesley.

Edwardson, S., & Giovannetti, P.B. (1987). A review of cost accounting methods for nursing services. *Nursing Economics, 5,* 107–117.

Edwardson, S.R., & O'Grady, B.V. (1988). The impact of prospective payment systems on nursing care in community settings. In *The impact of DRG's on nursing—Report of the Midwest Alliance in Nursing* (NTIS Publication No. HRP-0907178, pp. 60–78). Bethesda, MD: Division of Nursing.

Fries, B.E., & Cooney, L.M. (1985). Resource utilization of groups: A patient classification system for long-term care. *Medical Care, 23,* 110–122.

Giovannetti, P. (1978). *Patient classification systems in nursing: A description and analysis* (DHEW Publication No. HRA 78-22). Washington, DC: U.S. Government Printing Office.

Jelinek, R.C., & Dennis, L.C. (1976). *A review and evaluation of nursing productivity* (DHEW Publication No. HRA 77-15). Bethesda, MD: Health Resources Administration.

Maibusch, R.M. (1988, December). The Nursing Minimum Data Set: Benefits and implications for clinical nurses. *National League for Nursing,* pp. 127–131.

McCloskey, J.C. (1988, December). The Nursing Minimum Data Set: Benefits and implications for nurse educators. *National League for Nursing,* pp. 119–126.

Werley, H.H., & Zorn, C.R. (1988, December). The Nursing Minimum Data Set: Benefits and implications. *National League for Nursing,* pp. 105–114.

Chapter 20

COMMES: Using a Computerized Consultant in Professional Practice

Helen Hoesing, Janet Cuddigan, and Sue Logan

The authors of this chapter describe the COMMES system, which is a computerized educational consultant. This system is an integral part of professional practice at Nebraska Methodist Hospital. This chapter outlines its specific uses. The authors also discuss how the COMMES system increased quality of patient care and nurse satisfaction.

The purpose of this chapter is to explain how COMMES (Creighton Online Multiple Modular Expert System), an artificial intelligence–based computerized consultant, can provide an essential component to an automated nursing information system and enhance the work environment for nurses. Nebraska Methodist Hospital was a pilot site for the development of this computer system. The hospital's experience in utilizing and evaluating the system will be discussed.

The object of instituting the COMMES system at Nebraska Methodist Hospital was (1) to improve patient care and patient outcomes, and (2) to improve nurse satisfaction by enhancing the work environment.

DEFINITION

COMMES is a computerized consultant designed to facilitate management of the nursing knowledge needed to provide quality patient care. COMMES captures the knowledge of nursing experts on a broad range of patient care problems and makes it available via computer to nurses planning patient care. In effect, COMMES permits nurses using the system to "consult with" the nursing experts contributing to the COMMES system. When successfully used, it extends and supports the efforts of hospital-based consultants such as clinical specialists and staff development instructors. Although used to enhance a preexisting nursing information system at Nebraska Methodist Hospital, COMMES can be utilized as a consultant system in health care settings with or without existing computer systems.

DEVELOPMENT

COMMES was developed in response to the knowledge explosion in professional nursing. Over the past 2 decades, it has become increasingly difficult to stay current on how to manage even the most common patient problems. More recently, nurses have been confronted with additional challenges as the complexity of patient care has increased and the length of stay has decreased. Very complex care must be planned and delivered in a relatively short period of time. Time to consult the professional literature to support care planning is a luxury few nurses can afford. Just as hospital information systems were designed to facilitate access to patient-specific data, COMMES was designed to facilitate access to the professional nursing knowledge necessary to plan quality patient care.

The COMMES system is the result of 13 years of research and development. Originally designed as a computerized BSN curriculum, the COMMES nursing knowledge base provides a detailed description of what a generalist nurse needs to know to provide safe, comprehensive care. Based on the recommendations of clinical users, the COMMES knowledge base has been expanded to include selected specialty content. COMMES currently contains the world's largest computerized nursing knowledge base.

In the process of creating and maintaining this extensive knowledge base, a technological bridge has been built between nursing education and nursing practice. The early development of COMMES in a university setting provided a unique opportunity for nursing educators to reach beyond the classroom. Nurses using COMMES in clinical settings have responded by sharing their expertise and knowledge with the nursing educators at Creighton University who routinely review and update the COMMES knowledge base. As a result, the COMMES nursing knowledge base combines some of the best efforts of nursing education and practice.

The system's knowledge is validated through references to current nursing literature. It was formally validated in a content validation study funded by the Division of Nursing of the U.S. Public Health Service. In this study, a nationwide panel of 106 clinicians and educators compared protocols produced by the COMMES computer system to protocols produced by master's and doctorally prepared nurse experts. This panel of evaluators considered the quality of the COMMES protocols equal to or better than those produced by the experts (Cuddigan, Norris, Ryan, & Evans, 1987).

DESCRIPTION

The COMMES system differs from traditional hospital information systems. Most systems are designed to facilitate the flow of information related to the management and delivery of patient care. They perform a variety of functions, ranging from patient billing to care planning and automated charting.

The COMMES system can be classified as a computer decision support system, a relatively new kind of computer system used to support nurses as they make decisions in an increasingly complex and challenging health care environment. Such systems are designed to promote a higher quality of decision making without replacing the decision-making power and authority of the nurse (Brennan, 1988).

As a computer decision support system, COMMES was designed to address the problem of knowledge acquisition in order to improve patient care delivery. It allows nurses using the system to get expert consultation on a broad range of health care topics and thereby meet a variety of needs. In essence, it serves as a broad-based, multipurpose consultant available 24 hours a day, 7 days a week.

COMMES responds to a nurse's request for information by using its artificial intelligence capacity to intelligently select information from its expert knowledge base. When accessing this information, nurses can utilize two "nursing consultants" within the COMMES system, the Nursing Protocol Consultant and the Minicurriculum Consultant.

Nursing Protocol Consultant: Care Plan and Standards of Care Guidelines

The most frequently used consultant is the Nursing Protocol Consultant. This consultant provides detailed guidelines for care on a broad range of patient care problems. Using a nursing process format, it reminds the nurse of current knowledge related to assessments, nursing diagnoses, goals, interventions, and discharge teaching for each patient care problem. See Exhibit 20-1 for a protocol produced in response to a nurse's request for information on the care of the pneumonia patient.

The Nursing Protocol Consultant provides the nurse with the advice of nursing experts during the planning of care. The nurse uses this advice to support (but not dictate) his or her patient care decisions. The NPC can be used as a comprehensive basis for writing care plans, standards of care, and quality assurance auditing tools.

Minicurriculum Consultant: A Learning Guide

The Minicurriculum Consultant provides a personalized study guide for nurses seeking instructional assistance. Each study guide identifies specific

Exhibit 20-1 Protocol for Patient with Pneumonia

CLINICAL PRACTICE PROTOCOL[a]

THE PATHOGENESIS AND RESULTING SYMPTOMATOLOGY
OF PNEUMONIA.

In PATHOGENESIS OF PNEUMONIA, consider:

Infectious inflammation	involves bronchioles
involves alveolar space	often caused by bacteria
often caused by virus	rarely caused by fungus
rarely caused by mycoplasma	rarely caused by parasites

In OXYGENATION ASSESSMENT OF PNEUMONIA, consider:

rales	cough	hypoxia
dyspnea	tachycardia	tachypnea
cyanosis		pale skin
shallow respiration		nasal flaring
bronchial breath sounds		use of accessory muscles
decreased breath sounds		positive sputum culture
fremitus		discolored sputum
foul-smelling sputum		increased sputum production
yellow sputum	green sputum	rust-colored sputum
increased sed rate		leukocytosis

In FLUID AND ELECTROLYTE ASSESSMENT OF PNEUMONIA, consider:

shaking	perspiration	fever
low sodium level		low chloride level

In SENSORY-PERCEPTUAL ASSESSMENT OF PNEUMONIA, consider:

headache	aching pain	chest pain
referred pain to shoulder and abdomen		
referred pain to flank		general malaise

CONCEPTS REGARDING RELIEF OF AIRWAY OBSTRUCTION,
EXERCISE TOLERANCE, AND ANTIBIOTIC THERAPY IN PLANNING
MEASURES FOR THE CARE OF THE CLIENT WITH PNEUMONIA.

In DESIRED OUTCOMES FOR PNEUMONIA, consider:

adequate expectoration of secretions	improved ventilation
adequate oxygenation of tissues	increased comfort
normal vital signs	normal arterial blood gases
dry pink warm skin	electrolyte balance
clear lung sounds	normal white blood cell count
negative sputum culture	

Exhibit 20-1 continued

In INTERVENTIONS FOR INEFFECTIVE AIRWAY CLEARANCE IN PNEUMONIA, consider:

monitor vital signs	assess lung sounds	
cough and deep breathe		suction
chest physiotherapy		ippb
input & output	force fluids	
assess electrolytes	iv fluid	oral hygiene
sputum culture and sensitivity		expectorant
aminophyllin	antitussive	range of motion
anxiety reduction		

In INTERVENTIONS FOR ALTERATION IN COMFORT IN PNEUMONIA, consider:

rest	cautious sedation	prevent pleurisy
cautious analgesia	keep warm and dry	oral hygiene

In INTERVENTIONS FOR IMPAIRED GAS EXCHANGE IN PNEUMONIA, consider:

cough and deep breathe	oxygen	intubation
ventilator	prevent respiratory arrest	prevent pulmonary edema
prevent heart failure		bed rest
assess arterial blood gases		antibiotic

In INTERVENTIONS FOR KNOWLEDGE DEFICIT IN PNEUMONIA, consider:

prepare patient for bronchoscopy   medication teaching

In INTERVENTIONS FOR INFECTION IN PNEUMONIA, consider:

isolation	antibiotic	antipyretic
prevent sepsis	prevent spread of infection	

In DISCHARGE TEACHING FOR PNEUMONIA, consider:
cough and deep breathe every 2 hours
force fluids if not contraindicated
medication teaching
complete course of antibiotics

flu vaccine	avoid contact with those having flu
avoid contact with those having upper respiratory infections	
pneumonia vaccine	adequate nutrition adequate rest
pace activities	stop activity if have dyspnea on exertion
routine follow-up with md	good handwashing technique
report increased temperature	report increased dyspnea
report increased or discolored sputum	

ª Information on nutritional assessment, interventions for alteration in nutrition, and the list of appropriate nursing diagnoses have been omitted.

learning goals. Each learning goal is linked to specific bibliographic references indicating precisely where the needed information can be obtained. A copy of all referenced information can be provided under the terms of the COMMES licensing agreement. See Exhibit 20-2 for an example of a minicurriculum on the syndrome of inappropriate antidiuretic hormone.

The Minicurriculum Consultant can expand the capability of an institution's educational offerings. It can also be used by staff nurses to meet their individual educational needs.

USE

Goals

The system is currently being used as a decision support tool at five clinical sites and four academic sites in the United States and Canada. Although use of the system may vary according to the unique needs of each institution, Nebraska Methodist Hospital purchased COMMES as a part of an overall effort to maintain a high quality of patient care. It was assumed that a more knowledgeable nurse develops better care plans and

---

Exhibit 20-2 Minicurriculum on the Syndrome of Inappropriate Antidiuretic Hormone

---

A MINICURRICULUM FOR THE FOLLOWING GOAL:

---

1. Syndrome of inappropriate antidiuretic hormone: Describe the effects of water intoxication due to retention of fluid caused by the syndrome of inappropriate antidiuretic hormone—SIADH.
(2.5; 2.5; 3.0; *; 10M/20M)   012601-0044

YOU CAN ACHIEVE THE GOAL BY COMPLETING THESE SUBGOALS USING THE RESOURCES CITED:

1.01. Water intoxication: Explain why the serum sodium falls when the patient develops water intoxication resulting from SIADH.
(2.5; 2.5; 3.0; *; 5M/10M)   012601-0045

Luckmann & Sorensen, Med-Surg. Nursing, 1987, pp. 1474–1475.

1.02. Interventions: Explain why accurate intake and output, daily weight, and head positioning are important interventions for syndrome of inappropriate antidiuretic hormone and describe a plan of care.
(2.5; 2.5; 3.0; *; 5M/10M)   012601-0046

Luckmann & Sorensen. Med-Surg, Nursing, 1987, pp. 1474–1475.

in turn provides better patient care. The COMMES system would be particularly beneficial in supporting nursing decisions related to unusual or nonroutine problems. As has been said, we often don't know what we don't know. The hope was that exposure to COMMES protocols on even routinely encountered problems would provide new insights and approaches to improving patient care.

The adoption of the COMMES system at Nebraska Methodist Hospital was also part of an overall plan to meet staff development needs. The COMMES system provides ready answers to staff nurse questions. This gives the staff nurses a sense of competency and confidence in their knowledge and abilities. It also frees supervisors and clinical specialists from having to serve as sources of information and allows them to deal with more complex problems. Investment in the COMMES system helps create an environment that values professional knowledge and that nurtures and supports the professional growth of the nursing staff.

COMMES and the Automated Nursing Practice Model

COMMES has been used to guide care planning in settings with or without preexisting computerized nursing information systems. Nebraska Methodist Hospital saw COMMES as an essential component of a totally automated and integrated system for nursing. Figure 20-1 depicts the nursing process as the core of nursing decision making, with an automated information system at the bedside. In this model, once the initial assessment information is obtained, knowledge about the patient's illness is needed to develop the care plan. This is where COMMES plays an essential role—by providing professional knowledge that suggests a standard for care. A nurse cannot be expected to know every updated aspect of care for a patient's illness, especially since most acute care patients have multiple diagnoses and some diagnoses may only be encountered once every 2 or 3 years. A nurse needs a knowledgeable consultant at the bedside 24 hours a day, 7 days a week. COMMES is available at every moment to each nurse on each patient care unit.

Use of COMMES at this initial stage can positively impact the rest of the model shown in Figure 20-1. The benefits of this model include the following:

- Readily available automated standards of care from the COMMES system
- More accurate and higher quality care plans from using the COMMES standards to guide care planning
- Accurate, quality care plans result in:

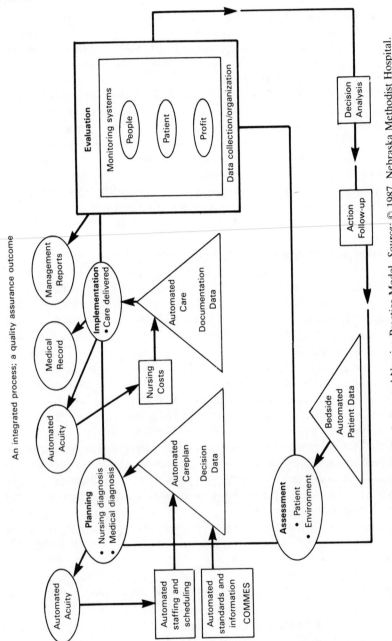

Figure 20-1 Nebraska Methodist Hospital's Automated Nursing Practice Model. *Source:* © 1987, Nebraska Methodist Hospital.

- a more accurate basis for an automated acuity system
- a more accurate staffing and scheduling system using a care plan-based acuity system
- a more accurate determination of nursing costs based on patient acuity
- a more complete, better organized medical record
- more accurate and efficient evaluation of staff performance, patient outcomes and profits
- improved quality of patient care

IMPLEMENTATION

Change theory was utilized in implementing the COMMES system (Bennis, 1969). Prior to implementation, a change agent responsible for coordinating implementation and evaluation of the system was designated. A task force was formed representing the staff nurses and nursing managers selected to pilot-test the system. After being oriented to the COMMES system, members of the task force identified facilitating and inhibiting factors that might affect implementation of the system. Implementation plans were then developed that maximized facilitating factors and minimized or compensated for inhibiting factors. For the actual implementation, a train-the-trainers approach was used, with the change agent and task force members serving as trainers.

EVALUATION

Evaluation of the clinical efficacy of the COMMES system is an ongoing process at clinical user sites. Each user site has developed evaluation strategies to measure the goals for COMMES unique to its institution. As was mentioned before, the goals at Nebraska Methodist Hospital were (1) to improve patient care and patient outcomes and (2) to improve nurse satisfaction by enhancing the work environment.

Quality of Patient Care

The impact of COMMES on the quality of patient care was evaluated quarterly for each of two pilot nursing units. Four commonly encountered patient problems were selected on each unit. Unit A selected postoperative teaching for cholecystectomy patients, postoperative assessment of thyroidectomy patients, pain management with bowel obstruction, and post-operative assessment of diabetic patients. Unit B selected assessment of pneumonia patients prior to discharge, assessment of depression in cancer patients, and monitoring of steroid therapy and enteral feedings. Monitoring criteria (patient outcome indicators) for these patient problems were developed (see Exhibit 20-3). Quality of care was measured via chart audits prior to COMMES implementation and at quarterly intervals thereafter.

Chi square analysis was used to compare pre-COMMES audits with each set of quarterly post-COMMES measurements. Results indicated progressive and significant improvements in the quality of care following COMMES implementation (see Table 20-1 for a summary of these results).

Comparison of pre-COMMES data to first-quarter data showed minimal improvement; however, positive trends were noted. During the first quarter, nurses were still becoming acquainted with the system and protocols were not obtained on all patients.

Exhibit 20-3 Examples of Patient Outcome Indicators

INDICATOR	SAMPLE	CRITERIA
POST-OP TEACHING	10 consecutive patients having cholecystectomy without CDE.	Prior to dismissal, 100% of patients will demonstrate understanding of all elements below UNLESS home health follow-up arranged or requested by nurse. —dietary modifications —activity limitations —breathing exercises (wound splinting, deep breathing) —wound care (including incisional care and s/s infection)
INDICATOR	SAMPLE	CRITERIA
DISCHARGE ASSESSMENT OF PNEUMONIA	Dismissal day charting for 10 consecutive patients with primary or secondary diagnosis of pneumonia.	100% of patients will have assessment of cough, sputum, breath sounds, and activity tolerance unchanged or improved from day prior UNLESS nursing intervention evident (notification of MD)

Table 20-1 Comparison of Patient Outcome Indicators Prior to COMMES Implementation and at Quarterly Intervals Following Implementation.

Indicator	Pre-COMMES vs. 1st Qtr. χ^2/p	Pre-COMMES vs. 2nd Qtr. χ^2/p	Pre-COMMES vs. 3rd Qtr. χ^2/p
Postop cholecystectomy teaching	0.5/NS[a]	1.26/NS	5.01/.02
Thyroidectomy assessment	.56/NS	9.34/.001	17.69/<.001
Pain management	.10/NS	1.43/NS	2.67/NS
Diabetic assessment	NA[b]	NA	NA
Unit A analysis	1.33/NS	14.19/<.001	29.71/<.001
Pneumonia assessment	.23/NS	6.15/.01	14.46/<.001
Steroid therapy	NA	NA	NA
Depression assessment	NA	NA	NA
Enteral feeding	NA	NA	NA
Unit B analysis	.08/NS	4.47/.02	9.70/.001
Overall analysis (Units A & B)	1.45/NS	19.08/<.001	40.68/<.001

[a]NS = Not significant.
[b]NA = Not analyzed due to insufficient sample size. These indicators showed a consistently positive trend over the course of the project.

The second quarter revealed significant improvements in the quality of care for two patient outcome indicators and nonsignificant improvements in two others. By this time, user proficiency was improving and the level of usage had increased.

Higher levels of system utilization and further improvements in the quality of patient care were noted during the third quarter. Significant improvements were noted over pre-COMMES measurements for three indicators; one indicator showed nonsignificant improvement and four indicators could not be analyzed due to insufficient sample size. For the second and third quarter, significant improvements were noted over baseline measurements for each nursing unit and for the overall total.

A study funded by the National Institutes of Health Center for Nursing Research supports these findings. In this study, 150 nurses planned care for hypothetical patients under three conditions: (1) use of traditional resources for planning care, (2) use of COMMES protocols to support care planning, and (3) use of COMMES protocols and minicurriculums to support care planning. The results demonstrated significantly higher mean ratings of quality for care planned under both computerized decision support conditions (conditions 2 and 3) over the traditional condition (condition 1). Time on task was greater when computerized decision support was used (Norris, Cuddigan, Foyt, & Leak, in press).

Nurse Satisfaction

User satisfaction was also measured at Nebraska Methodist Hospital. As might be anticipated, user satisfaction increased each quarter as acceptance and proficiency improved. By the third quarter, 85% of the nurses who responded to the user satisfaction survey agreed or strongly agreed that COMMES was a valuable resource. Eighty-six percent of the nurses surveyed agreed or strongly agreed that COMMES improved their planning of care and provided them with confidence in the delivery of that care.

Cost-Benefit Analysis

At Nebraska Methodist Hospital, the benefits of improved patient care and nurse satisfaction outweighed the costs of COMMES implementation and use. Based on this analysis, COMMES became an essential component of the hospital's automated nursing practice model and was made available on all nursing units.

The cost of COMMES varies depending on the size of the institution, the extent of already existing automation, and the number of nursing units involved. Steven Evans at Creighton University in Omaha may be contacted for the specific institutional information needed to guide individual cost-benefit analysis.

Multisite cost-benefit analysis studies are currently underway (Norris, 1989). The costs of all resources expended on the acquisition, implementation, maintenance, and use of the system are being measured against its actual benefits. These studies have been designed to measure the effect of COMMES on quality of patient care and patient outcomes, length of stay, incidence of complications, nurse satisfaction, attitudes toward decision support systems, staff turnover, and personnel productivity.

SUMMARY

Because of its positive effect on nurse satisfaction and patient care, COMMES has become an essential component of Nebraska Methodist Hospital's total automated nursing practice model. The hospital feels strongly that this total automation plan will allow it to thrive rather than simply survive.

REFERENCES

Bennis, W.G. (1969). *The planning of change.* New York: Holt, Rinehart & Winston.

Brennan, P.F. (1988, November–December). DDS, ES, AI: The lexicon of decision support. *Nursing and Health Care, 9*(9), 501–503.

Cuddigan, J., Norris, J., Ryan, S., & Evans, S. (1987). Validating the knowledge in a computer-based consultant for nursing care. In W.W. Stead (Ed.), *Proceedings of the Eleventh Symposium on Computer Applications in Medical Care* (pp. 74–78). Washington, DC: Computer Society Press.

Norris, J. (1989). *COMMES utilization and evaluation guidelines.* Unpublished manuscript, Creighton University, School of Nursing, Omaha.

Norris, J., Cuddigan, J., Foyt, M., & Leak, G. (in press). Decision support and outcomes of nurses' care planning. *Computers in Nursing.*

Index

NOTE: Pages appearing in italics indicate entries found in artwork.

329

About the Editors

GLORIA GILBERT MAYER, RN, EdD, FAAN, is a private health care consultant specializing in patient care delivery systems, operational audits, patient classification systems, organizational behavior, and continuing education and staff development. She has published numerous articles in both nursing journals and popular magazines. Her books include *The Middle Manager in Primary Nursing* (with Katherine Bailey, 1982), *2001 Hints for Working Mothers* (1984), and *The Health Insurance Alternative* (with Thomas Mayer, 1984). She has given workshops on writing and teaches several writing courses. She has served on the editorial board of several nursing journals. Formerly, she held positions in both nursing administration and clinical nursing research. She currently makes her home in Huntington Beach, California.

MARY JANE MADDEN, PhD, RN, is currently a principal in Lawrenz, Madden & Associates, Inc. and an assistant professor at the University of Minnesota. Her expertise is in organizational effectiveness, and she has extensive experience in health care and corporate settings. She is the author of publications on communication, leadership, and career mobility. She lives in St. Paul, Minnesota.

EUNICE LAWRENZ, BNS, RN, is currently a principal in Lawrenz, Madden & Associates, Inc., a consulting firm specializing in health care leadership and organizational effectiveness. In addition to her years of experience in nursing administration, she has had extensive experience and done extensive research in innovative scheduling and staffing in hospitals. She publishes a bimonthly newsletter, *Perspectives on Staffing and Scheduling*, and is the author of a computerized scheduling system. She consults nationally and internationally and makes her home in Montclair, New Jersey.